Wages, Bonuses and Appropriation of Profit in the Financial Industry

The 2008 financial crisis led the whole world to ask questions of the financial industry. Why are wages in the financial industry so high? Are bonuses responsible for the financial crisis? Where do bonuses come from? Politicians and others urged people to believe that the crisis was the price of Wall Street's greed and blamed the "bonus culture" prevalent in the financial industry. However, despite widespread condemnation and the threat of tighter regulation, bonuses in the industry have proven remarkably resilient.

Wages, Bonuses and Appropriation of Profit in the Financial Industry provides an in-depth inquiry into the bonus system. Drawing on examples from France, the City and Wall Street, it explains how and why workers in the financial industry can receive such large bonuses. The book examines issues around incentives, morality and wealth-sharing among employees, including the rise of "the working rich" – those who have benefited the most from the high wages and large bonuses on offer to some employees. These people have achieved wealth through their work thanks to new forms of exploitation in our ever-more dematerialised economy. This book shows how the most mobile employees holding the most mobile assets can exploit the most immobile stakeholders. In a world where inequalities are rising sharply, this book is therefore an important study of one of the key contemporary issues.

It will be of vital interest to those studying finance, banking or political economy.

Olivier Godechot is codirector of MaxPo, Sociology Professor at Sciences Po and Research Professor at CNRS, France.

Routledge International Studies in Money and Banking

Wages, Bonuses and Appropriation of Profit in the Financial Industry

The working rich

Olivier Godechot

Translated by Susannah Dale

Routledge
Taylor & Francis Group

LONDON AND NEW YORK

First published in English 2017
by Routledge
2 Park Square, Milton Park, Abingdon, Oxon OX14 4RN

and by Routledge
711 Third Avenue, New York, NY 10017

First issued in paperback 2018

Routledge is an imprint of the Taylor & Francis Group, an informa business

First edition published in French by Éditions La Découverte 2007

British Library Cataloguing in Publication Data
A catalogue record for this book is available from the British Library

Library of Congress Cataloging in Publication Data
Names: Godechot, Olivier, author.
Title: Wages, bonuses and appropriation of profit in the financial industry: the working rich / Olivier Godechot; translated by Susannah Dale.
Other titles: Working rich. English
Description: Abingdon, Oxon; New York, NY: Routledge, 2017.
Identifiers: LCCN 2016010199| ISBN 9781138123960 (hardback) |
    ISBN 9781315648477 (ebook)
Subjects: LCSH: Floor traders (Finance)—Salaries, etc.
Classification: LCC HG4621 .G63513 2017 |
    DDC 331.2/8133264—dc23
LC record available at https://lccn.loc.gov/2016010199

ISBN 13: 978-1-138-34380-1 (pbk)
ISBN 13: 978-1-138-12396-0 (hbk)

Typeset in Times New Roman
by Swales & Willis Ltd, Exeter, Devon, UK

Contents

Figures

Tables

Preface
Understanding before regulating

The first version of this book was published in French in April 2007 (Godechot 2007). Financial markets were then booming at an exceptional rate. The Dow Jones index peaked at more than 13,000 points, 200 points above its millennium maximum. Bonuses in banks had reached record levels. Those given out on Wall Street at the beginning of that year amounted on average to 225,000 dollars. The ten best-paid employees of Société Générale, the leading French investment bank, simultaneously received nearly eight million euros each. While the press would occasionally comment on wages in the financial industry, I was one of the few social scientists venturing into this area at the time. Apart from Louise-Marie Roth's illuminating book (2006) on the extreme gender gap in finance, I found very few scientific studies, especially in the twin disciplines of economics and finance, which should be the most concerned by such phenomena. I remember that my critical approach to bonuses in an online chat organised by the newspaper *Libération* drew many bitter comments from financiers who did not accept me questioning the supposedly meritocratic dimension of their pay (Cori 2007; Godechot and Cori 2007).

Four months later, France's largest bank, BNP-Paribas, suspended the valuation of two funds invested in subprime securities. This was the first sign of a global financial crisis that climaxed with the spectacular bankruptcy of Lehman Brothers in September 2008, bringing the world's financial system to its knees. Within a few months, attitudes towards financial wages had changed radically. Accusations were made that bonuses fuelled *greed*. This inclination, once seen as the essential virtue of capitalism, was then labelled a deadly sin again. Public outrage soared when it was discovered that bailed-out firms, such as AIG in 2009, were paying hefty bonuses to its traders out of taxpayers' money. As well as expressing moral indignation, many commentators stated that bonuses were an incentive to take the kind of risks that had resulted in the massive subprime crash (Rajan 2008; Bebchuk 2010; Thanassoulis 2012). In short, bonuses had killed Wall Street. Jacques Attali, an economist who advised both President Mitterrand and President Sarkozy to adopt pro-market policies, proposed banning bonuses altogether (Attali 2009). Some neoliberal economists, brandishing a knife between their teeth for the occasion, were passing me on my left.

In order to avoid further financial meltdowns, financial regulatory institutions tried to limit risk-taking behaviours by several means: increasing the required capital for engaging in financial activities, outsourcing the riskiest activities, and, as an echo of the bonus scandal, regulating remuneration. The G20 Financial Stability Board (FSB 2009) called for sound compensation practices in the banking industry that would better account for all risks taken by setting all incentives on risk-adjusted notions of profit, place greater emphasis on the long term through deferrals and clawbacks, and diminish bankers' appetite for risk via a balance of remuneration that was more favourable to fixed wages. The United States and the European Union adopted divergent approaches to regulation (Lehmann 2014; Biedermann and Orosz 2015). In 2014 the United States implemented the Volcker rule, which forbids banks to carry out proprietary trading. However, it did little to restrict compensation. In contrast, the European Union has not yet adopted (early 2016) the European equivalent of the Volcker rule, but was quick to enforce strict implementation of the FSB regulation of remuneration through the 2010 Capital Requirement Directive (CRD) III. Under pressure from the European Parliament, the European Union went even further with the 2013 CRD IV Directive. A great novelty in capitalist market societies, it even introduced a bonus cap! From 2015, bonuses were not allowed to exceed 200% of the fixed wage.

So, are the bonus excesses of the financial industry about to be curtailed? Some may think that the combination of larger capital requirements, the ban on the most speculative activities, the banks being sued for misconduct and condemned to hefty fines, bonus deferrals and clawbacks, the bonus cap and a poor business climate in finance will finally lead bankers' compensation to fall to more ordinary levels and put an end to the four-decade-long finance wage premium.

A number of elements make this seem unlikely. First, the new regulations are restricted to too-big-to-fail banks and do not concern small banks or hedge funds. Second, the regulated sector is skilful at conforming to the new regulation through circumvention (for instance a massive increase in fixed wages) and categorical redefinition of its activity. Therefore, remuneration levels are still high and will probably remain so in the coming years. Moreover, the main hypotheses of bonus regulation have gone unchallenged. Regulators seem to believe that the only problem with pay in the financial industry is that incentives are badly designed: they favour excessive financial risk-taking, which leads to bankruptcy and bail-outs funded by taxpayers.

While regulators may have good reasons to target too-big-to-fail banks and retail banks covered by state guarantees, since the failure of those banks puts the economy and taxpayers at risk, limiting regulation to these firms overlooks two facts. First, as the long-term capital management (LTCM) bankruptcy proved in 1998 (MacKenzie 2003), the failure of large hedge funds can also fuel systemic risks. Second, competitive pressure from non-regulated finance sectors (such as alternative investment funds) will favour strategies for circumventing or downplaying such rules in the regulated sector.

The conception of the risks supposedly caused by the bonus culture in finance is also rather limited. The regulators' only concern is that traders embark on risky financial deals in order to maximise pay. They concentrate solely on activities where shareholder equity is in jeopardy. When other stakeholders are at risk, such as clients, which is especially the case in fee-generating (and bonus-generating) brokerage activities, deals are not considered as "risky". Some of the solutions put forward by regulators (generalisation of risk-adjusted notions of profit) also disregard the fact that bonuses contribute to the politicisation of risk measurement and therefore misrepresent the risks involved (Chapter 2). Third, regulators pay almost no attention to the fact that soaring inequalities (Chapter 1) may lead to high social risks both within financial firms (pushing employees to please the best-paying departments) and between financial firms and the rest of the population. The 2011 Occupy social movement and the rise of anti-finance populism both at the far left and the far right, as seen within the Tea Party and the French Front National, are related to the growing gap between Wall Street and Main Street, or between the "Parisian Bobos" and the Provinces (Godechot 2014).

Finally, regulators offer a biased view of incentives and pay design. According to their regulation principles, bonuses are the only incentive component of work and wages. The fixed wage is not considered to have an incentive dimension and is left out of regulatory constraints. Moreover, regulators seem to imagine that bonuses were introduced by short-sighted shareholders in order to solve a first-order shirking problem at work. First of all, this ignores the fact that activist shareholders are not so much the physical persons who invest, but largely asset managers from institutional investor firms who supposedly speak in the name of the shareholders they represent while having their own personal interests and of course their own bonuses (Jung and Dobbin 2016). Regulators have also overlooked the fact that shareholders and chief executive officers (CEOs) did not impose bonuses on lazy financiers but were largely claimed by the latter in order to obtain what they considered to be their legitimate share of profit.

Not everything is flawed in European bonus regulation. Bonus caps, deferrals, clawbacks and disclosure are certainly useful tools within a comprehensive regulatory approach. One of the great achievements of this ruling was to impose the idea that citizens, through their parliamentary representatives and the regulatory institutions they mandate, may now have a say on finance pay. However, the limitations I have highlighted show that there is a need for a profound and detailed understanding of what bonuses are, and of why and how they are granted.

In this book, I will not focus on the contribution bonuses made to the global financial meltdown or the accuracy of public policies adopted in the aftermath. Nor will I make a plea for any new, smarter regulations. Instead, I will do something quite different but no less essential to this regulatory debate. I will try to offer a general understanding of pay practices in finance and the resulting income inequalities. I will claim that the organisation of financial activity counts more than an employee's initial educational or social background. To prove my hypotheses, I will delve deeply into the balance of power within the financial firm.

Throughout my book I rely on qualitative material mainly collected before the 2008 crisis. However, I updated my resources after the crisis by various means (quantitative series and surveys, press releases, punctual interactions with informers, etc.) to guarantee its continued relevance. Therefore, this book is an updated translation of my 2007 opus. I hope it will constitute a reliable foundation for all readers wishing to understand, deregulate, criticise, defend, regulate, absolve or tame the finance industry.

My book is not merely about finance. It uses finance as a case for the emergence of the working rich phenomenon and for the generation of inequality at the workplace level (Avent-Holt and Tomaskovic-Devey 2014). In the United States, for example, the recent boom in the information technology (IT) industry has fuelled concerns over rising inequality in the San Francisco Bay Area (Silicon Valley Institute for Regional Studies 2015), discontent and even strong social protests which targeted Google buses in particular as a symbol of the new schism (Levy and Levy 2015). I believe that the model I coined for finance in the 2000s could also be very helpful for understanding the Google–Facebook–Twitter contribution to rising inequality in the 2010s.

Before venturing into wild new High Tech areas, follow me into the world of Finance.

References

Attali, J 2009, 'Altius, Fortius, Bonus, Malus', *L'Express*, 18 August.

Avent-Holt, D and Tomaskovic-Devey, D 2014, 'A Relational Theory of Earnings Inequality', *American Behavioral Scientist*, vol. 58, n°3, pp. 379–399.

Bebchuk, L 2010, 'How to Fix Bankers' Pay', *Daedalus*, vol. 139, n°4, pp. 52–60.

Biedermann, Z and Orosz, Á 2015, 'Diverging Financial Regulations After the Crisis? A Comparison of the EU's and the United States' Responses', *Financial and Economic Review*, vol. 14, n°1, pp. 31–55.

Cori, N 2007, 'Quand les financiers font recette', *Libération*, 2 June.

FSB 2009, *FSB Principles for Sound Compensation Practices. Implementation Standards*, 25 September, http://www.fsb.org/wp-content/uploads/r_090925c.pdf?page_moved=1, accessed 1 April 2016.

Godechot, O 2007, *Working Rich. Salaires, bonus et appropriation du profit dans l'industrie financière*, La Découverte, Paris.

Godechot, O 2014, 'Financialization and Sociospatial Divides' (Translation of: 'Financiarisation et fractures socio-spatiales', 2013), *L'année sociologique*, vol. 63, n°1, pp. 17–50.

Godechot, O and Cori, N 2007, 'Les salaires de la finance n'ont pas grand-chose à voir avec les compétences', *Libération*, 28 May.

Jung, J and Dobbin, F 2016, 'Agency Theory as Prophecy: How Boards, Analysts, and Fund Managers Perform Their Roles', *Seattle University Law Review*, vol. 39, pp. 291–320.

Lehmann, M 2014, *Volcker Rule, Ring-Fencing or Separation of Bank Activities-Comparison of Structural Reform Acts Around the World*, LSE Law, Society and Economy Working Papers n°25.

Levy A and Levy, D 2014, 'San Francisco's Income Gap Captures Wall Street Spotlight: Tech', *Bloomberg*, 28 January.

MacKenzie, D 2003, 'Long-Term Capital Management and the Sociology of Arbitrage', *Economy and Society*, vol. 32, n° 3, pp. 349–380.

Rajan, R 2008, 'Bankers' Pay is Deeply Flawed', *Financial Times*, 8 January.

Roth, LM 2006, *Selling Women Short. Gender Inequality on Wall Street*, Princeton University Press, Princeton NJ.

Silicon Valley Institute for Regional Studies 2015, *Income Inequality in the San Francisco Bay Area*, Research Brief, http://siliconvalleyindicators.org/pdf/income-inequality-2015–06.pdf, accessed 1 April 2016.

Thanassoulis, J 2012, 'The Case for Intervening in Bankers' Pay', *The Journal of Finance*, vol. 67, n°3, pp. 849–895.

Introduction

Finance as a working rich observatory

It's just a payslip. There's not much to see.

The contrasting colours of the bank's logo brighten the top left corner. It's a plain piece of paper, flat and smooth. At the top, under the company name, there's a job title: "trader". On the line below appears yet another term specifying the payment type: "annual bonus". Further down, 60 years of French social history is crystallised: "pension plan", "work accident insurance", "unemployment insurance". The only evidence of the silent struggles between government, unions and employers is a list of rates summarising the distribution of the welfare state burden: employer contribution, 8.2%; employee contribution, 6.55%. The few lines reserved for professionals ("AGIRC" and "APEC") are a reminder of the failure to fully unify the new Social Security system in the aftermath of World War II. The list ends with references to last-ditch attempts made to bail out the structural debt of a system functioning on borrowed time: "CSG" (generalised social contribution), "deductible CSG" and "CRDS" (contribution for the reimbursement of the social debt). These acronyms are impenetrable to anyone outside France, and yet so familiar here. The observer scans these lines and intermediary amounts, pausing only at the two boxes of interest at the bottom of the sheet: the gross amount promised and the net amount received. In the first box, a round number, the annual bonus: 1,000,000 euros. In the second, a calculated amount: 913,733 euros. It's just a pay slip. There's not much to see.

The return of wage inequality

The twentieth-century belief that in advanced market societies inequality is in a downward trend has been swept aside for good. Over the last 40 years, inequality has been on the rise in the United States. By some strange irony, the Marxist theory of the absolute impoverishment of unskilled workers under capitalism found its first empirical confirmation in the United States while intellectual Marxism was definitely declining: the real federal minimum wage fell by 33% between 1968 and 2006 (Bernstein and Shapiro 2006). Falling wages at the bottom of the pay scale are not, however, the only reason for its increasing length. The other end of the scale has also moved further away. In 1970, the top 1% of wage earners received 5.1% of the American wage bill. Forty years later, in 2007, the same fraction had increased its share to 12.2% (Piketty 2014).[1] During the same period, the share of those lying slightly further down the pay scale – the group belonging to the top 10% but not the top 5% (F90–95) scarcely increased. Its share went up from 10% to 10.5% of the wage bill.

The growth in inequality is due primarily to the increased salaries of a small elite group at the very top of the pay spectrum. This rise in the highest salaries has also changed the composition of wealth among the wealthiest classes. Whereas capital income was traditionally the main source of wealth and salaries constituted a minor share, salary income is in the process of becoming the dominant source of revenue among the highest-paid groups. Among the top 0.1% of American households with the highest incomes, the contribution of salary (fixed salaries, bonuses and stock options) to their wealth increased from 26% in 1970 to 44% in 2007 (Piketty and Saez 2003).[2] In the past, the rich were thought of as individuals with independent means. Now they are wage earners.

To describe this phenomenon, Emmanuel Saez and Thomas Piketty use the term "working rich" coined by *Forbes* magazine (Dolan 1998). The "working rich" category was constructed as a reverse mirror image of the other new category, "working poor". Just as it is possible for people to be poor, extremely poor or even homeless while in wage-earning jobs, so it is possible for people to be extremely rich thanks to their job. The working rich category thus highlights two facts: first, some individuals (such as company executives) earn incomes that position them within the wealthiest classes; second, the incomes of the wealthiest classes derive largely from wage income.

This explosion in the numbers of working rich is not limited to the United States. The same phenomenon can be observed in many developed countries, albeit on a smaller scale, particularly in the United Kingdom and Canada. In other countries such as France, Germany and Japan, however, income inequality in general and salary inequality in particular have been considered stable over the past 30 years (Piketty and Saez 2006; Charnoz, Coudin and Gaini, 2013). Is this contrast due to a significant difference in culture, social standards and labour market systems between free-market countries that are tolerant of social inequality and countries that give greater importance to equal conditions, or is it simply the delayed manifestation of a return to inequality in the context of contemporary capitalism?

Several factors make the first theory unviable in France. The most recent studies have shown that when the top end of income distribution is analysed, income and salary inequality began to increase noticeably from the mid-1990s (Godechot 2012). The share of the wage bill earned by the top 0.1% highest-paid employees almost doubled, rising from 1.2% of the wage bill to 2% between 1996 and 2007. CEOs clearly benefited from this increased inequality. Between 1994 and 2007, the salaries of the 100 highest-paid CEOs (excluding shares and stock options) rose from 870,000 euros to 3.2 million. This phenomenon does not only apply to CEOs. At lower levels of the hierarchy within major banks, high salaries have increased even more substantially. At BNP-Paribas, for example, the top 1% of employees received 12.5% of the wage bill in 2008, but only 6.3% in 2000.

In just nine years, inequality within this particular bank rose to a level that the entire American labour society took 20 years to reach.[3]

Although the phenomenon exists on a smaller scale than in the United States and the United Kingdom, these various factors show that in France, and more broadly in continental Europe, the highest wages are inflating and income inequality has made a sudden return.

Technological change and executive power?

The return of wage inequality has not gone unnoticed. It has given rise to multiple studies, particularly in economics, which have taken two main directions: on the one hand, a set of macroeconomic studies on the existence of skill-biased technological change; on the other hand, more limited studies focusing solely on executive pay.

From the first perspective, the shift from a Taylorist industrial society to a post-Taylorist services society brought about profound changes to labour demand and, as a result, to the pay differential between skilled and unskilled workers. Whereas the old Taylorist mode of production favoured the division and simplification of tasks, restricted design operations to a small group of individuals and maintained a steady demand for unskilled labour, the new mode of production – based on innovation, product differentiation, new technologies and maintaining commercial relations – increased the demand for skilled labour at a level that exceeded the production capacity of the education system (Katz and Murphy 1992). Added to this biased technological progress were the effects of lower transport costs, outsourcing and new competition from an unskilled labour force in countries with very different pay levels. This approach may help to explain the relative drop in unskilled labour costs in developed countries and/or the rise in unemployment in this category; however, it fails to account for the fact that the upper end of the pay scale moved further away. The observable differences in skill level between the top 1% (F99–100) and the group lying a little below (F90–95) do not appear sufficiently significant to explain this pay gap.

The increase in executive pay, particularly in the United States, is one aspect of the rise in inequality at the top of the wage hierarchy that has been analysed in the greatest detail. Across the Atlantic, CEO pay in listed companies has long been published in their annual reports to shareholders, which makes it possible to take stock of long-term developments. The top 100 CEOs earned an average of 60 million dollars in 2006 (fixed salary, bonuses, allocated shares and exercised stock options) as opposed to 1.7 million dollars in 1970 (in 2005-constant dollars), which is equivalent to an annual growth rate of 12% (Piketty and Saez 2003).[4] Free-market proponents put forward several arguments to account for the executive pay boom. In an unstable, ever-changing environment, shareholders need to recruit highly talented business leaders to manage their companies, individuals who show great composure and an ability to make complex, high-risk decisions on the spot. The shareholders of different groups fight over these very rare individuals, which drives up their salary. The form of pay (made up of bonuses and stock options) is designed in the best possible way so as to strike a balance between the interests of shareholders and those of the CEO (Jensen and Meckling 1976). Moreover, according to Xavier Gabaix and Augustin Landier (2008), a simple market mechanism is enough to bring about considerable pay differentials, without invoking the exceptional talent hypothesis. All that is needed is for the largest firms to compete for the best CEOs. Slightly higher productivity among CEOs is magnified by the size of the firms that employ them, leading to payment of high salaries to the CEOs of the largest firms. However, the excesses of the 1990s and the successive setbacks to the post-2002 and 2008 economic downturn caused even the staunchest free-market proponents to have their doubts.[5] Many studies have shown that, on the contrary, shareholders have little control over their CEOs, who in fact have plenty of leeway to set their own salaries (Bebchuk, Fried and David 2002).

Two categories have therefore captured the attention of economic theorists: the macro-category of skilled workers and the micro-category of CEOs. The working rich have emerged as an intermediate category that is both narrower than the first group and broader than the second. The payment of very high salaries to those employees who are specifically *not* CEOs is striking. While even economists who are the most favourable to free-markets concede that CEOs who hold their shareholders captive succeed in accumulating unwarranted earnings, they maintain that subordinate employees are kept in line by the CEO, who has an interest in paying them market-level compensation that both protects from risk and encourages productivity. Analysing salaries based on external global standard variables involves focusing on the market-based, individualistic explanation with regard to talent. To be sure, the working rich are usually more highly educated than other employees. But is this sufficient to explain the scale of the phenomenon? Should we not question the collective exchanges that underpin the accumulation of individual skills within a firm? If we are to understand the salary levels of the working rich, we must look beyond the standard variables of wage equations (age, seniority, education, status) and go inside the firm in order to analyse the specific exchange relations that form between employees and understand how their value is constructed and imposed in these professional exchanges.

The working rich of finance

The financial markets are a sector in which the emergence of very high salaries has taken place under the watchful eye of the media and public. In the mid-1980s, a new character – the "golden boy" – was presented to the public through newspaper articles, documentaries, essays, films and novels. The media, showing a combination of envy, revulsion and fascination, focused primarily on the pay levels of these young people and the effects of their sudden exposure to wealth. On the one hand, the golden boy (a male) was intriguing. He earned a lot of money. People envied him and wanted to know his secrets. On the other hand, his financial standing gave him a level of power that he was unable to wield.

He was nothing but a *nouveau riche*. If he was from a working-class background, he was most likely vulgar and flashy, frittering away his cash to acquire the most conspicuous symbols of his new social status – and therefore the least credible to those with old money.

Oliver Stone's film *Wall Street* (1987), along with the novels *The Bonfire of the Vanities* (Wolfe 1987) and *American Psycho* (Ellis 1991), focus on the way in which monetary wealth gives men new-found power over the things that can or must be acquired: suits, paintings, apartments, women. Wolfe and Ellis provide few details of the financial operations engaged in by their characters or the effects of these. In the work of both writers, the heroes perform non-stop mental accounting of their environment and have a heightened awareness of possessions and their brands, market value, place of purchase, whether or not they are in line with the latest fashions and so on, as if the characters were continually exploring the omnipotence of money and its limits: "I go into the bedroom and take off what I was wearing today: a herringbone wool suit with pleated trousers by Giorgio Correggiari, a cotton oxford shirt by Ralph Lauren, a knit tie from Paul Stuart and suede shoes from Cole-Haan. I slip on a pair of sixty-dollar boxer shorts I bought at Barney's . . . " (Ellis 1991, p. 72) Tom Wolfe's hero frequently becomes absorbed in calculations of his future income, fretting and reassuring himself over the very fantasy of his profession.

> If you weren't making $250,000 a year within five years, then you were either grossly stupid or grossly lazy. That was the word. By age thirty, $500,000 – and that sum had the taint of the mediocre. By age forty you were either making a million a year or you were timid and incompetent. *Make it now!* . . . Boys on Wall Street, mere boys, with smooth jawlines and clean arteries, boys still able to blush, were buying three-million-dollar apartments on Park and Fifth. (Why wait?)
>
> (Wolfe 1987, p. 58)

In 1985, with a salary of 980,000 dollars, the 38-year-old hero, a Yale graduate, flirts at last with the dream figure of 1 million dollars and feels himself becoming one of the rare members of the "masters of the universe", a cast of 300 to 500 people on Wall Street.

After the eclipse that resulted from the stock market troubles of the late 1980s and early 1990s (1987 crash, the Gulf War, housing market crash), the public figure of the golden boy made a return in the mid-1990s, this time in a less flashy and more civilised fashion, less *nouveau riche* and with more sophistication. In Denys Arcand's film *The Barbarian Invasions* (2003), Sebastian is a maths graduate and the son of a history professor. As a trader or financial engineer (the film does not specify) in the field of swaps and derivatives on petroleum products, he is able to use his high salary ("Money's no problem") to arrange a refined and peaceful death for his father, who has terminal cancer.

Money can be surprising! Naturally, the spending of it provides narrative material, both real and unreal, for novelists and film directors. The origin of that opulence, however, is somewhat less novelistic but no less astounding. For a long time, economic studies on finance (and to a lesser degree sociological studies[6]) have shown little interest in the issue of compensation, and have priority to the question of rationality and the efficiency of these new financial intermediaries. However, when one reads the accounts given by operators and former financial operators such as Michael Lewis (1989 and 1991), Manuel Rozan (1999), Nassim Taleb (2001) and even Nick Leeson (1996), it is clear that the question of pay is of vital importance in the financial industry. Bonuses, and more generally compensation, appear in those accounts to be the sun around which the financial world revolves. These operators and former operators devote almost as many pages to discussing bonuses, salary relations and the rhythm of the job market as they do to exposing the inner workings of the securities market.

The finance sector is exemplary. It may be a small sector in France, but its members are firmly established among the richest strata of employees.[7] By its extreme nature, finance is an excellent laboratory in which to dissect the explosion in high salaries and working rich. Describing the high salary levels in finance and dwelling on their psychological and social effects is one thing. Analysing their origin is quite another. One reason for taking on this task is not only to study the way in which the spoils are shared out on the little desert island of the financial markets. It is also to bring to light the wage formation mechanisms that are in place in other sectors and configurations, but which often function in a more diffuse and attenuated way. An analysis of finance thus provides an insight into the reshaping of inequality in post-Fordist societies. The capital–labour relationship has lost some of its importance on account of the increased fragmentation of wage labour and the rise in power of the wage elite, who are sometimes referred to by the hagiographic terms "creative class" and "manipulators of symbols" (Reich 1991; Florida 2002).

Avoiding simple ideas, entering the bank

The mere mention of particularly high bonuses – 5, 10 or 20 million euros – is enough to leave anyone unfamiliar with finance wages speechless.

Why are some people paid so much? A series of simple, incontrovertible answers can quickly be asserted to put an end to the scandal surrounding such excess. These good reasons make reference to relative scarcity market mechanisms, considerations in terms of human capital, differences in compensation or incentive. a) It is the game of supply and demand. b) They are very "good". c) They work extremely hard. d) It motivates them to earn more money for the company. These ready-made responses in turn give rise to a number of questions. a) Why, in the finance industry, have wages remained so high in comparison with other sectors? b) What are these people so "good" at? Are they better than aeronautical or nuclear engineers? What are their skills? Why are skills worth more in finance than elsewhere? c) Do they really work more than professionals in the industry[8] (for example, 20 times more)? d) Why do people need such strong incentives in finance? Why do incentives cost so much? Are workers in gold or diamond mines offered comparable incentives?

We should therefore be wary of "simple ideas" (Lordon 2000). Each one can be countered with the question: why in finance but not elsewhere? And, within finance, why some people but not others?[9]

Not only do investment bankers earn high wages, they also seem particularly mobile. They go from bank to bank. They spend three years here, six months there, a year somewhere else, forever on the lookout for a better offer. They appear to dictate their conditions to companies. This leads to a new series of questions. How does this labour market function? Are we looking at a market that is close to the ideal? What is exchanged on this market? Why does the system seem so favourable towards its employees?

High wages and a high level of mobility – this all seems very "market-orientated". Supply, demand and an equilibrium. We must not get ahead of ourselves, however. Financiers do not go out into a market place where the finance work is done by open outcry; rather, they carry out a series of bilateral negotiations – negotiations between the employee and the headhunter, negotiations between the employee and the company seeking staff, which itself is not a collective abstraction but is represented by a line manager, also an employee, who recruits a subordinate. Not everything is predefined before the negotiation process begins. There is an art involved, and actors need to know how to play their cards right.

That is not all. Compensation is not only determined by outside options on an over-the-counter market, which opens when the company doors close. It also depends on internal relations within the company: relationships between employees; relationships between line managers and subordinates, because the former evaluate the latter and the latter judge the way in which they are being judged; relationships between subordinates themselves, because it is by talking, comparing each other and acknowledging – or not – the fate that awaits them that they form and strengthen their notions of justice, which, if violated, may be a decisive factor in their having recourse to the external market.

Furthermore, wages are not only decided at specific moments set aside for their negotiation, such as performance evaluations or the awarding of annual bonuses and wage increases; rather, they are an issue throughout the year. In companies where very high variable wages depend, albeit indirectly, on financial results within internal departments, all decisions regarding organisation, division of labour, task assignment (portfolio allocation, etc.) and accounting have *ipso facto* an effect on wages. The massive and extraordinary case of fraud involving the rogue trader Nick Leeson, who drove Barings Bank to bankruptcy after initially attempting to cover up a trading error and thereby protect his bonuses and those of his team, provides an example of a situational reversal: here, paid wages did not serve the proper functioning of the financial firm; rather, it was the functioning of the financial firm that came to depend on the wage-payment mode. In order to understand wages, therefore, one must also open the business organisation's black box and analyse the "wage-labour nexus" on a micro level (Boyer 1990).

Wages are not merely a price. They are also an operation in which wealth is redistributed and shared out.[10] This division of wealth is not simply a sharing of the value added among an abstract collective of shareholders and employees, but also – particularly in finance – a sharing of the wage bill among employees by employees. To understand this division, we must of course look at external anchors, but also plunge back into the interpersonal relations between employees and discover what makes that division possible and tenable.

From haves to power

Let us consider, as an entry point, the wage gap between, on the one hand, engineers who graduate from top universities that lean towards finance, and on the other hand, those who work in another economic sector; also, within the first group, the disparity between those with front office positions such as traders and sales people, and those with other types of jobs (risk control, back office positions, even financial engineering). How can one explain the fact that "minimal differences in talent" result in major disparities in income (Menger 2002, p. 45)? Menger's comparison for the world of entertainment between the artist and the capitalist entrepreneur is instructive: an artistic career provides the support needed for artists to carry out a capitalist-style accumulation of wealth that is the origin of considerable inequalities.[11]

Attributing wage disparity to a process of accumulation makes it possible to avoid implausible essentialist explanations that are difficult to refute, based on talent and the innate ability to generate large sums of money on the markets – which can only be revealed (both to the individual and to the employer) by entering the financial industry.[12] Merely by emphasising the way in which the financial operator's trade is learned by experienced senior employees, market observers are able to counter this notion of talent (Lewis 1989, pp. 204–217; Schwager 1992, pp. 137–148).

Perceiving the professional career as a process of accumulation allows us to emphasise the fact that financial operators appropriate goods, which for the most part they have not bought and from which they yield a profit. Traditionally, this was knowledge and expertise, but also many other elements, as I will show, such as securities and client portfolios, etc. The origins of the division of the fruits of labour among employees during the annual bonus distribution lies in another more sustained, imperceptible and diffuse division of activity.

To understand this division, I shift from a traditional notion of property rights as an absolute, real right towards a more medieval and more English notion of property as a personal, limited right – the right of use of goods granted to an individual by the other community members; in doing so, I characterise this division as an allocation and/or an enshrining of rights over the company's assets: by sharing work, portfolios, clients, and machines between themselves, employees claim rights of use over material or immaterial assets, rights that may not be guaranteed by law but which are nonetheless relatively long-term, exclusive and monitored. The key to understanding the division of the fruits of labour may be understanding this sharing of rights.

There are two advantages to this point of departure. First, it provides an understanding of the basis for the legitimacy of the share-out. If a balance can be established between profit and a particular type of asset over which a category of employees is granted right of use, then those workers will benefit from a relatively stable and solid base from which to demand all or part of the profits and criticise any allocation that fails to respect the division of assets. Second, it enables an understanding of the recurrent tests of strength that impose a division. Employees to whom the most moveable and removeable assets are allocated can take advantage of this situation in order to successfully threaten to move the assets internally (within the company) or externally (to a competitor).

Basing this analysis on the division of assets thus gives a new perspective on pay inequality. This is no longer the mere fruit of natural disparities in gifts and talents, the consequence of social stratification or of family, economic and cultural heritages that are unequal and the result of differing educational investments. Indeed, they are also caused by the unequal distribution of assets by employees and among employees.

Finally, this standpoint provides clarification of my conception of power relations. The notion that ownership is the origin of power is a traditional and fairly common one. It occurs in Marx (1990), where ownership of productive capital leads to the exploitation of labour, and in Bourdieu (1984), where the ownership of capital (both economic and cultural) within a field is the root cause of domination. Here I will extend this concept beyond the sphere in which it is traditionally formulated in order to define capitalist relations within wage labour, characterise a relationship of exploitation between employees[13] and conceive the accumulation of capital (to be defined) by employees over the course of their professional career.

This extension also functions as a shift away from these traditional approaches. First of all, the shortened concepts of "capital" and "capitalisation" do not provide a satisfactory description of the way in which employees acquire assets throughout their professional career, in so far as the routine use of these terms tends to diminish the acts of exploration, devolution, selling, negotiation, conquest and recognition that specifically enable employees to extend themselves within their working environment. Similarly, the phenomena of domination are too easily taken for granted by these approaches. They offer little in the way of answers to free-market criticisms of domination theories. Such criticisms reject the notion that domination can result from a contract – particularly an employment contract – that has been freely entered into by both parties. These criticisms thus invite me to provide a more rigorous definition of the conditions under which ownership of an asset can transform into power, in other words, actually forcing others to act in favour of the owner's interests.

Empirical materials

In order to develop this abstract approach, I carried out empirical studies between 1997 and 2015 (see boxed text) during which all methods available in social sciences were used to explore a subject that is sensitive, taboo and often difficult to access: interviews, observations, questionnaires, databases, documentary sources, archives, etc. Its exploration demanded an extended investigation and, in order for this to be validated, it was necessary to track down all corroborative elements of varying status, ranging from specific anecdotes – difficult to verify second-hand but often highly evocative – to statistical correlations that were more scientifically correct but often lacking in informative content, as well as detailed interviews and observations focusing on a few cases or individuals. It would be absurd to try to establish a hierarchy for these different sources of knowledge. They all helped to paint a general picture. Becoming immersed in the world of finance is by no means easy. It is a complex, often esoteric environment on account of its sophisticated division of labour, abstruse financial products, and advanced accounting and management systems.

The study was only made possible because certain interviewees – some of whom were earning low salaries in low-ranking positions while others earned very high incomes from management roles – agreed to talk about their salaries, work and companies. They took the risk of opening up and discussing a highly sensitive subject, and I am truly grateful to them. I had to preserve their anonymity as rigorously as possible. In order to limit cross-referencing, I did not even give fictional names to the interviewees and I generally only refer to their profession and bank. When the data referred to was not public, I named the financial institutions after stars: names of planets and moons from the solar system were used for French banks and the names of more distant stars for Anglo-American institutions. In some cases, the same bank may be referred to under several different names in order to prevent it from being identified too easily.

The book begins with a first descriptive part in which I provide a number of elements against which bonuses can be measured, and I give a detailed account of their specific distribution procedure. Part II continues with an analysis of the property rights implicit within the organisation and on which the distribution of bonuses is based. In Part III I finish with an analysis of the functioning of the labour market in which some actors acquire the power to hold up their company.

The study

This book is based on research conducted between 1997 and 2015.

It draws on the information gathered for a study carried out in 1997 and 1998 as part of a Master's degree (Godechot 1998), which was later used for the publication of *Traders* (Godechot 2001). The study comprised:

- Four months of participant observation in the equity derivatives trading room of a major French bank referred to at the time as "Universal Company", during an internship as assistant trader (developing programming routines for traders and middle office staff on the securities lending and borrowing desk).

- Around ten interviews with financial operators from other banks.
- A questionnaire survey in the trading room, focusing on market behaviour and symbolic hierarchies in the room (95 respondents).

The qualitative fieldwork that fuels the core of the book was conducted for my PhD between 2000 and 2002 (Godechot 2004). It was constituted of the following elements:

- Three and a half months of participant observation in the human resources department of a large French bank, Saturn Bank, as part of an internship focusing on bonus budgeting specifications for banking market support functions.
- Around 70 interviews with a variety of actors (traders, sales people, financial engineers, directors-general, accountants, back office staff, trade unionists, human resources professionals, consultants, headhunters, etc.) in the financial industry, of which 50 were recorded and transcribed. Approximately ten of these interviews took place in the City of London.
- A questionnaire survey at Neptune Bank (80 respondents) on the subjective perception of bonuses.
- Consultation of the salary files at Jupiter Bank (Godechot 2011a).

It was completed with the following materials throughout the period:

- Consultation of the social reports of major French banks.
- The systematic gathering of articles from the French and Anglo-American press on the subject of bonuses.
- Consultation of the financial reports of major banks.
- Gathering and consultation of personal accounts published by actors in the financial world, including those of Lewis, Rozan, etc.

After my PhD and the publication in French of the first version of this book (Godechot 2007), I tested some of the causal mechanism essentially through a quantitative approach. To that aim, I conducted the following studies that enable to substantially update the current version of this book:

- A questionnaire survey launched in 2008 with efinancialcareers.fr, a financial website, on networks and turnover among French financiers (Godechot 2014b).
- A study of France exhaustive pay files in order to measure finance's contribution to inequality (Godechot 2011b, 2012 & 2014a).
- A study of the role of financialisation on inequality in the OECD countries (Godechot 2015).

Notes

1 In other words, the top 1% of the highest-paid employees earned 5.1 times the average salary in 1970 and 12.2 times the average salary in 2007.
2 Updated series are available on Saez's webpage: http://eml.berkeley.edu/~saez/, accessed 1 April 2016.
3 Statistics for BNP-Paribas were compiled from social reports. Cf. Chapter 1. The two entities are, of course, of vastly different size (40,000 employees as opposed to 150 million). Inequality on a global level is not increasing at the same pace as within individual firms and sectors.
4 A large part of this increase stems from the allocation and exercise of stock options. If we look at "cash" alone – 1,416,000 dollars in 1970 as opposed to 5,297,000 dollars in 1999 – the increase remains stable at 4.4% throughout the period. If we expand this to *Forbes 800* CEOs, their "cash" compensation increased from 25 times the production worker's wage to 90 times it in the same period (Murphy and Zábojník 2004, p. 192).
5 Murphy and Zábojník accept that CEOs may try to extract rents but continue to support the validity of the market theory to explain the long-term changes to CEO pay (Murphy and Zábojník 2004). The Gabaix and Landier model has been widely criticised, particularly for not being consistent with the data (Frydman and Saks 2010).
6 Many books in the area of social studies of finance deal with the question of compensation, grasping the importance of what is at stake and providing new insight into the issue. However, compensation is often merely one element among many in a much broader picture of finance work (Godechot 2001), the finance community (Zaloom 2006), the downsizing of capitalism (Ho 2009) and even financial confidence (Abolafia 1996). Roth published a book on gender-based pay inequality on Wall Street (Roth 2006). The mechanisms of gender-based salary discrimination are analysed with greater detail and precision than in my research. On the other hand, Roth focuses less on the functioning of the financial market as a whole.
7 When the socio-professional categories were reformed in France, the National Institute of Statistics and Economic Studies (INSEE) introduced a new profession, "financial market professionals". Based on the *Déclarations Annuelles des Données Sociales* (Panel DADS – French Social Security wage data for the private sector), their number could be estimated at 10,000 in 2007, that is, 0.1% of employees in the private sector. However, they make up 7% of the 1000 highest-paid employees (Godechot 2011b).
8 Throughout the book, when I use the term "professional", I refer to the French notion of *cadres,* a group well rooted in French social history that enjoys a specific status (Boltanski 1987). It is larger than the population who de facto manage. In ISCO-08, it corresponds to the two first groups: 1. Managers, 2. Professionals. In 2014, this group constituted around half of the employed workforce in large French banks.
9 When faced with ready-made, strong reasons that explain and justify working rich wages, we must provide benchmarks in order to assess their significance: employees with the same type of degree and a similar workload. This operation by no means consists of identifying a sectorial essence of finance that would make the sector out to be a highly specific, remote island, but rather, on the contrary, of bringing out a series of clear disparities between working rich and ordinary workers, differences that are obvious here but valid more generally. In my investigation, the comparative approach taken will be applied above all within the world of finance.
10 Avent-Holt and Tomaskovic-Devey (2014) developed a "relational theory of inequality" that is similar to my approach to the labour market.

11 Although Menger reiterates his comparison with the capitalist model, he only rarely explains the strategy of accumulation by artists. He uses the expression "portfolio worker" to refer to the "rationalised management of personal capital" by the working artist (Menger 2002, p. 80) and suggests a possible strategy of the accumulation of reputation capital: a series of happy pairings in collective projects that work (Menger 2002, p. 45). The idea is not developed fully, however, because the explanatory mechanism used centres primarily on the characteristics of a supply that focuses on the particularities of the entertainment world and which causes the artistic labour market to function as a lottery in which the winner takes all.

12 This theory of talent is indeed unscientific. It can be argued that any wage differential is rooted in disparities in innate ability (especially when the differential cannot be explained by education, as is the case here). Much like the invocation of the soporific powers of opium, this is a lazy approach, in part irrefutable and unfalsifiable. Although it is often mobilised if not by neoclassical theory itself then at least by its free-market vulgate as a way of explaining wage disparities, it contradicts the theory of efficient markets. Presupposing the same rationality among all market operators, the neoclassical theory concludes that none of them can beat the market in the long term. Their compensation is therefore either the fruit of chance (a view developed by Taleb (2001)), or the fruit of privileged information, which in both cases leads further away from the ideology of talent. My response to this ideology of talent and the myth of the financial superhero will not be based on its own terms (how can there be an indicator of personal talent?) but rather by constructing a credible alternative.

13 This approach was also strongly influenced by the redefinition of exploitation provided by Boltanski and Chiapello (2006, pp. 373–376).

References

Abolafia, M 1996, *Making Markets. Opportunism and Restraint on Wall Street*, Harvard University Press, Cambridge MA.

Avent-Holt, D and Tomaskovic-Devey, D 2014, 'A Relational Theory of Earnings Inequality', *American Behavioral Scientist*, vol. 58, n°3, pp. 379–399.

Bebchuk, L, Fried, J and David, W 2002, 'Managerial Power and Rent Extraction in the Design of Executive Compensation', *The University of Chicago Law Review*, vol. 69, pp. 751–846.

Bernstein, J and Shapiro, I 2006, 'Nine Years of Neglect', *Center on Budget and Policy Priorities, Economic Policy Institute*.

Boltanski, L 1987, *The Making of a Class: Cadres in French Society*, Cambridge University Press, Cambridge UK.

Boltanski, L and Chiapello, E 2006 *The New Spirit of Capitalism*, Verso, London.

Bourdieu, P 1984, *Distinction: A Social Critique of the Judgement of Taste*, Harvard University Press, Cambridge MA.Boyer, R 1990, *The Regulation School: A Critical Introduction*, Columbia University Press, New York.Charnoz, P, Coudin, E and Gaini, M 2013, 'Une diminution des disparités salariales en France entre 1967 et 2009', in *Emploi et salaires*, Insee Références, Paris, pp. 75–86.

Dolan, K 1998, 'The World's Working Rich', *Forbes*, 6 July, pp. 190–252.

Ellis, BE 1991, *American Psycho*, Vintage, New York.

Florida, R 2002, *The Rise of the Creative Class: And How It's Transforming Work, Leisure, Community and Everyday Life*, Perseus Books Group, New York.

Frydman, C and Saks, R 2010, 'Executive Compensation: A New View from a Long-Term Perspective, 1936–2005', *Review of Financial Studies*, vol. 23, n°5, pp. 2099–2138.

Gabaix, X and Landier, A 2008, 'Why Has CEO Pay Increased So Much?', *Quarterly Journal of Economics*, vol. 123, n°1, 2008, pp. 49–100.

Godechot, O 1998, *Transformation des métiers et des pratiques de la bourse. Les enjeux de la rationalisation*, Social Sciences Master (DEA) dissertation under the supervision of Rémi Lenoir, ENS-EHESS, Paris.

Godechot, O 2001, *Les Traders. Essai de sociologie des marchés financiers*, La Découverte, Paris.

Godechot, O 2004, *L'appropriation du profit. Politiques des bonus dans l'industrie financière*, Doctoral thesis in sociology under the supervision of Michel Lallement, CNAM, Paris.

Godechot, O 2007, *Working Rich. Salaires, bonus et appropriation du profit dans l'industrie financière*, La Découverte, Paris.

Godechot, O 2011a, 'Le capital humain et les incitations sont-ils les deux mamelles des salaires dans la finance ', *Revue d'économie financière*, n°104, pp. 145–164.

Godechot, O 2011b, *Finance and the Rise in Inequalities in France*, Working Paper n°2011-13, Paris School of Economics.

Godechot, O 2012, 'Is Finance Responsible for the Rise in Wage Inequality in France?', *Socio-Economic Review*, vol. 10, n°2, pp. 1–24.

Godechot, O 2014a, 'Financialization and Sociospatial Divides' (Translation of: 'Financiarisation et fractures socio-spatiales', 2013), *L'année sociologique*, vol. 63, n°1, pp. 1750.

Godechot, O 2014b, 'Getting a Job in Finance. The Role of Collaboration Ties', *European Journal of Sociology*, vol. 55, n°1, pp. 25–56.

Godechot, O 2015, *Financialization is Marketization! A Study on the Respective Impact of Various Dimensions of Financialization on the Increase in Global Inequality*, MaxPo Discussion Paper n°15.3.

Ho, K 2009, *Liquidated. An Ethnography of Wall Street*, Duke University Press, Durham NC.

Jensen, M and Meckling, W 1976, 'Theory of the Firm: Managerial Behavior, Agency Costs and Ownership Structure', *Journal of Financial Economics*, vol. 3, n°4, pp. 305–360.

Katz, L and Murphy, K 1992, 'Changes in Relative Wages, 1963–1987: Supply and Demand Factors', *Quarterly Journal of Economics*, vol. 107, n°1, pp. 35–78.

Leeson, N 1996, *Rogue Trader: How I Brought Down Barings Bank and Shook the Financial World*, Little, Brown & Company, London.

Lewis, M 1989, *Liar's Poker*, Hodder and Stoughton, Coronet Books, London.

Lewis, M 1991, *The Money Culture*, WW Norton & Company, New York.

Lordon, F 2000, 'La force des idées simples. Misère épistémique des comportements économiques', *Politix*, vol. 13, n°52, pp. 183–210.

Marx, K 1990, *Capital. A Critique of Political Economy*, Penguin Books, London.

Menger, PM 2002, *Portrait de l'artiste en travailleur*, Seuil, Paris.

Murphy, K and Zábojník, J 2004, 'CEO Pay and Appointments: A Market-Based Explanation for Recent Trends', *American Economic Review, Papers and Proceedings*, vol. 94, n°2, pp. 192–196.

Piketty, T 2014, *Capital in the Twenty-First Century*, Harvard University Press, Cambridge MA.

Piketty, T and Saez, E 2003, 'Income Inequality in the United States, 1913–1998', *Quarterly Journal of Economics*, vol. 118, n°1, pp. 1–39.

Piketty, T and Saez, E 2006, 'The Evolution of Top Incomes: A Historical and International Perspective', *American Economic Review, Papers and Proceedings*, vol. 96, n°2, pp. 200–205.

Reich, R 1991, *The Work of Nations: Preparing Ourselves for 21st Century Capitalism*, Alfred A. Knopf, New York.

Roth, LM 2006, *Selling Women Short. Gender Inequality on Wall Street*, Princeton University Press, Princeton NJ.

Rozan, JM 1999, *Le Fric*, Michel Lafon, Paris.

Schwager, J 1992, *The New Market Wizard*, John Wiley and Sons, New York.

Taleb, N 2001, *Fooled by Randomness. The Hidden Role of Chance in the Markets and in Life*, Texere, New York.

The Barbarian Invasions 2003, film directed by Denys Arcand, Astral Films, Canada and France.

Wall Street 1987, film directed by Olivier Stone, American Entertainment Partners, USA.

Wolfe, T 1987, *The Bonfire of the Vanities*, Farrar, Straus and Giroux, New York.

Zaloom, C 2006, *Out of the Pits: Traders and Technology from Chicago to London*, University of Chicago Press, Chicago IL.

Part I

Bonus practices

1 The size of bonuses

It would be trite to say that wages are high in the financial industry. From the novels of Zola and the escapades of Michael Milken to the tales of the legendary golden boys and the financial articles commenting on the quality of the annual batch of bonuses, all seem to make the same observation: there is a link between financial activity and the flow of high wages. During the subprime crisis, commentators repeated this ad infinitum, seeing it as the root of all the evils that had descended upon the global economy. This truism is often accompanied by a second cliché: wages in the financial industry are mysterious and secret! These two observations do not sit well together. For is it not true that wages in finance are scrutinised more closely than in other sectors? The remuneration consultancy firms organise annual surveys, headhunters compile the results of their activities as intermediaries, banks regularly monitor their compensation levels, financial operators continually discuss their pay and journalists are always after inside information that will help them write their annual article on the unbelievable and enigmatic wages of traders. Just because their pay levels are so high, they are considered mysterious and thus awaken our curiosity.

I shall now make an initial overview of these pay levels. Using the data available in the social reports of French banks, the complete wage data for France as found in administrative sources (Godechot 2012) and the data provided by the Office of the State Controller in the United States, I shall try to reconstruct the major trends in the Paris and Wall Street financial markets. I will then be in a position to analyse the part played by finance in the current rise in inequality. Using private data on pay provided by informants from a major bank, I shall try to uncover late 1990s pay structure (Godechot 2011a). This incursion will provide an opportunity to step inside an investment bank and analyse the division of labour. This limited data will nevertheless allow us to rule out a rather common interpretation of remuneration as a system that provides maximum incentives and enables banks to maximise their profit.

Finance's "working rich"

French banks' highest wages

In the social reports, there are a number of elements that allow us to assess changes to wages within large banks. The law passed in France on 12 July 1977 required all firms with more than 300 employees to publish a social report with information on employment, working conditions, training, professional relations and wages. Among the statistical indicators published there is one particularly valuable figure: the sum total of the ten highest wages.[1] Unfortunately the difficulty involved in collecting information – the social reports are not public but reserved for shareholders, social partners, labour inspectors and accounting firms – and in making comparisons – they are written for firms in the strict legal sense and exclude subsidiaries and foreign operations – mean that the studies that draw on this resource are rare (Allouche 1993; Ferrary 2002). I managed to gather the social reports of a few of the largest French financial institutions. I completed these trends with series established thanks to the *Déclarations Annuelles de Données Sociales* (DADS), an exhaustive administrative dataset on individual wages in France (Godechot 2012).[2] This data has been available since 1994 and gives an accurate picture of wage distribution.

Figure 1.1 details the ten highest-paid wage earners of France's three largest commercial banks, Société Générale, Banque Nationale de Paris (BNP), Crédit Lyonnais, and of one its famous investment banks, Indosuez as well as the 100 best-paid finance executives in France.

Figure 1.1 shows some particularly striking changes. At the start of the period, all three banks paid remarkably similar wages to the ten highest-paid employees: an average salary of around 280,000 euros between 1978 and 1982.

Whereas the ten highest wages of Crédit Lyonnais and BNP fell slightly between 1978 and 1988, Société Générale distanced itself from its competitors in 1983 and began a regular wage increase of 8% p.a. until 1993. After rising sharply in 1994 then falling again in 1995, the ten highest wages began to steadily increase once more between 1995 and 2001, at a far more sustained average rate of 40% p.a. The curve representing Société Générale has an exponential shape on a logarithmic scale. In 2001, the ten best-paid wage earners were paid an average of 7 million euros. The economic downturn reduced that amount to 4 million euros in 2002 and 2003. In 2007, the recovery enabled the top ten from Société Générale to beat their 2001 record and earn an average of almost 8 million euros each. The spectacular losses that resulted from the misappropriations of rogue trader Kerviel followed by the subprime crisis, as well as a less sustained financial activity, markedly reduced the wages of the top 10, who nonetheless received an average salary of 2.5 million euros each. In addition, in order to monitor these wages, which were considered by many to encourage excessive risk-taking, the French Government and the European Union asked the banks to allocate part of the wages (between one-third and one-half) as securities or stock options. However, firms were not required to include security-based compensation in the statistics of their social report. It is thus highly likely that the overall compensation of the top ten earners was severely underestimated after 2008.

From 1994 onwards, the wages of the top 10 earners of Société Générale placed them firmly among the 10,000 highest-paid French wage earners. By 1998, these employees belonged to the "two hundred families" described by Piketty,

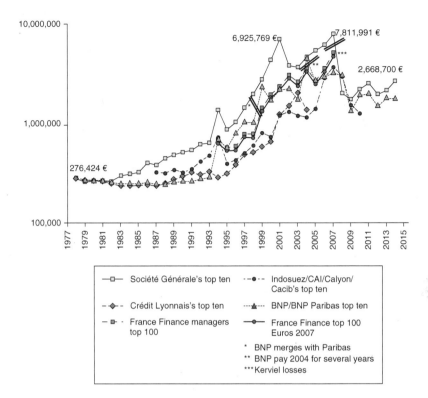

Figure 1.1 Average highest wages from 1978 to 2014 (constant 2014 euros)

Note: The average of the ten highest wages at Société Générale was 276,000 euros in 1978 and 6,926,000 euros in 2001.

the 0.01% of the population at the top of the wage distribution scale who earned an average income (in all forms) of 1.2 million euros (Piketty 2001). In 2001, they were earning close to the wages received by a number of football stars.

Similar changes took place in the other banks, albeit belatedly and less emphatically. Although Indosuez closely followed the curve of Société Générale's top ten, it fell behind in the 1995 economic decline. At BNP, compensation levels did not take off until 1994 and rose more unevenly. At Crédit Lyonnais, the upward trend only became apparent after 1996.[3] Nevertheless, the gap between Société Générale and its competitors narrowed in the 2008 crisis.

The average wage of the 100 highest-paid finance executives in France calculated between 1994 and 2007 using DADS, was confirmation of the progression already established for these four institutions (Godechot 2012). It lies between the curve for Société Générale and that of the other banks. It rises steadily (particularly in the latter half of the 1990s): between 1996 and 2007, the wages of this elite group increased 8.7 times, rising from 580,000 euros to 5 million

euros – a much faster rise than for the top 100 executives in non-financial sectors
(× 3.6), the top 100 CEOs or the top 20 professional athletes (× 3.3).

The first question to be answered is: who are these individuals earning the
highest pay in finance? Are they CEOs or market operators? The social reports
sometimes contain a *nota bene* explaining these developments. In 2002, for example, the social report of Société Générale reads, "the recipients of the 10 highest
wages are essentially market specialists". At the economic peak of 2001, therefore, the CEOs of the bank were probably no longer among its ten highest-paid
wage earners, as I know that they earned 3 million euros and 1.5 million euros
respectively in 2001 – although these figures do not include stock options or
allocated shares (Société Générale 2004, p. 22). Other sources such as press disclosures and information gathered for the survey show that these ten wage earners
mostly include heads of trading room and heads of desk, particularly heads of
equity derivatives trading rooms (Chocron and Pinson 2001).[4]

The second question to be answered is: why is there such a marked difference
between these three large banks, which are of similar size and activity? The press
reported bonuses higher than 10 million euros for 2000, paid in 2001, in each of
these banks (Chocron and Pinson 2001). The difference is rooted in their distinct
histories and legal structures. Société Générale, well ahead of its competitors,
chose to develop its activity internally and in Paris, rather than through subsidiaries or centres abroad. Therefore, most of the bank's heads of trading room
(securities, fixed income, equity derivatives, etc.) are included among its top ten
wage earners. In contrast, BNP and Crédit Lyonnais allowed subsidiaries, brokerage firms and foreign subsidiaries to develop their financial activities. The highest
wages are thus only partly featured in the social reports. The annual accounts of
BNP-Paribas Arbitrage (a subsidiary of BNP with 330 employees), which contain
little detail, give an insight into the scale of this misrepresentation. In 2000, the
gross average salary was 560,000 euros, whereas at the parent company it was
only 63,000 euros according to the same source.[5] The curve of the top ten earners
at Société Générale is therefore particularly illustrative of the effect of the sudden
emergence of these market professionals in the traditional world of banking.

The rise in inequality in the French banking sector

What does this top wages trend allow us to conclude as regards the evolution in
inequality in the French banking industry? The first consequence is that the share
of the overall wage bill allocated to the ten highest wages rose sharply. During the
1980s, at Société Générale the top ten wages were generally eight times higher
than the average wage in corporations. This ratio rose to 13 in 1991, 138 in 2001,
156 in 2007 and dropped back down to 50 in 2014. In a firm employing between
30,000 and 35,000 staff depending on the year, the share of the wage bill allocated
to the top ten rose from 0.2% at the start of the period to almost 4% in 2001 and
2007 and shrank back to 1% in 2014.

Is the rise in inequality resulting from these inflated elite wages limited to
the higher wages of these very specific individuals, or is it merely a symptom

of the changes taking place in wage distribution as a whole? The social reports must contain some indicators of inequality in pay distribution. In 1998, the 10% highest-paid were paid four times more than the 10% lowest-paid at Société Générale, and 3.5 times more at BNP. These ratios increased steadily, reaching 7.3 at Société Générale and 5.4 at BNP in 2013.

I would take this interpretation further: the social reports also contain a distribution of wages in categories (minimum six) freely defined by the firm. Using probability distributions that accurately describe wage distribution, it is possible to identify, from these heterogeneous and unstable groups, stable thresholds enabling a comparison of average salaries by fractile.[6]

Between 1978 and 1987, the share of the top decile of the wage bill fluctuated between 18% and 22% among the three main banks (Figure 1.2). The rate of inequality measured here is therefore similar to that observed among French

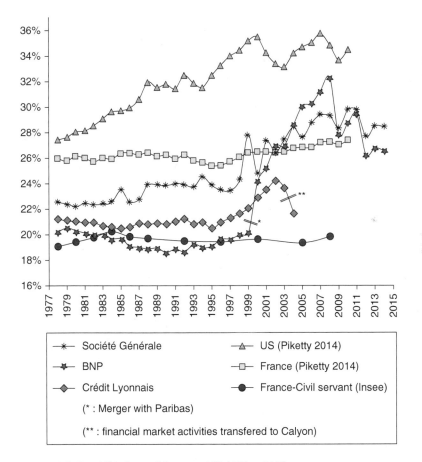

Figure 1.2 Top 10% share of the wage bill 1978 to 2005

Note: In 2008, the top 10% of the best-paid BNP-Paribas' employees earned 32% of the wage bill.

Government officials (INSEE, 1978–2000) and was a great deal lower than for private sector wages as a whole, which remained stable at 26% (Piketty 2001). Société Générale was the first to move away from this model. The inequality ratio of the bank made a two-stage increase between 1987 and 2002: from 22% to 24% between 1989 and 1998, then an uneven increase from 24% to 28% between 1998 and 2008.[7] The rate of inequality at BNP was very similar to that of the civil service until it merged with Paribas, an average-sized investment bank where wages were higher. This rise in inequality was by no means a one-off, and it continued after the shock of the merger subsided. In 2008, the top 10% of wage earners received 32% of the wage bill. Having started out with a particularly low level of inequality, Société Générale and especially BNP exceeded the French average (27%) and seemed to be on their way to matching the level of inequality in the United States (35% in 2008) (Piketty 2014).[8] The subprime financial crisis put a stop to this lopsided dynamic, albeit temporarily.

What can be said of the rise in inequality in finance outside of these two institutions, which are nonetheless highly illustrative? The DADS data once again gives an insight into the way in which the concept of "working together" in the financial sector underwent a major and sudden transformation. In less than ten years French finance saw an increase in inequality (with the top 1% rising from 6% to 12% of the total wage bill) similar in scale to that experienced by the whole of the United States during a period of over 35 years (with the top 1% of wages going from 6% to 12% of the total wage bill between 1965 and 2000 (Piketty and Saez 2003)). Although the two phenomena differ, with a single sector on the one hand and an overall wage-earner society on the other, this comparison at least shows the great speed of the increase in inequality in the French financial sector.

Insights from Wall Street and elsewhere

Is the change observed limited to France? Was France simply catching up with the rest of the field or is this change representative of international developments in the financial sector? After the financial crisis, researchers have taken a keen interest in wages in finance and the development of wage bonuses in the sector (Kaplan and Rauh 2010; Philippon and Reshef 2012; Boustanifar, Grant and Reshef 2014). These studies show a sharp increase in the wage gap between the financial sector and other sectors, even when controlled by the qualification differential, especially in the United States but also Canada, the Netherlands and Germany. However, as they are based on sectorial statistics, they cannot provide an accurate breakdown of the part of the development that is linked to the financial markets and to traditional retail banking activities. In order to provide a context for French statistics, I am therefore proposing to analyse the progression of bonuses in New York based on data compiled by the Office of the State Comptroller.[9] Given the major role played by the financial markets in New York and the dominance of the bonus as a form of compensation in the sector, I believe this will provide an understanding of the changes in finance wages in the United States.

Between 1989 and 2006, the average bonus on Wall Street increased 8.9 times, rising from 25,000 dollars to 225,000 dollars (Figure 1.3). The financial crisis took its toll, as it did in France, with bonuses falling by 50% between 2006 and 2008. Nevertheless, the bonus showed remarkable resilience. By 2014 it had risen back up to an average of 173,000 dollars, which was higher than the record in 2000 and only exceeded by three years (2005, 2006 and 2007) during the period.

The average bonuses, although high, do not make it possible to size correctly the top of the distribution. In the aftermath of the 2008 crisis, the State of New York attorney general Andrew Cuomo (2009) led an investigation into bonus distribution among the nine banks that were the original recipients under the United States Government Troubled Asset Relief Program (TARP) bailout plan (Table 1.1). Although banks were performing poorly in 2008, and some – for example Citigroup, Merrill Lynch and Well Fargo – were facing

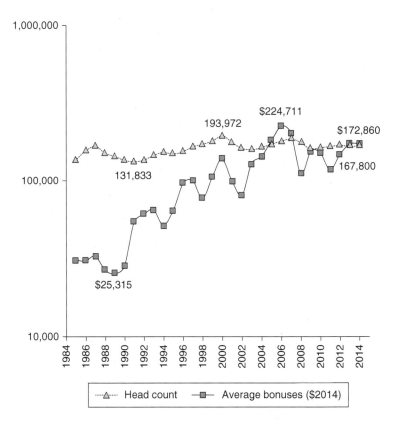

Figure 1.3 Average bonus awarded in New York between 1985 and 2014 and number of staff compensated (constant 2014 dollars)

Note: In 2014, the average bonus granted to Wall Street's 167,800 financial employees amounted to 172,860 dollars.

Table 1.1 2008 bonuses among the nine original TARP recipients

Bank	Net income (M$)	Number of employees	Average bonus ($)	No. > $1M	No. > $3M	No. > $10M	Mean bonus > $10M (M$)	Mean top four bonus (M$)	TARP (M$)
Merrill Lynch	-27,600	59,000	61,017	696	149	14	17.86	30.25	10,000
JP Morgan Chase	5,600	224,961	38,642	1626	>200	10	14.55	18.70	25,000
Morgan Stanley	1,707	46,964	95,286	428	101	10	14.68	18.26	10,000
Goldman Sachs	2,322	30,067	160,408	953	212	6	11.28	11.48	10,000
Bank of America	4,000	243,000	13,580	172	28	4	16.00	16.00	45,000
Citigroup	-27,000	322,800	16,512	738	124	3	11.29	10.92	45,000
State Street Corp	1,811	28,475	16,471	44	3	0	–	4.47	2,000
Wells Fargo & Co.	-42,933	281,000	3,477	62	7	0	–	4.32	25,000
Bank of NY Mellon	1,400	42,900	22,028	74	12	0	–	–	3,000
All nine banks	-80,693	1,279,167	25,495	4793	≈910	47	14.68	14.30	175,000

Source: Cuomo (2009).

Note: In 2008, Merrill Lynch suffered a loss of 27 billion dollars. It had 59,000 employees to whom it paid an average bonus of 61,017 dollars. In that bank, 696 employees earned more than 1 million dollars, with 14 of them earning more than 10 million dollars. These 14 earned on average 18 million dollars and the top four received 30 million dollars. Merrill received 10 billion dollars from the Government as part of the 2008 rescue plan.

significant losses, they continued to grant very substantial bonuses to a fraction of their employees. In those nine banks, 4,800 employees received more than 1 million dollars each, 900 received more than 3 million and 47 received more than 10 million. Although suffering a loss of 27 billion dollars, Merrill Lynch offered on average 30 million to the top four. The head of the bank's compensation committee explained: "Merrill had suffered substantial losses largely related to one unit of the corporation. . . . We had to balance that with the need to pay our employees in units that performed" (Cuomo 2009, p. 3).

These American examples can be compared with remuneration paid in the European Union, also recently monitored by the European Bank Authority (EBA 2015). In a benchmarking survey representing around 60% of European banking system between 2010 and 2013, EBA found around 3,100 to 3,500 financiers earning more than 1 million euros in total remuneration. 60% of this population worked in investment banking, two-thirds were located in the United Kingdom, 17% in Germany and 7% in France. 354 earned more than 3 million euros and nine, all working in the United Kingdom, earned between 10 and 19 million euros.

Bonuses under regulatory pressure in the European Union

With the 2008 financial crisis, many observers blamed bonuses for favouring risk-taking (Rajan 2008; Bebchuk, Cohen and Spamann 2010; Cheng, Hong and Scheinkman 2015). As a result of the bonus outrage, financial regulators prompted new regulations that would both limit the levels of the bonuses, especially in banks bailed out by taxpayers, and diminish the risk-taking dimension. In 2010, France and the United Kingdom experimented with a one-off 50% tax on banking bonuses (Gatinois and Renterghem 2009). The G20 FSB made the following recommendations (FSB 2009): bonuses should be based on risk-adjusted notions of individual, business line and firm performances; 50% should be awarded in shares or share-linked instruments; 40 to 60% should be deferred over a period of at least three years; guaranteed bonuses should be limited to one year for newly hired staff; deferred bonuses should be subject to malus or clawback arrangements in the event of future negative results or misbehaviour. While those principles were very lightly applied in the United States (Ferrarini and Ungureanu 2011; Chon 2014; Biedermann and Orosz 2015), they were strictly implemented in the European Union in 2010 with the CRD III Directive (2010/76/UE).

Moreover, the European Parliament tightened bonus regulation considerably in 2013 with the CRD IV Directive (2013/36/EU). A great novelty in market societies, it imposed a bonus cap! "The variable component shall not exceed 100% of the fixed component." Member states may also allow shareholders to extend this cap to 200%. This bonus cap became mandatory in 2014 even in the United Kingdom, which was at first very reluctant to implement this new directive.

Many believe that this bonus cap is a major shift that will substantially reduce incentives to take risks and wages in the European financial industry. It is still too early to measure its full impact. However, several limitations suggest that the shift is not as radical as first thought.

First, only banks covered by the CRD IV are bound by the bonus caps. Mutual funds and alternative investment funds under Alternative Investment Fund Managers Directive (AIFMD), Undertakings for the Collective Investment of Transferable Securities (UCITMS) or Markets in Financial Instruments Directive (MIFID) regulations or even some small banks do not have to comply with any bonus cap.

Second, banks did not recover pre-crisis profitability in Europe after 2008 and the labour market is now less active than before. Therefore, for the moment applying the new rules is not as constraining as some feared.

Third, in order to conform to the new regulation without diminishing total salaries, European banks substantially increased fixed wages (Murphy 2013). Even before the application of the CRD IV bonus cap, fixed wages were already on the rise. The average fixed wage of the "identified staff", around 30,000 bankers in Europe whose professional activities have a material impact on the institution's risk profile, increased from 132,000 euros in 2010 to 172,000 euros in 2012, while the ratio of variable to fixed remuneration decreased from 208% to 108% (EBA 2015). The application of the bonus cap in 2014 also led to another sharp increase. Fixed wages for these identified staff increased by 73% in Société Générale's market activities, by 52% in BNP's investment bank and by 46% in Barclays.[10] Up to now, therefore, this policy does not seem to have reduced the level of pay in market activities.[11]

Fourth, they tried to circumvent this regulation by inventing a new form of pay: "role-based allowances" paid either every month or every trimester (EBA 2014). Admittedly, the EBA required role-based allowances that are not predetermined (such as those linked to the family situation) to be reclassified as variable pay. However, the national competent authorities still need to implement this additional requirement. This example shows that many banks, especially in the United Kingdom, are willing to explore new payment methods (like some form of flexible fixed salary) in order to continue paying bankers as previously.

For the moment, banks and financiers try to maintain pay levels and structure in line with previous practices. Only time will tell whether or not the regulatory change will finally lead to significant developments.

Finance, the catalyst for the inequality dynamic

The remarkable levels of compensation received by financial workers are not simply an exotic phenomenon, feeding the press's curiosity about the unexpected, blatant and ill-wielded power conferred by sudden access to financial wealth. It is a phenomenon that increases inequality not only within financial firms and the financial sector, as seen previously, but one that also transforms them more broadly within societies as a whole. As shown in the highly detailed studies by Piketty, Atkinson and Saez, inequality – in terms of assets, income or wages – has been on the rise in developed nations for the last 40 years (Piketty and Saez 2003; Atkinson 2008; Piketty 2014; Saez and Zucman 2014). This phenomenon has been particularly visible in the United States and the free-market

"Anglo-American" economies. Meanwhile, European countries seemed to have been spared – at least until recently.

The complete individual wage data contained in the DADS allows us to make a very accurate assessment of the changes in inequality in France and to decompose them in order to measure the part played by finance (Godechot 2012). Contrary to the view put forward by social scientists, who generally consider France to be a good example of stability in inequality during the last 30 years, especially when measured with the D9/D1 ratio, the DADS data shows a sharp surge at the very top of the wage distribution in the mid-1990s. The top 0.1% increased its share of the total wage bill by 0.85 percentage points, moving up from 1.1% in 1996 and 1.95% in 2007. Half of this increase is for the top 0.01%.

In order to decompose this increase, I calculated the evolution of the overall wage share earned by people belonging to France's top 0.1% working in finance, service to business, entertainment and other sectors. I find that finance contributed to 48% of the rise in the share of the top 0.1%, whereas service to business and other sectors each contributed nearly 23%, and entertainment to 8% of the rise (Figure 1.4). When moving into the top 0.01%, I find that finance made a contribution of 57% to the increase in the share of the working rich. The impact of finance on the increase of the top 1% remains high, with a contribution of around 40%.

My figures for France lie in between those calculated by Bakija, Cole and Heim (2012) for the United States and those found by Bell and Van Reenen for the United Kingdom (2013). In all three countries, finance played a major role in the return of wage or income inequality, contributing to one-third (United States), one-half (France) and three-quarters (United Kingdom) of the rise of top wages.

Is this movement specific to these few countries? I can now respond by relating aggregate data on inequality such as the Word Top Income Database and macroeconomic data on financial activity produced by international agencies (Godechot 2015).

This new study focuses on 18 OECD countries for which I have measures of both inequality and financialisation.[12] Thanks to ordinary least squares panel regressions with country and time fixed effects, I can measure the impact of various financialisation measures on various inequality measures, while controlling also for GDP per capita, unionisation and globalisation.

As dependent variables I used the OECD inequality decile ratios D5/D1 (ratio of the median to the upper threshold of the bottom 10%), D9/D1 (ratio of the lower threshold of the top 10% to the upper threshold of the bottom 10%) and D9/D5 (ratio of the lower threshold of the top 10% to the median) and from the World Top Income Database the top 10%, 1%, 0.1% and 0.01% of income shares.[13] The increase in inequality over my sample has been general and obvious since 1980: from 1980 to 2007, the ratio D9/D1 multiplied by 1.1, moving from 2.9 to 3.2, the top 1% income share multiplied by 1.6, moving from 6.5% to 10.2% and that of the top 0.01% multiplied by 2.7, moving from 0.5% to 1.4%.

At first glance, financialisation can be approximated by the share of economic activity (i.e. GDP) achieved in the financial sector (comprising both finance

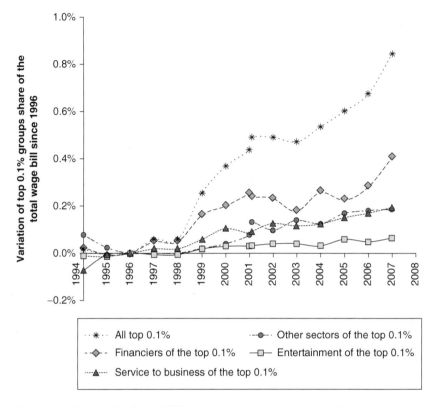

Figure 1.4 The contribution of different sectors to the rise in inequality in France

Note: Between 1996 and 2007, the top 0.1% increased its share of the total wage bill by 0.8 percentage points. During the same period the financiers belonging to the top 0.1% increased their share of the total wage bill by 0.4 percentage points.

and insurance) in industry national accounts gathered and standardised by the OECD. First, the most iconic financial transformations of financialisation (like the financial markets boom) occurred precisely in this sector. Second, most financial transformations taking place outside the financial sector also translate into financial transactions and therefore contribute to the value added of this sector. Financialisation has no effect on the D5/D1 ratio but increases the D9/D5 and D9/D1 ratios. One standard deviation of finance increases by 0.12 standard deviation the top 10% share, by 0.23 the top 1% share, by 0.28 the top 0.1% share and by 0.41 the top 0.01% share. These first results show that the unequal impact of financialisation grows stronger as one moves up the income distribution scale. To put this another way, if one focuses on the 1980–2007 sequence of rising inequality, based on my regressions, I can estimate that one-fifth of the increase of the top 1% share, one-quarter of that of the top 0.1% share and 40% of that of the top 0.01% share result from financialisation (Table 1.2).

Table 1.2 Contribution of financialisation to the 1980–2007 period of increasing inequality in 18 OECD countries

	1980	2007	Evolution	Counterfactual 2007 level in the absence of financialisation	Contribution of financialisation to the increase in inequality
Finance/GDP	4.66	6.59	1.93		
D5/D1	1.65	1.66	–	–	–
D9/D5	1.71	1.89	0.19	1.87	15%
D9/D1	2.83	3.17	0.34	3.10	20%
Top 10% share	28.96	34.48	5.52	33.81	12%
Top 1% share	6.46	10.23	3.77	9.47	20%
Top 0.1% share	1.61	3.62	2.01	3.07	27%
Top 0.01% share	0.50	1.37	0.87	1.01	41%

Note: I use the aforementioned regression parameters to calculate the average evolution of inequality for 18 countries (17 for the top 0.1% and 12 for the top 0.01%) that would have prevailed in the absence of financialisation between 1980 and 2007. Between 1980 and 2007, the top 1% share increased from 6.5% of income to 10.2%, that is, a 3.8 percentage point increase. If finance's share of GDP had remained constant, the counterfactual share of finance would have been 9.5% according to my model. Financialisation therefore accounts for 20% of the evolution of this inequality measure.

When I decompose this financial sector effect, I find that this evolution was mainly driven by the increase in the volume of stocks traded in national stock exchanges and by the volume of shares held as assets in banks' balance sheets. On the other hand, the financialisation of non-financial firms and households does not play a significant role.

Ultimately, the Occupy social movement of 2011 – which condemned inequalities with the slogan "We are the 99%" and occupied sites that symbolised financial power (Zuccotti Park next to Wall Street, Saint Paul's cathedral in London, La Défense in Paris) – was "right" to target finance as the catalyst and main symbol of the contemporary rise in inequality. My analyses clearly show that finance has made a powerful contribution to its recent increase. Finance encourages polarisation both in financial firms and the financial sector as a whole, in global financial cities and between these cities and their hinterlands (Godechot 2014), and in national economies as well as between these economies, and thus constitutes a threat to social cohesion. Of all the risks incurred by the payment of bonuses in finance, the social risk is no doubt the most overlooked but certainly not the least important.

Pay structure at Jupiter Bank

An analysis of the social reports and bonus budgets that are included in the general information provided to shareholders and social partners gives an insight into the scale of compensation. Unfortunately, this data is imprecise. During my fieldwork, some informants granted me access to Jupiter Bank's remuneration files, and I was able to carry out statistical processing and thus measure compensation.

To that end, I merged a set of heterogeneous files that had a range of different purposes in order to obtain the most complete view possible of the wages of capital markets managers. However, precise information was often lacking. The degree studied by professionals was specified in only half of cases. Unfortunately, there is no detailed description of the activity of employees other than a vague job title and position in the organisation chart. Nothing is known of portfolio results (profit and loss or P&L) or of the limits placed on financial operators (objectives, risk limits, types of interventions, etc.).

Despite its shortcomings, this unique dataset provides an interesting picture of the composition of pay in 1998 by department and profession. Before analysing the results, I shall first summarise the activities of its main actors.

An overview of finance work

Let us take a brief look inside a trading room and give an overview of the division of financial labour.[14] Financial institutions generally adopt the same organisation of work. They distinguish between activities involving daily interventions in the financial markets such as trading and brokerage, mergers and acquisitions (M&A – sometimes referred to as corporate finance), and the more traditional activities of business financing. In general terms, all of these activities bring into opposition a much-valued advanced guard, the front office, which makes decisions regarding financial transactions, and a rear guard which assists the front office and is usually referred to as "support functions" or simply as "operations".

The trading room front office professions generally include traders, salespeople and, on the fringes, financial engineers, and research and development (R&D) engineers. Traders are responsible for increasing the value of a securities portfolio allocated to them. This core group is divided into several types of trading professions depending on the type of strategy, product and interaction with other employees. Some traders are responsible for continuously displaying bid and ask prices on particular securities, and they are known as market makers. Others, called arbitragers, use arbitrage opportunities to exploit the price differences between very similar products. Another group is known as "prop traders" (short for proprietary trading, or trading for oneself), who carry out more speculative and independent trades which involve developing one or more generally formalised scenarios for forecasting future prices.

Although it is difficult to make an accurate estimate, it would appear that the most common type of trader is a market maker, if not in the strict sense (registered as such with market institutions, with discounted transaction costs and obligations to display prices) then at least in practice. Market makers are responsible for optimising and implementing arbitrage strategies on securities portfolios that are largely sustained by clients' transactions. In the derivatives market, the profession is increasingly restricted to engineering graduates on account of the complex mathematical relations required to establish the prices of derivative products in relation to the price of simple products. However, the computer and mathematical equipment used is such that in practice they do not need to have a command of sophisticated mathematics. In addition, the mathematical models that link the prices of products in the same family do not always eliminate the more subjective and less formalised forecasting of future price characteristics (Beunza and Stark 2004).[15]

Salespeople, often known simply as "sales", are less renowned than traders, managing client portfolios rather than securities portfolios. They stay in regular contact with their clients to offer them financial products (the pricing and arbitrage of which always falls to the trader). They are generally organised by client type, whereas traders usually specialise by product type. Financial engineers invent new products whose modelling and computerisation are entrusted to R&D engineers. An important component of this activity is financial mathematics (top mathematicians and physicians may be recruited as "quants", who are experts in financial mathematics), but there is also a legal and fiscal element as well as a sales side to the role (products must be adapted to suit clients' needs).

The front office financial operators (i.e. traders and salespeople) could not operate without considerable logistical support, which makes their transactions materially possible. The back office takes care of the confirmation, settlement, delivery, follow-up and accounting of financial transactions. This monitoring process has become increasingly complex: assistant traders, known as the middle office, serve as intermediaries between back office and front office. Over the past few years, risk control, which measures and verifies the risks taken by the front office, has become firmly established (Power 2005). Market IT specialists develop software that gives faster access to electronic stock exchanges and enables the portfolio status to be visualised; market organisation engineers, meanwhile, develop information systems to aid communication between front and back office. The support functions, along with back office and IT services, also include accounting and human resources (HR), which work exclusively in the service of the capital markets bank.

These are some of the chief professions in market finance, particularly finance that focuses on derivative products. Financial analysts may be partly included in this group, but they are usually found working in brokerage firms proposing trades to private investors or firms. Their advice and analysis are sent to clients. They also help salespeople specialising in the sale of cash equities (and more rarely derivatives salespeople) to develop the arguments they will use to persuade customers to enter into transactions (which are subject to brokerage fees). Analysts also intervene to some degree to support the operations of the M&A department. Indeed, they are closer to corporate finance than to trading rooms.[16] In Jupiter Bank's corporate finance department, some employees put together major financial operations for their customers, which are large firms: origination (issuing new securities on the market), and M&A. Although financing activities (traditional financing, export financing, structured financing, issuance of bonds) are usually distinct from M&A, they are similar in the type of work and pace of work involved. In these corporate finance professions, the type and pace of work are different from those encountered in trading rooms: these workers are organised into project teams working on a few major contracts throughout the year, whereas in pure market activities, employees work individually, managing a flow of activity from day to day, week to week and even month to month.

These professions all demand technical and general skills. While some jobs require more skill than others, for example financial engineers compared to back office administrators, and the professionals/technicians ratio is much higher in the front office and in corporate finance compared to support services, the proportion of professionals with a university degree or even graduates from the *Grandes Écoles* is very high in all professions. There are graduates of the elite *École Polytechnique* and the *Écoles Centrales* working as traders, salespersons, financial engineers as well as back office administrators.

A pay hierarchy dominated by traders and salespeople

Table 1.3 shows the pay distribution for a number of professions at Jupiter Bank in 1998. Traders and salespersons dominate the pay hierarchy, earning an average of 376,000 euros and 352,000 euros respectively. They are way ahead of financial engineers (217,000 euros), even though the latter are often more highly qualified. One notch below them, on a salary of around 130,000 euros, we find analysts and some corporate finance specialists. And if we go down even further, at around 80,000 euros, we find financing jobs and most of the support staff: IT, back office and risk control.

Most of the pay differences are a result of the different bonuses paid to the various professions. The average bonus of traders and sales is four times higher than the average fixed income. This ratio falls to 2.5 for financial engineers, 0.8 for analysts and drops steadily in line with the hierarchy of total compensation, reaching 0.34 for risk controllers.

The higher the expectation of a bonus, the higher the standard deviation. The standard deviation is twice the average among traders and salespeople, whereas it is generally equal to the average in the other professions, with the exception of analysts, where it reaches a maximum (2.33). High incomes are thus linked to

Table 1.3 Wages earned by professionals at Jupiter capital markets bank in 1998

	Trader			Salesperson		
Thresholds	*Fixed '98*	*Bonus '98*	*Total '98*	*Fixed '98*	*Bonus '98*	*Total '98*
P25	54,695	28,787	92,502	56,614	33,584	95,323
P50	78,684	67,170	153,530	76,765	76,765	158,328
P75	103,632	291,706	391,500	100,274	230,294	319,534
P90	120,905	777,244	896,230	118,985	849,211	975,873
P95	133,379	1,823,164	1,932,554	130,577	1,477,722	1,602,466
Average	80,562	340,884	421,446	79,765	314,226	393,990
Standard deviation	29,328	766,250	778,149	29,191	685,124	696,367
Number of staff	215	215	215	144	144	144

	Financial engineer and R & D			Financial analyst		
P25	51,817	47,979	99,844	48,971	4,798	59,876
P50	64,290	76,765	163,126	63,697	19,191	95,956
P75	84,441	191,912	305,141	115,147	57,574	172,721
P90	103,632	422,206	506,648	147,773	124,743	268,677
P95	113,229	671,692	736,942	163,164	268,677	422,206
Average	69,141	174,572	243,713	86,462	67,655	154,116
Standard deviation	21,883	243,826	253,163	53,109	158,166	199,834
Number of staff	71	71	71	85	85	85

	Mergers and acquisitions professional			Market IT specialist		
P25	57,574	19,191	76,765	55,655	19,191	74,846
P50	84,441	34,544	130,500	61,412	28,787	88,280
P75	105,552	71,008	168,883	69,088	47,979	115,147
P90	134,492	130,500	264,992	80,603	67,170	142,015
P95	153,607	182,317	345,595	86,361	84,441	159,288
Average	86,429	56,488	142,918	63,577	36,007	99,584
Standard deviation	35,738	57,562	87,363	13,917	31,285	42,823
Number of staff	61	61	61	63	63	63

	Back office administrator			Risk controller		
P25	46,594	6,717	54,145	47,918	5,758	54,006
P50	58,927	11,515	72,279	59,493	7,676	74,846
P75	74,098	28,787	95,956	76,765	19,191	92,410
P90	93,078	61,412	153,530	85,046	38,382	122,824
P95	107,471	105,552	198,629	90,199	57,574	151,611
Average	62,770	26,327	89,097	62,897	21,517	84,416
Standard deviation	21,176	46,497	60,891	19,900	39,058	53,797
Number of staff	82	82	82	41	41	41

Note: 25% of the 212 traders at Jupiter Bank earned fixed wages below 54,695 euros (2014 euros). The upper threshold of the bottom quarter was 28,787 euros for bonuses and 92,502 euros for total compensation. I have eliminated the few rare individuals who had a bonus of zero because I do not know whether they received nothing or their bonus was not recorded. The heads of trading room have been divided into their original fields, trading or sales.

very high levels of inequality among front office employees. Similarly, the ratio between the threshold of the last decile and the median is very high among traders and sales: the P90 threshold earned bonuses 11 times higher than the median, whereas this ratio is only 6.5 for analysts, 5.5 for financial engineers and back office administrator, and around three or four for other professions.

This inequality is partly due to the strongly hierarchical nature of bonuses. By making an imperfect reconstruction of the hierarchy with the aid of an organisation chart, I draw a distinction between the "bottom" level of employees who have no junior staff below them (level zero), their line managers (level one), their managers' managers (level two), and so on. Level zero varies significantly from one department to the next: 358,000 euros for "bottom-level" traders and salespeople in the equities front office; 85,000 for the fixed income front office; 65,000 for analysts; 39,000 for market IT support; and only 6,700 for the back office. On this very uneven playing field, pay scales vary considerably. In finance professions, the level two professions in the hierarchy often earn around eight times that of level zero: this is the case for the fixed income front office (8.47), financing (8.25) and structured products. Analysts, corporate finance and equities front office (if levels two and three are combined) are even less equal: the upper levels earn nine to ten times the base wages. In equities and equity derivatives front offices, the hierarchy is as follows: 360,000 euros for level zero; 1 million for level one (small heads of desk); 2.8 million for level two (large heads of desk, heads of sales and of trading); and 5.1 million for level three (heads of trading room). In the support functions, not only are base bonuses lower but also pay scales are also shorter. The upper level receives 6.9 times the base bonus of the back office, and generally three times the base bonus of other support departments.

An analysis of the statistics for trader and sales bonuses by product and by year enables a better understanding of some of the reasons behind the inequalities described above. Traders and salespeople working on equity products and equity derivatives earn considerably more than their counterparts in charge of fixed income, fixed income derivatives, foreign exchange and commodities. In 1997, the hierarchy appeared as follows: equity traders and their equivalents earned 454,000 euros; equity salespeople and their equivalents earned 314,000; and fixed income traders and salespeople earned 221,000 and 216,000 respectively. A divergent economy widened the gap between the world of fixed income trading and that of equities: 1998 and 1999 were very good years for equities, and the incomes generated by these activities increased substantially, whereas 1998 was a bad year for fixed income trading (Asian crisis) and 1999 was an average year (affected by the rise in interest rates). As a result, the bonuses of fixed income traders and sales staff halved in 1998 then recovered the following year. Even though these employees made a significant loss (in relative terms) on account of Jupiter Bank's poor results in these activities, they remained at the top of the hierarchy and only the financial engineers came close.

Optimal incentives?

The incentive provided by such levels of compensation is one of the arguments used to justify these wages, by finance professionals and economists alike.[17] Ultimately, "if bonuses drive employees to make ten times more money, the firm is happy," some say. Although measuring the effort made by employees is not an exact science, it is nevertheless in the firm's own interests, according to the theory of incentives, to develop an optimal incentives formula that encourages employees to make maximum effort at minimum cost. Offering a combination of a fixed income and a bonus proportional to a performance indicator could be the solution to resolve this "moral hazard" issue (Holmstrom and Milgrom, 1987; Lazear 1995).

Excessively high fixed wages

Seen from afar, financial operators' wage formulas may resemble the theoretical model. Even if individual formulas are rare, some operators claim they can expect a certain percentage (5%, 8%, 10% depending on their profession and product) of the results of their portfolio. These results depend on many different factors such as economic conditions and the product in question, but it is true to say that they are partly the fruit of the employee's effort and commitment: time spent at work, vigilance and monitoring of potentially costly mistakes, careful planning and inventiveness in order to identify profitable transactions, and so on. Financial operators do not work alone, they say. A whole system is required to obtain profitable transactions in conjunction with IT specialists, back office administrators, risk controllers, etc. Why do these employees receive smaller bonuses? Once again, the economic theory of incentives provides answers, along with companies' good economic sense. The closer the correlation between the performance indicator, as well as the financial result, and the employee's effort, the more profitable it is for the firm to use them to vary that employee's compensation (Holmstrom 1979). HR professionals are thus the first to explain that support staff have less responsibility for results than financial operators. What is more, they fulfil roles for which there is usually no other indicator to reflect their commitment level as accurately. It is therefore logical that their bonuses are not linked so closely to an accounting results indicator. Does this assessment help to explain pay structure through the theory of incentives and its framework of maximum effort incentives?

One characteristic of bonuses is that they are always positive or zero.[18] In the event of a loss, employees are guaranteed to at least earn their fixed wages, which cannot be reduced by a negative bonus.[19] This detail is of theoretical significance. It means that, in contrast with the usual case of incentives theory, variable income is not a linear function of the performance indicator. Employees can only gain from obtaining a higher bonus expectation. Their income is less predictable but this inconvenience is more than offset by the added utility conferred by a higher income. Therefore, if we compare two employees with similar training, seniority, technical skill, etc., the one who works in a job where effort is more closely correlated to the performance indicator should, according to the theory of incentives, have both a higher bonus expectation and a lower fixed wage. In other words, the theory of incentives takes greater account of the variability and structure of compensation (the share of fixed income and that of variable income) than of the amount.

So what does Table 1.3 reveal? Employees who receive the highest bonuses do not receive the lowest fixed wages: traders and salespeople earned a fixed income of 80,000 euros, well above that of back office administrators, risk controllers, etc. They are only overtaken by analysts and M&A professionals (86,000 euros). In addition, in the latter two professions the employees were often older, which may explain the pay gap.

Are these initial descriptive results enough to conclude that the high fixed wages of traders and salespeople constitute a serious violation of the theory of incentives? Not entirely. Although there are experienced, well-qualified staff working in all of these professions, there are slightly more *grandes écoles* graduates (*École Polytechnique*, *Écoles Centrales*, *École des Hautes Études Commerciales*) among financial operators than among other groups. In other words, a high fixed income could be seen as a result of superior human capital and not as a violation of the theory of incentives.

In order to prove that the theory of incentives does not provide a satisfactory explanation for pay structure, I shall first show that, all things being equal, the fixed wages of traders and salespeople are higher than the rest. Using the available variables, I made a linear regression. I regressed the fixed wage logarithm on age, gender, seniority, category of collective agreement and degree type. I then analysed the structure of the residuals by profession.

All things being equal (within the limits of the available control variables), traders and salespeople earn the highest incomes of all managerial staff in an investment banks. Those of equivalent age, degree and seniority earn 20% more than the other investment bank professionals and 7–8% more than analysts and M&A professionals. This difference does not apply to just a few. The different distribution thresholds of fixed wages in these two professions are almost always higher than those of their colleagues.

The fact that, all things being equal, the professions benefiting from the highest bonus expectation are also those in which employees earn the highest wages casts serious doubt over the optimality of the wage formation system. It is not so much the fact that these compensations are not incentivising but rather that these incentives are too costly. In this kind of situation, the theory of incentives projects models that are equally incentivising but less costly, for example with more malus clauses and fewer bonuses. Traders and salespeople have the good fortune to be given strong incentives without having to pay anything in return. They neither rent nor buy their raffle ticket, that is, the position offered to them.

Wages too closely tied to the observable economic situation

It is common to hear employees themselves say that compensation is paid in line with the global economic situation. The 1998 Asian crisis, for instance, caused Société Générale to suffer major losses and resulted in noticeably smaller bonuses for both traders and salespeople working in fixed income. Similarly, the 1999–2000 boom and the 2001–2002 dip in the equities markets led to a global rise then fall in the bonuses awarded to employees responsible for these products. However, this correlation between elements of an exogenous observable economic situation runs contrary to certain projections of the theory of incentives.

The effort made by employees is generally difficult to measure accurately and it is both difficult and of little use to specify it in employment contracts. In order to maximise it, the economic theory of incentives shows that compensation must be indexed to a results indicator that is as close as possible to employee effort (Holmstrom 1979).[20] If compensation is indexed to a results indicator that is loosely linked to employee effort and has a high level of randomness, then a less incentivising compensatory structure is obtained: employees who are less certain of the result of their effort are less incentivised, the incentives are more costly for the firm, which must pay for its employees' risk aversion, and the rate at which compensation is indexed to the results indicator is lower. An entrepreneur has every interest in using any information available in order to deduce from the results indicator those hazards that are not linked to variations in employee effort. For example, if employees know that the results of their activity are highly dependent on an exogenous, measurable economic variable, such as the volume of transactions on the derivatives market, an entrepreneur can offer a compensation framework in which, using an identical results indicator, bonuses are smaller when the volume rises and larger when the volume drops. In that scenario, compensation depends more closely on employee effort and skill. The entrepreneur would be compensating an employee's own contribution rather than the economic situation.

The interest of the notion of observability lies in the fact that it allows us to test the question of the optimality of compensation agreements. Marianne Bertrand and Sendhil Mullainathan have shown that executive pay is usually correlated to economic indicators that are unrelated to their own contributions, such as the price of oil for oil companies or, more broadly, average sectorial results or industry exchange rate fluctuations (Bertrand and Mullainathan 2001). This means that boards of directors do not use all the information available when setting the compensation levels of CEOs in American firms. They are paid more on the basis of luck than their own contribution.

What about the situation in finance? I shall analyse the correlation since 1988 between the curves of the top ten at Société Générale and the top 100 finance professionals in France, which tend to be representative of the wages and bonuses of the main heads of desk and heads of trading room during this period, and financial indicators for price levels and transaction volumes (Figure 1.5).

There is a strong correlation between the wages of the financial elite and the representative market index, but the correlation with transaction volume is even more marked. French finance, which specialised in intermediation through developing and selling derivative products, was particularly sensitive to volumes of activity. During the period 1994–2007, therefore, when the transaction volume increased by 1%, the wages of the French financial elite increased by the same rate. From 1996 to 2000, the continued rise of the top ten wages at Société Générale strictly followed the rise in transaction volume on equities products, and it is highly likely that these elites included the majority of heads of equity activities. Finally, the downturn of 2001 and 2002, followed by the recovery of 2003 and 2004, was due to the economic turnaround in the equities market. At Société

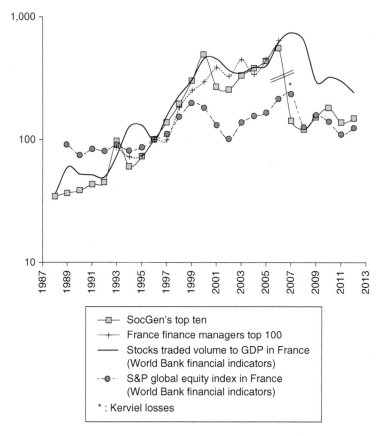

Figure 1.5 Comparison of the evolution of Société Générale's top ten, the top 100 finance
professionals in France and indicators of stock market activity in France

Note: In Figure 1.5, the curves of Société Générale's top ten and the top 100 finance professionals in
France are moved back by one year to reflect the year on which the bonuses were paid rather than the
year of payment. All the curves are set at 100 in 1996.

Générale, the year 2008 (paid for 2007 results) should have been a record year
both in terms of results and compensation had it not suffered the surprise discovery in January 2008 of Jérôme Kerviel's massive fraud. The drop in transaction
volume then brought down the amounts allocated for the bonuses of Société
Générale's elite.

  With the very imprecise data I have available, my statistical demonstration
cannot be as rigorous as it was in the previous section. Nevertheless, both the
convergence of the compensation curves with those of financial indices and
the numerous accounts given by actors (which call to mind the notion "in the
right place at the right time") suggest that the link between compensation and
transaction volume is proven. Furthermore, recent studies show that transaction

volume is a good indicator of financialisation and is particularly correlated with the rise in inequality (Kus 2013; Dünhaupt 2014; Godechot, 2015). This means that compensation schemes are not conceived in such a way that employee performance is maximised at minimum cost. Financial workers are compensated not so much for their efforts and talents as for their good fortune to be engaged in an activity that is enjoying rapid growth, for which they are in no way responsible.

***

This initial overview does not provide a full understanding of compensation in the financial industry, but it does allow us to take stock of the situation. Compensation is very high, certainly; it is increasing and has made a significant contribution to the contemporary spiral of inequality. This first glance also enables me to rule out simple explanations. These exceptional levels of compensation are not merely a question of optimal performance incentives. The fixed part is too high and the variable part is correlated too closely with the observable economic conditions to be able to equate these compensation schemes with the optimised piecework wages of the manufacturing industry. This overview suggests that I am dealing with what economists refer to as "rents", that is, the portion of earnings in excess of the minimum amount needed to attract a worker to accept a particular job or a firm to enter a particular industry (Milgrom and Roberts 1992, p. 269).[21] Financial operators generally receive compensation that is far higher that what they would expect in another job (back office, retail banking) and higher than what seems strictly necessary to incentivise their performance. This observation therefore leads me to step inside a financial firm in order to understand the process that leads to such distribution.

Notes

1 The definition of "salary" for both social reports and DADS includes fixed wages, bonuses and benefits in kind, but excludes stock options, incentives and profit-sharing.

2 Access to the data was obtained through the Secure Access Data Centre (CASD) dedicated to researchers and authorised by the French *Comité du secret statistique*.

3 The social reports of Crédit Lyonnais are only available up to 2003, when the bank was bought by Crédit Agricole and incorporated into it. The financial activities of Crédit Lyonnais merged with those of Crédit Agricole Indosuez, forming Calyon (then CACIB).

4 Derivatives are second-class financial securities. They are generally standardised contracts that define the terms of delivery of classic first-rate securities, such as stocks, currencies or bonds, at future dates and at a price agreed in advance. There are two major categories of products: options – derivatives whose delivery is subject to the completion of a clause in the contract (usually the crossing of a current price level) – and futures – derivatives whose future delivery is not conditional.

5 Source: *Bulletin des annonces légales et officielles*, http://balo.journal-officiel.gouv. fr/, accessed 1 April 2004. The markedly different averages found in the social reports are due to different boundaries. The social reports only include employees working in France.

6 The bottom of the distribution curve (0–90%) is well modelled by a lognormal distribution function, and the top (10% highest-paid) by a Pareto distribution function (Piketty 2001). Empirical distribution thresholds included in the social reports could be used to calculate the parameters of the distribution functions.

7 The uneven rise is no doubt due to the lack of detail (for high incomes) published by Société Générale with regard to distribution. By combining wage distribution and the ratio between the average wages of the top and bottom deciles, I obtain a rather different picture: an increase that is both more regular and more marked (the share of the top decile reached 30% in 2005).

8 Some of these figures can be found in the electronic appendices of Piketty's book.

9 Every year, the State of New York publishes the following reports:
   Cf. http://www.osc.state.ny.us/press/releases/feb10/bonus_chart_2009.pdf, and http://www.osc.state.ny.us/press/releases/mar15/nyc_security_avg.pdf, both accessed 1 April 2016.

10 These figures are estimated thanks to mandatory *Pillar 3 Disclosure Reports* that are downloadable on the respective websites of these three banks. CRD IV defines in 2014 a larger perimeter for the staff identified as "Material Risk Takers" than CRD III, adding all staff paid more than 500,000 euros in total pay, all staff in the top 0.3% and all staff with a remuneration greater than that of the lowest senior management. I therefore probably underestimate the true increase in fixed wages.

11 Although I find a 13–14% reduction of total pay among the "Material Risk Takers" staff of Société Générale and BNP-Paribas, this evolution is not reliable as the perimeter of this staff changed, increasing the monitored population of these banks by 40%.

12 I used the following countries: Australia, Canada, Denmark, Finland, France, Germany, Ireland, Italy, Japan, the Netherlands, New Zealand, Norway, Portugal, Spain, Sweden, Switzerland, the United Kingdom, and the United States. The top 0.1% share is not defined for Finland, nor is the top 0.01% share for Finland, Ireland, New Zealand or Norway.

13 Cf. http://topincomes.parisschoolofeconomics.eu/, accessed 1 April 2014.

14 The division of labour described here is greatly simplified. More details can be found in Godechot (2001). Finance is constantly evolving and inventing new professions every year.

15 One of the major challenges of options trading is predicting future price volatility.

16 When carrying out my research, I met more financial markets professionals than corporate finance workers, and so my conclusions for the latter group are not as clear-cut or as certain.

17 For a more in-depth discussion, cf. Godechot (2011a).

18 Some financial theorists rightly see bonuses as a free option allocated to employees in addition to their securities portfolio (Ahn *et al.* 2002). The recent introduction of the clawback clause to limit risk-taking does not really affect the analysis. Indeed, it is not the bonus that becomes negative, but rather the deferred bonus that is reduced. Moreover, banks use this measure sparingly in order to avoid disputes.

19 The risk of an individual being fired for individual losses beyond a certain threshold is by no means negligible. Even so, it should not be exaggerated and is not systematic. Dismissals take place most frequently when an overall activity ceases to be profitable (such as the impact of the Asian crisis on emerging markets or the downturn of 2001–2001 in the equities market).

20 Any information available that enables employees' specific contribution to be better defined may be used to improve contracts. This indexing of contracts is a "Pareto improvement": it improves the situation of at least one of the two parties, principal or

agent, without worsening that of the other party. The profit derived from the improvement of the contract is shared between the principal and the agent according to the respective bargaining power of the two parties.
21 Tomaskovic-Devey and Lin have proposed a means of measuring the scope of financial rent in the United States (Tomaskovic-Devey and Lin 2011). Oyer (2008) clearly demonstrates that there are rents by comparing the income prospects of former elite MBA students according to whether they entered the financial employment market during an economic boom or a crash.

References

Ahn, H, Dewyne, J, Hua, P, Penaud, A and Wilmott, P 2002, 'The End-of-the-Year Bonus: How to Optimally Reward a Trader?', *International Journal of Theoretical and Applied Finance*, vol. 5, n°3, pp. 279–307.

Allouche, J 1993, 'Les rémunérations salariales, une analyse de 255 bilans sociaux d'entreprises (1979–1991)', *Revue de gestion des ressources humaines*, n°8, pp. 52–61.

Atkinson, A 2008, *The Changing Distribution of Earnings in OECD Countries*, Oxford, Oxford University Press.

Bakija, J, Cole, A and Heim, BT 2012, *Jobs and Income Growth of Top Earners and the Causes of Changing Income Inequality: Evidence from US Tax Return Data,* Discussion Paper, Williams College, Williams Town.

Bebchuk, L, Cohen, A and Spamann, H 2010, 'The Wages of Failure: Executive Compensation at Bear Stearns and Lehman 2000–2008', *Yale Journal on Regulation*, vol. 27, n°2, pp. 257–282.

Bell, B and Van Reenen, J 2013, 'Extreme Wage Inequality: Pay at the Very Top', *American Economic Review*, vol. 103, n°3, pp. 153–157.

Bertrand, M and Mullainathan, S 2001, 'Are CEOs Rewarded for Luck? The Ones without Principles Are', *Quarterly Journal of Economics*, vol. 116, n°3, pp. 901–932.

Beunza, D and Stark, D 2004, 'Tools of the Trade: The Socio-Technology of Arbitrage in a Wall Street Trading Room', *Industrial and Corporate Change*, vol. 13, n°2, pp. 369–400.

Biedermann, Z and Orosz, Á 2015, 'Diverging Financial Regulations after the Crisis? A Comparison of the EU's and the United States' responses', *Financial and Economic Review*, vol. 14, n°1, pp. 31–55.

Boustanifar, H, Grant, E and Reshef, A 2014, *Wages and Human Capital in Finance: International Evidence, 1970–2005*, Working Paper, University of Virginia.

Cheng, I, Hong, H and Scheinkman, J 2015, 'Yesterday's Heroes: Compensation and Risk at Financial Firms', *The Journal of Finance*, vol. 70, n°2, pp. 83–879.

Chocron, V and Pinson, G 2001, 'Grogne autour des bonus record versés par les banques', *La Tribune*, 29 May.

Chon, G 2014, 'US Bank Bonus Curb Hit by Regulatory Squabble', *Financial Times*, 14 August.

Cuomo, A 2009, *No Rhyme or Reason: The 'Heads I Win, Tails You Lose' Bank Bonus Culture*, The Attorney General of the State of New York Report, New York.

Dünhaupt, P 2014, *An Empirical Assessment of the Contribution of Financialization and Corporate Governance to the Rise in Income Inequality*, IPE Working Paper 41/2014, Berlin School of Economics and Law, Institute for International Political Economy.

EBA 2014, *On the application of Directive 2013/36/EU (Capital Requirements Directive) regarding the principles on remuneration policies of credit institutions and investment firms and the use of allowances*, 15 October https://www.eba.europa.eu/documents/10180/534414/EBA+Report+on+the+principles+on+remuneration+policies+and+the+use+of+allowances.pdf, accessed 1 April 2016.

EBA 2015, *Report on Benchmarking of Remuneration and on High Earners 2013*, 7 September, http://www.eba.europa.eu/documents/10180/950548/Report+on+Benchmarking+of+Remuneration+and+on+High+Earners+2013.pdf, accessed 1 April 2016.

Ferrarini, G and Ungureanu, MC 2011, 'Lost in Implementation: The Rise and Value of the FSB Principles for Sound Compensation Practices at Financial Institutions', *Revue trimestrielle de droit financier*, n°1–2, pp. 60–65

Ferrary, M 2002, 'Mécanismes de régulation de la structure des qualifications et spécificité du capital humain. Une analyse du capital social des conseillers bancaires', *Sociologie du travail*, vol. 44, n°1, pp. 119–130.

FSB 2009, *FSB Principles for Sound Compensation Practices. Implementation Standards*, 25 September, http://www.fsb.org/wp-content/uploads/r_090925c.pdf?page_moved=1.

Gatinois, C and Van Renterghem, M 2009, 'Paris et Londres scellent leur réconciliation sur la taxation des bonus bancaires', *Le Monde*, 10 December.

Godechot, O 2001, *Les Traders. Essai de sociologie des marchés financiers*, La Découverte, Paris.

Godechot, O 2011a, 'Le capital humain et les incitations sont-ils les deux mamelles des salaires dans la finance?', *Revue d'économie financière*, n°104, pp. 145–164.

Godechot, O 2011b, *Finance and the Rise in Inequalities in France*, Paris School of Economics, Working Paper n°2011–13.

Godechot, O 2012, 'Is Finance Responsible for the Rise in Wage Inequality in France?', *Socio-Economic Review*, vol. 10, n°2, pp. 1–24.

Godechot, O 2014, 'Financialization and Sociospatial Divides' (Translation of: 'Financiarisation et fractures socio-spatiales', 2013), *L'année sociologique*, vol. 63 n°1, pp. 17–50.

Godechot, O 2015, *Financialization is Marketization! A Study on the Respective Impact of Various Dimensions of Financialization on the Increase in Global Inequality*, MaxPo Discussion Paper n°15.3.

Holmstrom, B 1979, 'Moral Hazard and Observability', *Bell Journal of Economics,* vol. 10, n°1, pp. 74–91.

Holmstrom, B and Milgrom P 1987, 'Aggregation and Linearity in the Provision of Intertemporal Incentives', *Econometrica,* vol. 55, n°2, pp. 303–328.

Kaplan, S and Rauh, J 2010, 'Wall Street and Main Street: What Contributes to the Rise in the Highest Incomes?', *Review of Financial Studies*, vol. 23, n°3, pp. 1004–1050.

Kus, B 2013, 'Financialisation and Income Inequality in OECD Nations: 1995–2007', *The Economic and Social Review*, vol. 43, n°4, pp. 477–495.

Lazear, E 1995, *Personnel Economics*, Massachusetts Institute of Technology, Cambridge MA.

Milgrom, P and Roberts, J 1992, *Economics, Organization and Management*, Prentice-Hall, Englewood Cliffs NJ.

Murphy, K 2013, 'Regulating Banking Bonuses in the European Union: A Case Study in Unintended Consequences', *European Financial Management*, vol. 19, n°4, pp. 631–657.

Oyer, P 2008, 'The Making of an Investment Banker: Stock Market Shocks, Career Choice, and Lifetime Income', *The Journal of Finance*, vol. 63, n°6, pp. 2601–2628.

Philippon, T and Reshef, A 2012, 'Wages and Human Capital in the US Finance Industry: 1909–2006', *Quarterly Journal of Economics*, vol. 127, n°4, pp. 1551–1609.

Piketty, T 2001, *Les Hauts Revenus en France*, Grasset, Paris.

Piketty, T 2014, *Capital in the Twenty-First Century*, Belknap Press, Cambridge MA.

Piketty, T and Saez, E 2003, 'Income Inequality in the United States, 1913–1998', *Quarterly Journal of Economics*, vol. 118, n°1, pp. 1–39.

Power, M 2005, 'Enterprise Risk Management and the Organization of Uncertainty in Financial Institutions' in *The Sociology of Financial Markets*, eds K Knorr Cetina and A Preda, Oxford University Press, Oxford, pp. 250–268.

Rajan, R 2008, 'Bankers' Pay is Deeply Flawed', *Financial Times*, 8 January.

Saez, E and Zucman, G 2014, *Wealth Inequality in the United States Since 1913: Evidence from Capitalized Income Tax Data*, National Bureau of Economic Research Working Paper n°20625.

Société Générale 2004, *Rapport annuel 2003 – Groupe Société générale*, Société Générale, Paris.

Tomaskovic-Devey, D and Lin, KH 2011, 'Income Dynamics, Economic Rents, and the Financialization of the US Economy', *American Sociological Review*, vol. 76, n°4, pp. 538–559.

2   The distribution of bonuses

Due to the legal safeguards that surround them, changes in the fixed wages of capital market banks are like the progress of a large ocean liner that can only be diverted from its course slowly and laboriously. Every year only minor inflections are observed, caused by potential increases – in themselves highly structured – or the impact of employees leaving and joining the firm. On the other hand, the allocation of variable wages usually undergoes a radical overhaul from one year to the next, and the distribution of bonuses is constantly supervised by all actors. The process that leads to the distribution of bonuses at the start of the year (December–January in Anglo-American banks; February–March in French banks) in actual fact lasts the entire year.

No sooner are bonuses distributed than the heads of department must renegotiate the future bonus formula that will enable them to calculate the collective bonus budget for the following year. During the spring, the HR department completes the wage surveys and forwards them to a remuneration consultancy firm.[1] Several months later, they receive the results and are able to compare each employee's salary with that of their counterparts in other banks. During this period, the accounting department puts together the mid-year results and begins to prepare the future bonus budget. Some provisional amounts are established. In order to divide the total bonus pool into sub-budgets for the different units and divisions, the heads of those departments are asked to submit their requests. To do so, they usually ask their subordinates about their expectations. When activity resumes in September, the first decisions are sent back to the heads of departments. Armed with the scenarios drawn up by HR, the main departments' budgets are agreed on but can be revised at the end of the autumn according to how financial results develop. Once the final bonus budget is set and broken down for the various sections of the organisation, heads must propose a distribution at individual level. They assess their employees, sometimes in a meeting, and propose a bonus distribution that must be approved by the next level of the bank's hierarchy. The sharing of the bonus pool can then begin.

Bonuses are the centre of gravity around which not only the allocation process itself revolves but essentially the bank's entire management system. In this chapter, I will focus on a few striking points of bonus distribution: the emergence and significance of bonus pool formulas; the flexibility of the arguments exchanged when bonus budgets are being set; and the economic and moral strategies used during individual distribution.[2]

Accounting, bonus pool formulas and appropriation of created value

In most major banks, during the late 1990s the bonus budget was calculated with a formula according to the results of a business line, in other words a centre of activity, usually global, that managed relatively homogeneous products. These business lines may have had up to 200 financial operators (i.e. traders and salespeople) and constituted the unit of accounting for results. In an economic climate marked by considerable financial risks, which banking leaders were beginning to take into account (following the collapse of Barings Bank, for example), by the rising importance of a shareholders' discourse focused on a "minimum income" for shareholders (Lordon 2000a), by inflated bonuses in finance and by employees' strong negotiating power in the sector, employees and entrepreneurs came to an understanding so that bonuses would only be paid out of the "value created". This solution raises numerous questions on the nature and means of determining value created or profit. As a former head of desk at Neptune Bank recounted, "The banks posted objectives [return on equity] of 10%, 15% . . . As soon as those objectives have been met at bank level, some sectors – especially traders, but also the entire M&A department and, to a lesser extent, asset management – who say 'Wait a minute, we've had results that are way above 15% profitability'." Once the shareholders have been compensated for capital and risk, the value created is really an ownerless commodity whose distribution between shareholders and employees, and particularly between employees themselves, is not fixed.

The formula used by Saturn Bank to calculate the base on which the rate is applied and the bonus pool established

Net banking income (banking equivalent of sales turnover)
(-) General costs (direct and dedicated)
(-) Structure costs (fixed)
(-) Risk provision (compensation, country)
(-) Cost of equity

= NET PROFIT (Profit before bonuses and taxes)
* Bonus rates

= BONUS POOL

Let us examine the formula used at Saturn Bank (boxed text). It is used to establish net profit, the basis on which a part – a percentage – will be deducted and distributed among financial operators. The starting point is the net banking income, a banking equivalent to sales turnover, from which a number of general and dedicated costs and risk provision costs are deducted thanks to the increasingly sophisticated use of cost accounting. Lastly, a line is deducted which may seem mysterious to the uninitiated: the "cost of equity". The bank, which is at the forefront in the characterisation of risks incurred by capital, can successfully calculate, for each of its departments, the risk taken on shareholders' capital and therefore the payment (interest rate + risk premium) that can compensate for that exposure. The bonus is therefore calculated on the basis of a net profit before tax but after deducting return on equity (return on capital adjusted by an interest rate and risk rate). This net profit generally corresponds to value created; this value, supposedly created "for the shareholders", is added, whereas there has already been a return on these two vital economic functions: the provision of equity capital and risk-taking.

This bonus formula makes visible the political role of accounting. Any operation that is likely to shape an organisation's final results may have an impact on bonuses. A single accounting decision contributes in the end to establish the causal relationship between profit flows at one end of the firm and costs at the other end.[3] In short, the accounting department states who is costing whom. This is a formidable task in which costs are divided up and certain entities are made responsible for profit. This common operation is closely monitored by the front office. The equity derivatives department of Saturn Bank has its own independent financial controllers who check internal billing operations. "They [equity derivatives] follow it closely," acknowledges a head of financial control. "They stay ahead, certainly, they look at things and fight with each other. They don't want to be billed for things unfairly." Similarly, any risk assessment operation poses a challenge. It helps internally to establish the "use of shareholders' equity", in other words, the degree to which shareholders' money is exposed in the event of loss. It therefore makes it possible to measure a department's profitability once the risks have been taken into account (Power 2005). A deputy chief executive explained this in the following way: "We fight over the *smile*. As you know, the *smile* is the volatility that increases when you move away from standard option theory. So we really fight over the methods for calculating the VaR and use of equity capital." By bringing into play the calculation of risks and profits, all the parameters for these complex indicators can be found at the intersection of financial mathematics and best interests.

As a consequence of their impact on bonuses, accounting and risk measurements are not just truth instruments that enable the firm to establish a "true and fair view" of its activity. They are also profit-sharing instruments between different units in the firm trying to maximise their bonus pools by all means. The bonus formulas therefore contribute to a strong politicisation of accounting and risk measurements that may conflict with their truth objectives. During the 2008 crisis, it was often claimed that bonuses favoured too much risk-taking (Rajan 2008; Cheng, Hong and Scheinkman 2015). Therefore, the regulators insisted that bonus pools should be calculated on returns adjusted for "the cost and quantity of capital required to support the risks taken" and "the cost and quantity of the liquidity risk assumed in the conduct of business" (FSB 2009). Concrete solutions put forward were based on "best practices" in the financial industry such as those already in place at Saturn in the early 2000s. Such principles were finally implemented in the European Union in the CRD III Directive (2010/76/EU). While it is true that calculating bonuses on a notion of income that does not take into account risks may lead the front office to maximise risk, tying bonuses to risk may also have a perverse effect. My analysis shows that it can lead to a misrepresentation of risks (Godechot 2008). This will be true particularly for the most complex products where the evaluation of risks rests essentially on internal models based on ad-hoc hypotheses. Bonus concerns may lead financiers to opt for over-optimistic hypotheses (MacKenzie 2011). If a trader takes too many risks and those risks are well measured, the firm can still react appropriately. It will not be the case when the risks are misrepresented.

Moreover, a bonus system based on accounting paves the way for a second turnaround. It portrays value created as a vacant good open to the rival appropriations of employees and shareholders. Furthermore, the bonus rate is not fixed; rather, it can be renegotiated at the beginning of every year (March–April) for a bonus that will be distributed in February of the following year. Its negotiability on a decentralised scale allows for a high level of heterogeneity and adapting the rule to local power relations between business lines and the bank's management, which are very different from one another. The rate varies significantly according to business lines. It might go down to 5% for treasury management and go up to more than 30%, even 35% at Saturn Bank, for derivatives, especially equity derivatives. Forex, fixed income and commodities, on the other hand, lie somewhere in the middle. According to a head of desk at Neptune Bank, "this point is arguable, whether or not it's harder to make money from some market activities than from others, because it's more risky, more technical, more volatile, because there are fewer clients or, on the contrary, more clients, and so on".

The flow of arguments and the shaping of bonus distribution

Tension and power struggles are an inevitable part of the meetings and processes that result in the distribution of bonuses, for example when the bonus pool formula is reviewed, and even in situations that seem to have less of a direct impact, such as when internal pricing costs are set or when risks are calculated. These are situations in which practical matters are discussed and rational arguments are exchanged, and in which the dominant position of the most powerful and legitimate entities is revealed. Domination is always based on a seemingly rational argument such as "the results mean this" or "the market calls for that". However, these discussions depart from a functional exchange on two points: first, the strength of the arguments exchanged clearly varies according to the internal power of the unit proposing them; second, the arguments exchanged are not always entirely coherent.

The meetings in which bonus pools are determined, particularly those in which the distribution of a department's budget among its various units is decided, provide favourable conditions in which to observe these power relations and gain an overview of the arguments exchanged. Indeed, the formula is not the end of the matter. It only determines the amount at the general level of the "business line". The question of how the bonus pool will be divided up among subunits, teams, etc. is then urgently raised.

Budget-related arguments

The budget breakdown is a process that requires more negotiation than the calibration of the formula. It is formally organised by HR, although their role as orchestrators does not bring them a great deal of power. Instead, they are restricted to a dual role providing administrative service and advice. This approach consists partly in passing unit managers' requests on to higher management as well as in putting forward a number of allocation scenarios that adhere to certain criteria: past budget distribution (what was proposed the previous year with an equivalent structure); the market (bonuses paid to employees' counterparts according to wage surveys); results; and any potential equity objectives such as bringing the salary levels of different jobs into line. Consultation meetings are then held between HR, the relevant departments and senior bank management, enabling capital markets managers to decide the budget size based on the scenarios proposed.

The manner in which the bonus budget for IT support functions is established provides an excellent illustration of this process. In 2000, all of the IT functions in capital markets banking were grouped into an independent entity and incorporated into the support functions: the equity IT staff, whose bonuses were previously paid by the equity department, IT staff working on forex, fixed income and commodities, who were paid by the fixed income department, and back office IT staff, whose bonuses were paid out of the back office's allocated bonus envelope. The unequal treatment of these three groups of workers was striking. The bonus to fixed salary ratio in Paris was 40% for the first group, 30% for the second and around 10% for the last group. What is more, IT functions relied hugely on staff from external IT services providers who had been working exclusively for Saturn Bank for years and to whom the bank paid direct bonuses. For several years, however, the CGT union had denounced such bargaining practices and filed a lawsuit against Saturn Bank for illegal subcontracting.[4] The direct payment of bonuses without the intermediation of the services provider may have provided evidence that subcontracting had taken place. The bank tried to end such practices at all costs, both by hiring some of these service providers and stopping bonus payments to the remaining contractors.

Well before the bonus budgets were discussed, the director of this new entity prepared a PowerPoint presentation putting forward the following arguments: [results logic] many banks pay globally, and it is necessary for both the minimum bonus pool level to be separate from results and for its maximum level to take results into account; [market logic] the new economy is a threat to the current labour market; [logic of past distributions] first, bonuses have always been paid to subcontractors and this cannot be changed, second, employees should not fear being paid less when leaving the front office's sphere of influence; [logic of equity] employees feel they have not been treated equally.

The HR department where I was an intern was responsible for drawing up scenarios that would clarify the debate and the capital market bank's decision regarding the bonus budget for support staff in general and IT staff in particular. Several scenarios were put forward: [Market logic] What budget would be required to pay everyone at the level of the market average? And at the level of the first and third quartiles? [Logic of past bonus distributions] What bonus pool would be necessary to pay employees at the same ratio (bonus on salary) as last year? [Logic of equity] What bonus pool would be required to pay equivalent bonuses to equivalent functions? The logic of equity must be understood according to a very specific meaning in these market departments accustomed to plentiful and recurrent results. It does not simply consist in applying the logic of "Equal pay for equal work!", but rather in filling the gap with those who are paid the most. [Results logic] HR were also looking for a formula that would allow the support staff's budget to be aligned with results; however, at the time of my internship, they had not yet found a satisfactory solution. Despite this, they still used the results to determine the scope of what was possible, given that the IT budget, as for other support departments, was taken out of a budget that was around 10% of front office bonuses (which were a direct percentage of results).

At the final meeting between IT and HR, in which bonus scenarios were proposed, an initial simulation of past scenarios resulted in a bonus proposal of 26 million euros for the 2,100 staff employed in the IT department of the capital markets bank. Enforcing equity, which meant increasing back office IT bonuses to match those of the front office IT, resulted in a bonus budget increase of 50 million euros. The head of the IT department, a newly appointed British man who was somewhat disdainful and scornful of the HR department, which he saw as a kind of alternative trade union, read the second scenario and exclaimed jovially, "I love HR! Human Resources totally convinced me!" The head of HR, in view of the magnitude of the sum, suggested that the harmonisation could be done over a two-year period. "Why not make it in one year? Why not treat people equally? People in the back office information system have horribly suffered!" It is impossible to know the sincerity of his desire for justice. The argument he asserted while the budget was being put together could easily be overlooked or blocked in the distribution phase.[5]

My observation of the meeting between back office and HR also provides an example of a case in which different people present different arguments in turn. At this relatively cordial meeting, everyone had something to add. When the back office bonus budget of 10 million euros was mentioned, one of the members said mockingly, "The bonus of two traders!" When the issue arose of remuneration differences between Europe and Asia on the one hand and the United States on the other, another ventured, "Europe, Asia, same struggle." Market tensions, evidenced by departures even among technicians, were also mentioned. A few comments were made about the need for harmonisation between back and middle offices, which had two very different histories. The discussion, however, ended in results logic, or rather in a combination of results and equity. The HR professional who had designed the bonus formula system a few years before was asked whether his formula system could support current developments. And when he spoke of the possibility of introducing a formula tailored to the back office departments, a head of back office reminded him that they should not lose sight of the main point: "How are front office bonuses developing? At the end of the day, that is what matters. Do we continue to allow the gap between back and front offices to widen?"

Let us now look at the coherence of these arguments in more detail. First case: the results are "there to be seen". The argument based on the idea of "paying in line with results" works well for the front office but does not necessarily apply for the back office. It paves the way for further arguments. Aligning oneself with the labour market in order to keep a team together is an approach that can only be used successfully if the heads of team are able to put forward one or more arguments that make use of those market tensions (market surveys, departures, hear-say, specific cases, etc.). However, when the situation is reversed (employees are paid more than their counterparts in rival banks), which was the case at Saturn Bank, for example, it is still not possible to lower bonuses in order to improve profits. Why should a team be punished for an event (changes in their labour market) they had no part in, if the results are there to be seen? If the results are there, then employees can continue to be paid in line with past distributions and the existing order can be maintained. To enable employees to "work together" and to avoid a situation in which lower-paid employees use influencing strategies, feel frustrated or refuse to collaborate, people easily agree that "equity" must be established and equivalent functions and employees of similar merit must be paid in the same way. The argument has a certain weight, particularly given that the equity in question is not pure or free but rather is designed to enable production. However, in an environment like the back office, which is constantly being reorganised, there is a continual building and rebuilding of teams and groups of teams with different histories. Solidarity is limited a priori. Some teams receive new members of whom, only recently, they had no knowledge whatsoever. This is why equity only becomes a mobilising argument when the results allow it; when they enable a painless alignment that changes the historical position of some while preserving the advantages won by others.

Second, the results are not there to be seen. The structure of this line of argument and its effectiveness vary according to who is presenting it and whether they are from front office or support functions. In the front office, even when results are the basis for legitimacy, the absence or weakness of results is not automatically sanctioned by absent or low bonuses. Indeed, a lack of results is not a good enough reason to make lower payouts than those currently being made in the labour market. Bad performances can be attributed to external circumstances (exceptional market conditions, the Asian crisis, etc.), to the poor development of an activity, or even to the inappropriate actions of isolated employees. Ultimately they cannot be used to question the quality of employees, starting with their bonuses. The fear of staff leaving is ever-present. The idea that money is required to prevent departures tempers the lack of results, particularly when the failure is local and runs counter to results obtained by others. As long as the absence of front office results is seen as a mishap, pressure and credible arguments will continue to drive bonus payouts. On the other hand, if the idea takes hold that the economic turnaround is general and structural on the markets, then the labour market argument carries little weight and paves the way for a major review of past gains. In a way, the bank's upper management takes the upper hand, sometimes with a certain amount of private satisfaction, and at last imposes its remuneration policy.

When the results are not there to be seen, bonuses should, in theory, be maintained in the back office. Indeed, it is considered that their own performance has only a very indirect impact on the results attributed to the front office. Nevertheless, in practice the absence of results puts back office bonuses at serious risk. The front office may lead a crusade to "limit the damage" and pay out market bonuses regardless, even if only to the most important players – particularly given that some isolated front office operators succeed in obtaining good results that run counter to their department's performance as a whole, and that they anticipate being fairly compensated for that. Therefore, in order to save front office's bonuses, management and the front office may wage a cost-cutting campaign that targets the easiest costs to cut, in other words the bonuses of those employees who are the hardest to justify and the least essential, and the bonuses of technicians and low-level support functions.

The influence of organisational structures

While the manner in which arguments are linked and combined obviously has an impact on the outcome of the discussion, as outlined above, it would be unrealistic to make it the sole and unequivocal deciding factor in the conflict. The effectiveness of the argumentative structure depends on the power and legitimacy of the party defending it.

Indeed, strictly speaking, heads of capital markets have control and decision-making power over bonus allocation. They negotiate bonus budgets on behalf of the bank's executives, and ultimately shareholders, and must ensure the bonuses are not too high, in other words that they remain in line with competitors' payouts and do not undermine overall profitability and hence shareholders' compensation. However, this cost-cutting logic is counterbalanced by the design of the bonus pool. The envelope available to the management of capital markets, out of which heads will pay themselves as well as the support functions, is in fact taken out of the budget allocated to the front office. At Saturn Bank, 10–15% of the equity derivatives department's bonus budget provided bonuses for support functions and market professionals. As a consequence of the logical order of distribution, most of the front office's demands were met with sympathy. Nick Leeson, the trader who drove Barings Bank to bankruptcy, had the following say about his bank's management: "For various different reasons they all wanted to believe my profits were real. They all benefited from me, and in their different ways they all put me under pressure to create these profits" (Leeson 1996, p. 191). In the aftermath of the 2008 global financial crisis, the regulators partially addressed this inefficient alignment of incentives. The FSB required the bonus pool for risk and compliance employees to be determined independently from remuneration and performance of other business areas (FSB 2009, p. 2). The CRD III Directive (2010/76/UE) extended this requirement in the European Union to all control functions but did not include the head of capital markets management.

Similarly, the fact that the company is divided into centres of activity, and that those centres are categorised into profit centres and cost centres, is one of the main structural elements that enables some employees to be in a better position than others to appropriate profit. Profit centres are associated with results and quantitative standards, while it is much more difficult to assign quantifiable elements of evaluation to cost centres.[6] Adhering to expenditure budgets (investment, wage costs, etc.) or lowering costs is sometimes a component for evaluation (Hartmann 2000; Mottis and Ponssard 2000), but it is fundamentally ambiguous: everything depends on matching provisional budgets with activity. When they are underestimated, it is often much more effective (from an entrepreneurial perspective) to disregard them. "When the budget was exceeded because during the year the budgets had shot up like that, could I blame them?" asked a head of back office when evaluating the team leaders under his supervision. Similarly, the support unit will not necessarily be given credit for reducing the budget (cost reduction). In a way it is part of the normal, continuous activity of the support functions and cannot easily be rewarded. The head of trade execution explained this as follows:

> If I have 100 people in the department and if, in the course of the year, I reduce my headcount by 18 or by 20, they are not going to say, "Last year, you paid your people this amount in your group, this year, it's up 10%." They will say, "There's 80 people – this amount and this year, you can pay them up 10%." They didn't take into account all the cost-cutting you have done and how much more profitable you made the place because you cut expenses – which may or may not be fair!

Support functions, by improving the quality of services provided, increasing productivity and reducing costs, help to push profits up generally. However, as this contribution is global, it is difficult to trace and quantify. It results in little or no compensation in terms of bonuses for its units. This externality effect benefits the front office above all. Indeed, an important factor, particularly at Saturn Bank, in maintaining profit and a competitive edge has been the systematic industrialisation of transaction procedures, both in front and back offices.

And yet, through its profit formula, the front office captures the lion's share of the bonus volume generated by cost-cutting. A reductionist, individualistic form of cost analysis favours the appropriation of profit by the front office at the expense of the back office.

The process of establishing bonus pools is therefore subject to a dual power game. First, the more visible game involving the forces of argument (identifying the most effective line of argument as circumstances require) and the less visible game involving the forces of organisational structure (one could even call this "the organisational unconscious"): the processes of decision-making and division into entities contribute greatly to the legitimacy and effectiveness of each of the parties involved in the argumentative discussion and partly determine the outcome of the debate.

Individual distribution, between justice and opportunism

During discussions surrounding the determination of the bonus pool, considerations regarding the personal value of individuals constitute a relatively weak and unstable argument. Sometimes, certain ideas, for example the notion that equity IT support specialists are "better" than fixed income IT specialists, come under discussion and make an impact. However, this type of argument usually fails to convince people at an institutional level because it is hard to prove. How can one ascertain whether accountants, as individuals, are better or work more than HR professionals? The line managers of these units all have an interest in making people think their teams are good and work hard. Very few people have an overall idea of the merit of different individuals, which cannot easily be compared. It would be difficult to confirm or to refute the arguments put forward.

The discussion on individual merit usually takes place when a line manager has to distribute the bonus budget allocated to her among her staff. This task is far from easy. Some, particularly younger line managers, admit that they have trouble completing it successfully. More senior line managers, much like experienced teachers, fall back on their tried-and-tested evaluation techniques and tend to reuse them to establish an order on the value scales they were subjected to when they first started out in finance.

The merit of subordinates

The distribution of bonuses in finance must take employees' expectations into account. The more important employees are in the line managers' eyes, the more their line managers will consider their expectations. Managers would thus meet with them once or several times before the annual distribution, both to evaluate their work and find out their aspirations, frustrations, loyalties and likelihood to defect. At Neptune Bank, for example, 74% of front office professionals who responded to my survey had had an opportunity to discuss their bonus with their line managers, as opposed to 59% of support professionals and 25% of technicians.

When employees were questioned about the criteria that should guide an ideal bonus distribution, they usually highlighted meritocratic criteria. Compensation should depend essentially on two factors: results and workload. The proportions of those two components varied according to profession. Front office operators placed far greater importance on the former, whereas back office staff, especially technicians, valued the latter (Table 2.1). They all agreed that, compared with the actual practice of bonus distributions, these two meritocratic criteria were not sufficiently taken into account, while too much importance was given to hierarchical position.

Does this mean that they all agreed on the ideal of meritocratic compensation? Many authors in the fields of sociology, economics and philosophy have shown that it is extremely common to invoke the merit at work, particularly in the upper levels of the social world (Miller 1992; Kellerhals, Modak and Perrenoud 1997). Despite such unanimity, the instability of the notion of merit should not be overlooked, not only because there are several rival meritocratic dimensions (Boltanski and Thévenot 2006), such as workload and results in this case, but also because in a single referential the components of merit are unstable. Merit does not equal productivity. It is a moral value that increases in accordance with one's desire to do good, the effort one makes to achieve it, the difficulties encountered and the quality and quantity of the result. The awarding of merit depends on the prior attribution of abilities and handicaps to the person being assessed. Its singularity in space and time is unstable. It can be expanded or reduced as circumstances require. Past annual results and the unit's overall performance can, according to the configurations, be discounted from individual merit or, on the contrary, may be added to it. The invocation of merit is more efficient locally. Within a team doing the same type of work, with a stable framework of tasks, it becomes a significant standard. However, it struggles to become a truly effective

Table 2.1 Bonus criteria: the ideal and the reality

	Workload		Results		Value on the labour market		Hierarchical position		Seniority	
	Ideal	*Reality*	*Ideal*	*Reality*	*Ideal*	*Reality*	*Ideal*	*Reality*	*Ideal*	*Reality*
Front office professionals (n = 19/19)	2.14	1.63	5.80	3.89	1.18	1.21	0.41	1.95	0.46	1.32
Support professionals (n = 17/16)	4.06	1.73	4.06	2.99	1.12	2.18	0.41	2.48	0.35	0.61
Technicians (n = 43/36)	4.63	2.26	2.76	2.83	0.95	1.30	0.63	2.88	1.04	0.73
All (n = 79/71)	3.91	1.97	3.77	3.15	1.03	1.47	0.53	2.54	0.75	0.86

Note: Respondents were asked to distribute ten points between five criteria to describe the ideal bonus distribution on the one hand and real distribution on the other. Seventeen support staff from Neptune Bank awarded an average of 4.06 points to the "workload" criteria as an ideal, and 16 support staff (one non-response) awarded 1.73 points to "workload" as it is in reality.

transversal standard other than as an incantatory ideology. When front office computer engineers were confronted with the fact that the way in which their merit and compensation were assessed was far more advantageous to them than to their back office colleagues, it caused a feeling of unease that was not only based on a desire to defend their own interests. Ultimately, they did not feel responsible for others' misfortune and refused to see this as a sufficient reason to disrupt their own system for evaluating merit. They generally ended up reconsidering the terms of the comparison, highlighting unobservable differences in the quality or intensity of the work being done.

"Merit" as invoked by employees is therefore a somewhat malleable notion that can be redefined according to the issues and circumstances in question. Moreover, when employees see that distribution does not accurately match their meritocratic ideal and that it has an element of randomness, they feel justified in resorting to strategies that break with the notion of merit in order to make the most of their advantage. The idea is to "look good to the boss", "know how to yell", and do everything possible to be "in the right place at the right time", by working on the products that bring profit at a particular time, "getting the highest amount of capital" in order to obtain more results, even if, for some, this means taking more risks.

Opportunism even extends as far as changing results indicators to meet expectations. One trader told me that in the mid-1990s, traders at her bank declared fictitious sales in bad months – which they later cancelled – as a way of increasing the securities sales index, which was unsophisticated and did not take cancellations into account. One of the most common strategies for influencing one's line manager is to be careful not to appear satisfied with one's lot, as if one were on the verge of leaving, and to advertise the fact.[7] As a result, 58% of front office staff (traders, salespeople) at Neptune Bank, as opposed to 27% of support staff, had already complained to their boss about their bonus.

Reward or retention?

Line managers' first reaction when questioned about their methods for distributing bonuses is to show themselves in their best light. They are fair! "The bonus is a justice equation," asserted one of them solemnly. At first sight, fair distribution also enables economic efficiency, because it motivates employees at work and keeps them with the company.

However, a closer look shows that there is an apparent conflict between a bonus designed primarily to "reward individual performance in a job", as some HR professionals explained, or even more specifically, "pure performance at moment t", and a bonus that serves above all to retain employees within an active market: "We pay our guys so they won't up and leave," said one head of trading. "You always reason in terms of replacement costs," added the head of a sales team.

The two purposes most often associated with bonuses may appear very similar at first sight, if not the same. If subordinate employees are rewarded (as they expect to be) then they stay. How to keep them? By rewarding them for what they contribute. Nevertheless, specific conditions are required in order for these two motives to become fully aligned: a stable economic environment and long-term contracts. In the unstable, ever-changing world of finance, the two dimensions are not always in line.

One former financial engineer somewhat resentfully explained that the year he went on unpaid leave (prior to switching to an academic career), his boss decided not to pay him a bonus for the previous year.[8] At the risk of breaching the rules of merit, his line manager probably preferred to use the bonus budget to retain those he could rather than those he considered impossible to hold back. Elsewhere, a former financial engineer from Neptune Bank told me that the opposite was true in her team: bonuses were paid to employees who were sure to be leaving instead of using up the limited budget on those who were staying and keeping a threatened team alive. The difference between rewarding and retaining can be compared with the distinction drawn by Elster between the two criteria for distributing scarce goods: the criteria of merit and that of efficiency. "Merit is a past-oriented criterion. It implies prioritising the giving of the scarce resource to those who through their past actions have won the right to receive it." On the other hand, "efficiency is a future-orientated criterion" (Elster 1992, p. 18).

> A tragic story reported by newspapers also highlights the tension between the two distribution principles. On 11 September 2001, the brokerage firm Cantor Fitzgerald lost 700 of its 1,000 employees when the twin towers of the World Trade Center collapsed. Ten days later an argument broke out between the victims' families, the company's chairman and the employees who had survived. The chairman of the firm, which was financially shaken by the disaster, stated that it would not be possible to pay bonuses to the victims' families at the correct level on account of the immediate risk of bankruptcy. The victims' families were outraged and put pressure on the firm. Eventually, the missing accounts for broker transactions were pieced together from back-ups, the lists of bonuses distributed the previous year were taken as a guide and the victims' families were paid the bonuses. A total of 45 million dollars was paid out and they were promised one-quarter of profits over the following five years. According to newspaper reports (Clark 2001) the surviving employees, at a comparative disadvantage, criticised the fact that the dead were given priority over the living.

Even under normal circumstances, tensions between the two distribution principles run equally high. In the following example, the head of a sales team suggests that he was only able to retain his employee through a kind of iniquity: "someone who paid for him".

> Why did I pay the guy 2.2 million euros and 600,000 euros the following year when he'd made zero profit? I mean, he'd joined almost at the same time as me. He didn't really have a boss at the beginning. In the end, I became his boss and when I paid him 600 even though he'd made nothing I sent him to

be the boss of the New York platform. So I also paid him for that. If he'd left, I'd have been left with no boss for the New York platform and I'd have looked like an idiot.

Do you think you overpaid him?

No, not in relation to the market. He could have left for a similar price. But I had to get the money to pay him from somewhere else. Inevitably, I took it from guys who'd made money. In fact, I paid for it myself.

The decision to reward or retain also involves different evaluation methods. In the case of the reward bonus, a distinction must be drawn between the factors that deserve to be rewarded and those that do not. To do so, work or performance indicators must be identified and procedures for appraisals, criteria, scales, etc. must be established. It is necessary to filter out what comes from the job and the working environment and what comes from the individual. As the head of trading explained, "He might have made millions on the market. He helped make that profit, yes, but 80% of it came from previous generations. Someone who does well on Sweden, if I move him onto Ghana he won't succeed. People often don't realise that!" In the case of bonus retention, there is a particular focus on labour market conditions, on the departures that have taken place previously in the team, on what headhunters are saying and so on. Past contributions are checked, but they are only taken into account insofar as they help to assess the market value of what the person will contribute the following year.

The reward bonus is more focused on the individual, and in that sense it is more individualistic, whereas the retention bonus takes greater account of developments that do not depend on the individual's ability, such as the number of market competitors, the level of tension in the labour market, etc. The retention bonus may take into account individual elements that it would seem entirely illegitimate to consider in the context of a reward bonus. Indeed, in order to retain employees in an optimal way, it is important to take into account not only labour market activity and price trends but also the probability that the employee will leave, which depends on her confidence, risk aversion and transaction costs, particularly the cost of a departure. As a trader explains, "Ultimately, for me a bonus is the minimum amount someone must be paid in order to keep them and motivate them the following year. If you think someone will be happy with 100, there's no point paying them 150!" However, if one knows that certain employees are more modest or do not value themselves highly, should one deliberately take advantage and give them a lower bonus? If this question is put to a line manager, the answer is likely to be "I'm not unfair". Employees' weaknesses are not exploited in that way. "I've even asked for more [for them] that what they're asking . . . Because some guys are better than they think. Humble people do exist too. I have no interest in undervaluing one guy just to overvalue another."

And yet, as soon as the situation becomes more complicated, for example when the bonus budget is weak and makes it difficult to keep in line with the labour market, pressure increases and there is a temptation to take advantage of risk differentials for departures and, when the market value is equal, to pay more to those who are most likely to leave and less to those who are least likely. If some employees can be "happy with less" then it is simply "tough luck", and if their modesty allows a team to be kept intact by compensating a greedier employee who is quicker to look elsewhere, then why not take advantage of that (this iniquity is then subject to the legitimate motive of maintaining the team and its activity).

One of the reasons for the pay differential between men and women in finance, particularly in the area of bonuses, may stem from the fact that the level of departure risk is different in each case.[9] On the one hand, the division of housework between men and women generally makes mobility more costly for women than for men (with men forcing a move on women more often than the reverse). On the other hand, different upbringings and relationships with authority create different working relations. In the context of gender relations, demanding more and threatening to leave are usually male traits, and even a form of virility (Babcock and Laschever 2003).

In 2002, a court awarded a former financial analyst in London 1 million pounds in damages for sex discrimination (Martin and Barrow 2002).[10] From the news clippings it is difficult to grasp her bosses' reasons for awarding her 25,000 pounds in 1999 when they had given her 125,000 pounds in 1998, and that same year had awarded one of her male colleagues a bonus of 650,000 pounds. The bank told the court that Julie Bower's meagre compensation was due to her mediocre performance and the fact that she had been ranked last of all the analysts. However, the trial revealed that she had in fact been ranked 37th of 67 and not last, and that her boss had turned "sarcastic and threatening" when she complained about her bonus (Martin and Barrow 2002; Rumbelow 2002). It is possible that her boss may have considered, consciously or otherwise, that this woman of almost 40 years of age, married with a child, was not an individual with a high risk of departure and that by reducing her bonus he could allocate far more money to other employees at no risk.

The two principles of the reward bonus and the retention bonus were often mobilised alternately by the same people during a single interview. They swung readily from one form of logic to the other. In euphoric periods, when the budget is high, the compatibility of the two types of logic is less problematic. When the bonus pool shrinks, however, it often becomes necessary to make more tragic decisions.

A fairly common way for a boss to manage this tension between plural and potentially contradictory principles, as well as avoiding accusations of bias and favouritism, is to limit communication and comparison between recipients as much as possible. Despite preconceived ideas about the transparency of compensation in Anglo-American banks, the latter have a particularly strict secrecy policy. Revealing one's bonus to anyone other than one's partner and financial advisor constitutes professional misconduct. "My boss said to me, 'If I find out you've told people your bonus, I'll take it back!'" This is a way for them to counter "relative behaviour". As the head of a trading room explained, "relative behaviour is when someone can't say straight away whether or not they're happy. They have to ask 20 people before they can say, 'I'm not happy' or 'I'm happy'. It's such a childish way to behave!" A common basic strategy used is to say, "I recommend you don't talk about your bonus because the others got less than you!" Although widespread, this strategy is obviously fragile and risky because one leak can reveal the line manager's Machiavellian lies. And yet, by giving employees the impression that they are receiving a favour and that their own bonus may also be considered unfair by colleagues, it creates a complicity between employees and their boss and includes them in a policy of secrecy as regards compensation.

***

This descriptive incursion into the various phases of the bonus distribution process, be they collective and institutional (establishing and dividing up the budgets) or more interpersonal (individual distribution) gives an insight into the multiple tensions that run through this method of remuneration: tensions between principles that are not always compatible; and tensions between those principles and the balance of power. My next challenge is to understand in greater detail the principles of legitimisation, which are highly localised and cannot be fully reduced to the main moral principles of distribution, and the balance of power that shape this distribution of wealth. To do so, I must analyse the labour process in its entirety and explain how the appropriation of profit is ultimately rooted in work itself.

Notes

1 This highly laborious process is described in my article on remuneration consultancy firms (Godechot 2006).
2 A more in-depth analysis can be found in my PhD (Godechot 2004).
3 For example, the financial analysis department produces an assessment of listed companies, which it distributes, free of charge, externally to clients (to encourage them to make transactions) and internally to sellers, M&A professionals, and traders. How can one assign a "cost" of financial analysis to the companies whose profits are measured? For a sociological analysis of the problems caused by internal pricing see Eccles and White 1988.
4 Subcontracting or "labour leasing offence" is defined in Article L125–1 of the French Labour Code (Code du Travail) as a profit-making labour-supply operation with the effect of causing harm to the employee concerned or avoiding the application of the law, regulations or collective labour conventions or agreements (Pélissier, Supiot and Jeammaud 2000, pp. 137–138). Since 1982, it is also punishable with correctional sentences.
5 After 1998, there were efforts to harmonise the bonuses between middle offices, which were previously controlled by front offices, and the back office with which they were merged. This equity objective was reiterated in numerous HR memoranda. The argument often came up when the overall budget was being put together but, judging from the final allocations, tended to fade away during the budget distribution phase. The leeway given to the subjective evaluation of the quality of

teams (a quality that tends to be associated with the front office in the organisational life of the firm), personal relationships, various forms of pressure (exerted by both middle office and front office), and the logic of past distributions all limited the scope of this desire for equity.

6 As Burlaud and Simon observe, "The measurable is given much more weight than the immeasurable" (Burlaud and Simon 1997, p. 64).

7 On influence activities, cf. Milgrom and Roberts (1988).

8 He then sued the bank but lost his case. He was unable to provide supporting evidence of his contribution to the team's results or proof of stability and a recurrence of the relations between financial performances and bonuses.

9 Roth (2006) gives a more comprehensive overview of the origins of gender-based pay inequality on Wall Street.

10 In 2003 and 2004, there were several other court cases over sex discrimination in the industry. These were generally won by the female plaintiffs and resulted in equally large payouts (Butcher 2005).

References

Babcock, L and Laschever, S 2003, *Women Don't Ask: Negotiation and the Gender Divide*, Princeton University Press, Princeton NJ.

Boltanski, L and Thévenot, L 2006, *On Justification: Economies of Worth*, Princeton University Press, Princeton NJ.

Burlaud, A and Simon, C 1997, *Le Contrôle de gestion*, La Découverte, Paris.

Butcher, S 2005, 'Les affaires de discrimination sexuelle pourraient se multiplier en Europe', *efinancialcareers.fr*, 24 January.

Cheng, I, Hong, H and Scheinkman, J 2015, 'Yesterday's Heroes: Compensation and Risk at Financial Firms', *The Journal of Finance*, vol. 70, n°2, pp. 839–879.

Clark, A 2001, 'Cantor Fitzgerald Pleads for Work to Pay Relatives', *The Guardian*, 21 September.

Eccles, R and White, H 1988, 'Price and Authority in Inter-Profit Center Transactions', *American Journal of Sociology* vol. 94 (July), pp. S17–S51.

Elster, J 1992, 'Éthique des choix médicaux' in *Éthique des choix médicaux*, eds N Herpin and J Elster, Actes Sud, Arles, pp. 1–35.

FSB 2009, *FSB Principles for Sound Compensation Practices. Implementation Standards*, 25 September, http://www.fsb.org/wp-content/uploads/r_090925c.pdf?page_moved=1, accessed 1 April 2010.

Godechot, O 2004, *L'appropriation du profit. Politiques des bonus dans l'industrie financière*, doctoral thesis in sociology under the supervision of Michel Lallement, CNAM, Paris.

Godechot, O 2006, '"Quel est le salaire de marché?" Enquêtes de rémunération et mise en forme du marché du travail dans l'industrie financière', *Genèses*, n°63, pp. 108–127.

Godechot, O 2008, 'Les bonus accroissent-ils les risques?' in *La crise des subprimes*, eds P Artus, JP Betbèze, C de Boissieu and G Capelle-Blancard, La Documentation Française, Paris, pp. 203–218.

Hartmann, F 2000, 'The Appropriateness of RAPM: Toward the Further Development of Theory', *Accounting, Organizations and Society*, vol. 25, n°4–5, pp. 451–482.

Kellerhals, J, Modak, M and Perrenoud, D 1997, *Le sentiment de justice dans les relations sociales*, PUF, Paris.

Leeson, N 1996, *Rogue Trader: How I Brought Down Barings Bank and Shook the Financial World*, Little, Brown & Company, London.

Lordon, F 2000, 'La "création de valeur" comme rhétorique et comme pratique. Généalogie et sociologie de la valeur actionariale', *Année de la régulation*, vol. 4, pp. 117–170.

MacKenzie, D 2011, 'The Credit Crisis as a Problem in the Sociology of Knowledge', *American Journal of Sociology*, vol. 116, n°6, pp. 1778–1841.

Martin, N and Barrow, B 2002, 'Sexism in the City: Court Awards Record Payout', *Sun Herald*, 13 January.

Milgrom, P and Roberts, J 1988, 'An Economic Approach to Influence Activities in Organizations', *American Journal of Sociology*, vol. 94, Supplement, pp. S154–S179.

Miller, D 1992, 'Distributive Justice: What the People Think', *Ethics*, vol. 102, n°3, pp. 555–593.

Mottis, N and Ponssard, JP 2000, 'Création de valeur et politiques de rémunération', *Gérer et comprendre*, June, pp. 78–90

Pélissier, J, Supiot A and Jeammaud, A 2000, *Droit du travail*, Paris, Dalloz, pp. 137–138. Since 1982, this is a punishable offence.

Power, M 2005, 'Enterprise Risk Management and the Organization of Uncertainty in Financial Institutions' in eds K Knorr Cetina and A Preda, *The Sociology of Financial Markets*, Oxford University Press, Oxford, pp. 250–268.

Rajan, R 2008, 'Bankers' Pay is Deeply Flawed', *Financial Times*, 8 January.

Roth, LM 2006, *Selling Women Short. Gender Inequality on Wall Street*, Princeton University Press, Princeton NJ.

Rumbelow, H 2002, 'City on Spot over Sexism Charge', *The Times*, 12 January.

Part II

Property rights and power

3   Property rights in the firm

Despite the decline of Marxism, wage relations are often understood as the result of the core opposition between two groups, wage earners and shareholders, and, beyond that, between two legal statuses, ownership and wage labour. This representation has the advantage of highlighting an anomaly in the exchange relations between the two groups and introducing a hint of inequality. Ownership attracts something that is alien to it and which it does not produce itself, namely, profit, the origin of which must be sought on the side of labour, a factor that is far more "demiurgic" than capital (Marx 1990). The difficulties of the Marxian labour theory of value and the rationalisations of neoclassical market theory – according to which each factor (labour, capital) is remunerated according to its contribution – do not entirely dispel the impression, particularly when market imperfections create rents, that between ownership and labour force, equivalents are not always traded for equivalents.

However, by basing the standard perspective on a legal and financial demarcation between wage earners and shareholders, it becomes difficult to conceive inequalities and divisions within wage earners and the flows of profit that circulate inside this group. From this angle, the shareholders remain the legal, full and complete owner of the firm's assets. The purchase of labour force is merely the purchase of a service at its value. In this case, there is little place for on-lending of profit. At best, one finds modest profit-sharing measures or small wage premiums in the industry for productivity. Some may unconvincingly consider that professionals receive as part of their pay a fraction of surplus value in order to attach them to the capitalist class.

Let us now abandon this legalism and consider that wage earners are also, in a sense, owners of the firm's assets. Let us draw all the consequences of this perspective. Would ownership not constitute the basis for claiming and appropriating profits?

This approach has a two-fold advantage. First, it makes it possible to conceive wage relations also as a relationship between wage earners: the combination, in labour, of the organisation of asset ownership and the prescription of tasks constitutes the different facets of this relationship. Second, it allows for a questioning of the notion of "merit", which is frequently used to justify remuneration. Although it is very effective for gaining the upper hand in a normative discussion, the notion of merit itself is not very explanatory. As Rawls points out, merit can always be related to non-merit (Rawls 1971, p. 71). Does one deserve one's merit? Merit is a means of transmuting endowments and assets into being and thereby forgetting their origin. As Rawls explains, merit can be the transformation of natural endowments (being 6 feet 9 inches tall and playing basketball), social endowments (being gifted at music for those brought up in a family of musicians) or moral endowments (the will to make an effort), which are equally arbitrary and undeserved.[1] "Merit" can be based on inequalities in natural assets, inequalities in social assets, and here inequalities in assets particular to the field of financial entities. To be sure, unlike other social environments based on physical enhancement (sport, fashion), nothing here seems to reinforce the importance of the first category of inequalities. On the other hand, we can observe the major importance of the second category of inequalities and, even more so, those of the third category.[2]

Shifting our perspective on labour and ownership in this way presents a particular challenge. To what extent can we consider the organisation of labour to be an allocation of rights over company assets? It is important to show that introducing property rights where the law does not recognise any enables the working relations between wage earners to be properly characterised. As a first step, I shall raise the question of the legitimacy of using the vocabulary of property law in the social sciences, and then examine how these concepts characterise the division of financial labour.

Do we have the right to introduce rights?

The idea that some elements of the work environment may be subject to appropriation is by no means original, and has already been put forward repeatedly in the fields of sociology and labour history. The appropriation of company assets, in the illegal form of pilfering and moonlighting or the semi-legal activity of using salvaged materials, has been analysed by observers of the labour environment and in statistical surveys that focus on the employee world as a whole (Bozon and Lemel 1989).

Appropriation at work goes beyond this recycling of materials for personal use. It impacts the work environment itself. As people may use an old chair on a parking space to signal some unofficial entitlement (Ewick and Silbey 1998, p. 23), an employee may use "markers" to transform an impersonal workstation into a familiar, personal environment (Linhart 1981): photos, pictures, lack of order (or a very personalised order), etc. Moreover those markers may serve as a means of managing competition between employees. Assembly line workers paid at a piece rate, as shown in studies carried out by Donald Roy (1952), make a distinction between "gravy jobs" and "stinkers" according to how hard it is to earn more than the basic rate. One of the challenges for workers is then to claim ownership of a "gravy job" and leave the "stinkers"[3] to the rest. The appropriation of jobs, in the Taylorist context, is nonetheless severely restricted by the interchangeability and exchange of tasks (Naville 1962, pp. 383–385).[4] On the fringes of the Taylorist world (production workers, maintenance workers), establishing a stable monopoly over a particular job or task could nonetheless enable a worker to acquire considerable bargaining power.[5]

The economics of property rights that developed in the late 1960s systematically reworked the legal concepts involved in order to draw all the consequences from an economic theory standpoint (Demsetz 1967). Alchian and Demsetz note that property law must be seen as a "bundle" of rights over certain things: "What are owned are socially recognized rights of action" (Alchian and Demsetz 1973, p. 17). The property right is thus the right to take certain actions as regards scarce resources: "Property rights assignments specify the norms of behavior with respect to things that each and every person must observe in his interactions with other persons, or bear the cost for nonobservance" (Furubotn and Pejovich 1972, p. 1139). This definition matches that of Fichte, for whom the property right was conceived as "an exclusive right to *acts* not to *things*" (Fichte 2012, p. 92). These rights, by nature extremely heterogeneous (for example the right to cut one's lawn on a Sunday), in most cases are reduced by the authors to the principal rights defined by Roman legal tradition: right of use (*usus*), right to enjoy the fruit of (*fructus*) and the right to dispose of (*abusus*) or, more specifically, the right to be the residual claimant who "is to receive any residual product above . . . the marginal value of the other inputs" (Alchian and Demsetz 1972, p. 782).

One of the aims of this new institutional economics is to show that when these rights are combined and granted exclusively to one single individual, there is an increased incentive to make optimal use of them. This strategy thus makes it possible to internalise externalities and to counter the phenomenon of free-riding. The establishment of property rights over the hunting territories of the Montagnais Indians of Quebec and the enclosure policy of seventeenth-century England subscribe to this logic (Demsetz 1967). In order to avoid the tragedy of the commons, modifications in technique or production made it advantageous to switch from a system of collective property to a system of individual property, which prevented the overuse of common resources.

This reinterpretation of economic history has been strongly criticised as an ideological initiative to justify capitalism from a deliberately a-historical perspective that overlooks the social relations that already existed prior to the establishing of property rights (Berthoud and Busino 1981; Tartarin 1982). This genealogical reconstruction of property rights on a unilateralist and collective basis – a kind of communist foundation for capitalism – seems somewhat conciliatory and strangely lacking in realism. The appropriation dynamic is more often based on the private capacity to exclude (force) than the contractual and consensual division of common goods.

Nevertheless, the partisan dimension of these studies should not overshadow the contributions made by their approach. These come less from their evolutionist conception of property rights than from the conceptual advances made. Their first contribution: the relationship between a person and a thing is not one of absolute disposition but rather a bundle of rights that the other actors concede to the owner. Moreover, the socialisation of exclusion carried out by legal and state machinery is only one of the ways in which these rights can be organised. It is thus possible to identify rights where the positive law does not appear to recognise any. A second contribution, related to the first: the firm can be seen as a bundle of rights granted to the actors that occupy it. As Demsetz remarked, "what shareholders really own are their shares and not the corporation" (Demsetz 1967, p. 359).

The nature of property rights over the firm is one point that seems to pose the biggest challenge to this school of thought since they do not incorporate full individual property rights – those same rights that are supposed to provide maximum incentive.[6] This type of research then tries to characterise the rights granted to executives, particularly CEOs: setting the team's incentives and excluding employees (through dismissals) (Alchian and Demsetz 1972; Hart and Moore 1990). In an innovative article, Rajan and Zingales extend the demarcation of property rights beyond the entrepreneurial limit. They consider that the firm also grants ordinary employees with an implicit property right, namely the right to access a category of productive assets (Rajan and Zingales 1998).

In order to conceive the firm as a division of property rights between employees, it is perhaps necessary to abandon an overly demanding notion of the property right, which descends from Roman law,[7] as a strict division of individual rights. It may be necessary to revive a more medieval conception of property right and view the modern firm as the basis for a simultaneous ownership of assets by the firm's employees.

The financial firm allocates rights

In order to produce, the firm grants its employees access to productive assets. I shall show that the characteristics of this access closely resemble those of property right: freedom of action, attribution of intentionality, exclusivity, durability and transferability. To make this analysis, I will focus on the relationship between the trader and their securities portfolio.

The property rights of the trader

The first element that resembles property right without being so legally speaking, in the strictly demarcated environment of financial products, is the trader's considerable freedom to carry out a series of actions:

> Total [freedom]! Total insofar as my risks are monitored [by risk management] . . . The deals vary enormously. I don't know . . . between 30 million euros, 250, 500, a billion . . . But they are all monitored just the same.
>
> (Confavreux 2002)

Even if this kind of autonomy-exalting discourse appears to deny the constraints that limit "freedom", the feeling being expressed must be taken seriously and its origin reconstructed. Front office jobs (traders, sales) are granted a special status and a "magic barrier" separates them from middle office jobs (middle office administrators and, above all, assistant traders). Members of the front office are allowed to enter into deals on a category of securities, in other words the right to choose the compensation, price, volume and time of the transaction, whereas members of the middle office, particularly assistant traders, do not have the freedom to enter into deals without the specific approval of a member of the front office. In terms of daily practice, there is an imperceptible shift from relationships in which tasks are carried out exactly (the assistant trader executes the trader's order), partially (the buy-side trader executes the trader's order and only gets to choose the right moment), with backing (the assistant trader and junior trader suggest transactions that are backed by the trader), or under control (the head of desk controls whether or not the ordinary trader's overall transactions properly adhere to the rules of good trading), to a relationship of complete freedom for star traders. Daily conversations are often peppered with stories of interns who successfully concluded transactions over the summer, assistant traders who assert traders' prerogatives, and traders (often women) who still have to ask their head of desk for permission to conclude a transaction. Although the magic barrier between front and middle offices is in fact porous, it nonetheless has its own symbolic efficiency insofar as it establishes prerogatives. Much like positive law in everyday life, it *assigns intentionality and responsibility* to actors invested with the freedom to carry out transactions.

The freedom given to financial operators is considerable but it is also surrounded by limits. The trader must respect risk limits that are generally speaking obligatory (transgressions can result in dismissal) in terms of amounts and counterparties: "I've got very few clients at Danone . . . Vivendi and France Télécom, which I decided to deal with in 1997. Now I don't even know if I'd have lines of credit to do business with them," stated the head of a sales team bitterly in 2002.[8] However, the limits placed on their freedom to make transactions (amounts, counterparties), whose aim is related more to risk management than to managing competition between employees, are from that perspective less vital than qualitative limitations. The categories of securities on which financial operators can transact are clearly defined and their boundaries closely guarded:[9]

> One former forex trader wanted to "boost his results by investing 10% of his profits in options" in the event that he got a "good feeling". But his management never agreed, stating "everyone does their own job". This "little" forex trader, whose legitimacy was fragile on account of his inadequate training (a former sports teacher) and who was working in a business line that had been particularly discredited in the second half of the 1990s, was requesting to use options, a noble and sophisticated product, albeit speculatively, which may have seemed particularly presumptuous. Nevertheless, although boundaries are regularly crossed and challenged, they are still jealously guarded even in superior trading methods.

This policy of protecting boundaries is not merely a constraint for financial operators but also provides a guarantee against external incursions. In the trading room,

I sometimes witnessed disputes over allocation. The basket traders (working on arbitrage of index futures against cash equities) constantly needed the services of the securities lending and borrowing desk in order to borrow securities they had sold without actually having. They frequently complained about the prices of those "thieves" and threatened to conclude this type of transaction themselves. The head of the securities lending and borrowing desk took action with the head of the trading room, thereby reconfirming portfolio division, re-enabling the existing boundaries and silencing the threats. Even if the methods of organising the allocation of prerogatives are relatively homogeneous from one bank to another and from one trading room to another, there is a fairly general tendency to clearly divide financial activity and to attribute local monopolies that allow internal competition to be limited.

The tightest intra-organisational boundaries are those between major product groups[10] and major job categories. It is very difficult for someone trading fixed income products to also trade equity products (and vice versa). Similarly, it is difficult to cross the boundary between traders (who manage securities portfolios) and salespeople (who manage a portfolio of clients): a trader cannot pick up the phone and talk directly to clients and sell them products without going through the seller, just as the seller cannot suggest transactions that are not managed by the trader.[11] This local monopoly is allocated either to an operator or to a small team (the desks) who then collectively manage the domain of activity (even if this means sharing assets once the desk gains power). The head of equity derivatives trading at Mars Bank organised his team in such a way that there were "always at least two traders on a security". He admitted that this style of organisation, which was in fact quite original, sometimes created tension during the first six months. Between desks, however, there are very seldom any areas of overlap.

What might seem like a desire to establish a rational organisation of work and avoid duplications is therefore also a means of limiting competition between financial actors. As one trader commented, "In this bank we have a huge amount of freedom to do whatever we like with products. The limitation comes from my neighbour. My neighbour won't let me trade products that he's trading." As the boxed text below shows, disputing a product boundary is a serious undertaking requiring the intervention of the bank's top management.

Acquiring rights over others' portfolios

This fixed income exotic products trader at Mars Bank was, in 2002, a "big" trader in the bank's London trading room. His ever-increasing income reached a peak in 2001 at more than 1 million pounds. A science graduate of the elite Paris-based *École Normale Supérieure*, a lover of art and music with left-wing tendencies, he did not see himself as a "typical" trader. He shows sensitivity, at least during the interview, to the well-being of those around him at work, not just his peers (such as the junior trader on his desk) but also, more unusually, the middle office employee who values his trading book each day. He does not embody the figure of the egotistical trader, certain of his worth, greedy, competing constantly and indifferent to the fate of those who lose out. Even so, he campaigned to be allowed to trade his neighbour's products, an area which he claims sets a limit on his "own freedom".

Do you have the right to trade equities?

We did everything we could. Our desk was allowed to trade a small amount.

Why?

Because it's a business. The broader our range of products the more chance we have of selling and bringing in money. It's another product. The fixed income market is inversely correlated to equities. For me, it's important to trade them and to have a better understanding of my market. When I say equities, it's limited to the CAC and Dow Jones indexes.

Did your boss have to fight for it?

Not my boss. It was my boss's boss's boss who took the fight to the highest level, with the number two or three of the bank, to get a share of equities. It took a year of negotiation. "I want this." "All right, I'll give you this . . . "

Did you have to fight for it too?

Not at my level, but I had to present all the arguments to this person so he could defend it against the others. Even it doesn't actually bring us much business, it's always motivating to move forward, discover new products and markets . . . It's a constant adventure. Otherwise it would get repetitive and tiring.

Didn't the fact that equity derivatives were so profitable between 1995 and 2000 . . . ?

Yes it did. I'd been wanting to trade equities since 1998 at my level. But it took time to convince them. My boss probably didn't want to annoy [the CEO of Mars Bank]. It took me two years to convince them. It went on for a long time. It didn't happen until 2001.

Right when equities weren't as profitable . . . ?

That's it . . . No, but it's about having market access. We don't need it to survive. For my boss I think it's also a question of power.

The possibility of making free use of a portfolio is not only a guarantee against external incursions but also a guarantee for the future. The *durability* of use may not have the unlimited form of the property right. However, the very low level of mobility within this professional activity results in a stable relationship between employees and the assets they manage. Admittedly, these are extremely volatile environments, turnover rates are very high, dismissals, at least in Anglo-American countries, take place easily and frequently, and economic market cycles make and unmake positions like Borges's lottery (Borges 2000; Godechot, Hassoun and Muniesa 2000). Yet the fact remains that within the financial firm itself, mobility is low. Financial operators often stay for a long time in the same market, the same product, the same job. They increase their domain of activity from their original position, becoming senior trader, head of desk then head of trading room, but they rarely make a radical shift in their domain of activity.

> One trader I met who had spent his entire career with Neptune Bank had the opportunity to change his domain of activity. He had worked as a trader from 1990 to 1999, mainly trading the franc-mark and, to a lesser extent, the dollar-mark. He went to work in London for a few years but continued to trade the same currencies. The introduction of the euro on 1 January 1999 put an end to his domain of activity. For a year, he traded the dollar-yen with mixed success. In 2000, he had the chance to sell short fixed income products to the central banks and take advantage of an unexpected "retirement". In 2002, his boss moved from selling to central banks to selling to the corporate firms. He had the chance – another surprise – to follow his boss and handle a client portfolio that he considered to be more interesting.

Not all professional moves are as Lilliputian as this former trader's baby steps. Occasionally, traders have a radical change of product, moving from cash to options, from short to long fixed income products or even shifting from fixed income trading to equity trading. Some become salespeople (the reverse is extremely rare), move into risk control, financial engineering or the back office (in the latter three cases, the move is often seen as a demotion). Moreover, although changes in people's domain of activity are rare, they are nonetheless more common internally than externally because financial work is extremely compartmentalised (Gautié, Godechot and Sorignet 2005; Godechot, 2006).

In any case, mobility is more of an opportunity granted (or not) when a domain has been exhausted (or when its occupant has exhausted its possibilities) than a career path that is imposed. This is a marked contrast with support functions, retail banking and other sectors such as insurance. When I returned to Universal Company in 2000, three years after the first survey I conducted there (Godechot 2001), many financial operators were doing the same activity either at Universal Company or in another bank. On the other hand, many support staff, all of which had remained with Universal Company, had changed jobs, function, department, etc. The contrast was even more marked with the bank's central services and insurance roles where it was common to have a systematic policy of moving highly educated young professionals (for example three periods of six months spent in widely varying roles) and not attaching them to any particular domain at the start of their career.

The last characteristic of this form of ownership, albeit not as clearly defined as durability, is *transferabitily*. Hence, portfolios are transferable. Over the course of a day, temporary transfers of use take place in order to help out colleagues. If a member of the desk is absent when her client calls, a colleague will take a message and conclude the transaction in the best interests of the person responsible for that domain.[12] Likewise, securities portfolios and client portfolios are assigned to a colleague during the holidays, but this is more a case of temporary care than transfer. When a new person joins a team, the issue of the domain of activity that will be allocated to the new operator is raised. This division presents such a challenge that it sometimes encourages a kind of Malthusianism, a refusal to hire and the continued use of an underproductive structure (as regards overall opportunities to generate profit). The financial operator, whose activity increases to the point that she builds a team of two to three people, has the very real impression that she is yielding her own personal domain.

Let us illustrate the transferability of assets with an example in the area of statistical trading. This activity consists in looking for statistical correlations between past prices and using these figures to predict future correlations and thereby make a profit. When the trader specialising in this activity joined Proxima Bank, he first carried out research for the trader who had recruited him. After a few months, this trader gave him four of his books (i.e. securities portfolios), one of which "didn't work at all and had never worked" and told him, "Listen, if you can make money with this, it's yours!" For this new trader, it was the "only way to start". Two years later, when his boss left for another bank and he inherited all his books which had become available, he faced the same question of how large an area to allocate to the statistician he had just hired:

> [The portfolios] are *mine*. They *belong to me*, because they all existed before he joined. For the moment, this year he's just doing research. I was the same in the first year, I did research and *they belonged to the other guy*. The idea is that if he really does a good job in research this year, in other words, if he really helps me, has some important ideas for the models and discovers some interesting things, then next year *I'll give him* an area where he can make his own model and I'll help him get it started. So we haven't established where it will be yet, if it's an existing model that's on its way out, or a new idea, or something in another country. But we've agreed that the real reward for his success this year isn't really his bonus, it's the right to launch his own model next year . . . [Determining what he'll get allocated] is quite strategic, but as the markets are so dynamic we can't predict it a year in advance. You can give them a few decent investments . . . I'm *not going to give him something so tiny* that there's no money to be made from it.

In the case of this trader, and more generally in small teams where the boss remains actively involved and the skilled employee almost becomes her equal, the handing-over of domain of activity can take the form of a transfer of semi-personal assets. Generally speaking, however, it is more like a concession. Much like under Ancien Régime law, the boss retains a *droit de suite* over the domain that is conceded.

Let us summarise. The example of the securities portfolio shows how the financial firm assigns a *domain of activity* to its employees. By giving those employees the *freedom* but not the *obligation* to engage in a certain number of actions with those assets, it grants them a level of *freedom to dispose of assets*. This free disposal, which is partly *transferable*, is protected both in time (*durability* of allocations) and against competition from what other employees dispose of (underlying *exclusivity*). In doing so, the firm attributes *intentionality* and *responsibility*: the intention to derive value from those assets and the responsibility to derive value on the one hand and, on the other, to respect the boundaries and not encroach on others' domains. Within this framework, the organisation of labour can therefore be characterised as the granting of a *right over assets*, and even of a *property right*. These property rights are all the more important because they not only give free disposal of assets but also access to ideas and know-how, in short, to a space of vital immaterial assets in partial joint ownership.

Naturally, the rights characterised above are not positive property rights defined and protected by the French civil code, but rather a conceptual characterisation of work practice and of employees' "legal consciousness" (Ewik and Silbey 1998). These property rights are not absolute: their duration, transferability and exclusivity are limited. Their limits are not clearly established and do not take the material form of a security or piece of proof. Disputes over the allocation of these rights are not settled in a court, they are settled by management during a formal or informal negotiation, and not in a trial. They conclude with the modification or preservation of the allocation or sometimes with the employee's resignation or exclusion. Far from being subject to a "Roman" and "absolute" property right, a firm's assets may be seen as the basis for simultaneous ownerships, similar to those to which land was subject during the Ancien Régime (Patault 1989). When a suzerain transferred land to the vassal it did not involve a transferral of all rights but rather the provisional transferral of the use of a piece of land. Similarly, when a head of desk delegates a securities portfolio to a trader for her to trade or yield a profit, this does not mean that the whole portfolio is being transferred but merely a level of freedom to use the portfolio; furthermore, the feeling that the delegated securities portfolio inspires in the head of desk bears a resemblance to the lord's eminent property right.

Overlap and compartmentalisation of knowledge rights

I shall now analyse the structure of property rights over knowledge as a special case. Although portfolio allocation is fairly strict, it brings with it access to assets whose protection and demarcation are far less clear: knowledge and, in particular, know-how. These are often the logical additions to a domain of activity that are themselves clearly demarcated. Being allocated a portfolio (for instance a futures portfolio) leads to the acquisition of know-how particular to the management of this portfolio (such as cash and carry arbitrage in my example). In their model of power within the firm, Rajan and Zingales consider that attributing employees with a right of access to a productive asset (in other words, power over that asset) gives them an incentive to specialise and acquire the human capital needed for its manipulation (Rajan and Zingales 1998).

Property rights over knowledge are therefore related in some way to the division of labour and property rights over domains of activity (securities, clients, machines). However, the compartmentalisation and rationalised division of knowledge are less advanced. Even if the financial firm has a well-developed knowledge management policy (which most do not), directing acquisitions (learning prescription), transfers (training prescription) and overall structure (division of know-how), it cannot provide a truly effective guarantee of exclusion, protection of individual monopolies, full transfers, etc. The know-how and ideas that generate profit have multiple and indistinct origins. Financial actors like to imagine their know-how as a very personal characteristic or even as a gift. This ideology of personal charisma, of the "self-made man" or the "uncreated creator", similar in finance to that described by Pierre Bourdieu and Jean-Claude Passeron in the case of educational success (Bourdieu and Passeron, 1979), is better able to make financial success a *causa sui*, with the dual merit of the innate gift and personal effort. Although some actors such as the head of the fixed income room at Neptune Bank, who sees himself as a "survivor" in a "hostile jungle", learnedly state that a trader's qualities are "innate", it is possible to reconstruct the part played by the flow of information, ideas, know-how, techniques and knowledge by accumulating details of specific, insignificant examples. Even in the case of financial operators who claim to be self-taught, there is always some form of information flow involved. They did not invent or reinvent options arbitrage by themselves. They have sometimes acquired knowledge by reading manuals of financial theory, but more generally, financial operators usually owe everything to a senior employee who showed them the ropes and the "tricks" of the trade at the start of their career: identifying profitable arbitrages, not getting cheated and learning to recognise others' strategies.[13]

This passing-on of knowledge from the oldest to the youngest is by no means the only way to access know-how. On the contrary, it can take place in reverse, from operators to their superiors ("I get inspiration from all my colleagues' good ideas," stated one head of desk). Winning ideas in finance often emerge from an informal reticular structure, everyday conversations between several operators or established situations such as morning meetings (Collins 1998; Beunza and Stark 2004). Although the specialist in statistical trading – as described above – was "lucky" when his senior colleague left, enabling him to inherit his portfolios, he also added that his colleague's departure destabilised him because it put an end to their interaction, which had always been a source of ideas: "In fact, it was the interaction between us that led to new ideas. When you're alone it's hard to stay motivated. You go round and round in circles on the same idea."

Although attached to domains of activity that are meticulously compartmentalised (securities or client portfolios), know-how goes beyond that division, developing and renewing itself through interactions between actors. Collective products are not, however, managed collectively. They are not exclusive, and are made available provided that this disposal is possible. They are there for the taking, but through a form of individual grip: they are to be invented, combined and, most often, copied. Financial economics has often highlighted the role of imitation, mimicry and blind conformity as a factor that determines the formation of anomalies in the financial markets (Artus 1995; Orléan 1999). This blind conformity is not limited to the monitoring carried out by large speculators on the securities market. It goes far beyond that: when a bank moves forward with a particular range of derivatives products, another will be sure to follow a few months later and replicate that new product based on a very similar combination of mathematics, software, clients and even employees. Within the same structure, blind conformity may also happen among teams and employees in the room. One buy-side trader (a subordinate trader who executes another's orders) talked about his failed two-year stint as a proprietary trader (after which he returned to his initial position as a buy-side trader), explaining that there is a strong temptation to copy the strategies used by good traders. However, he was quick to point out the limitations of such behaviour: any replication that is too crude and too visible risks exposing the inanity of his own professional position and highlighting it as being no more than additional uncontrolled risk-taking. Moreover, given that the distribution of knowledge, while not actually divided up, is nonetheless monitored, and especially considering that access to ideas depends on the underlying structure of allocated assets, mimicry cannot be carried out instantaneously or generally, as one might imagine. Even in a given market, the actors (and assets) are too heterogeneous.

Although the use of know-how may not be entirely free, it is not completely controlled either. Its exclusive use is particularly difficult to assert given that use by one person does not prevent (other than through the profit margin) the use by another.

Apart from software, intellectual property rights are very difficult to assert and very poorly defended. One hedge fund executive I met was obsessed with this difficulty. As the former head of a capital markets department that was well ahead of its competitors, he saw them all "steal" what he considered to be "his ideas". Starting over again on a tiny hedge fund with the fervour of a believer, he sought unsuccessfully to patent his "revolutionary" options trading technique at all costs. In short, the characteristics of know-how as described here play a major role in financial sector economics. I will give further examples of this in the following chapters.

Amount, strength and distribution of rights

Variations in structure

The allocation of securities portfolios to traders can therefore be characterised as an allocation of rights, since it has similar characteristics to those of property right. What about the domains attributed to other professions? The allocation of client portfolios to salespeople can be conceived in exactly the same way. The characteristics of client portfolios remain the same as for securities portfolios: availability, durability, exclusivity, transferability and responsibility. Only some details differ. The division of client portfolios is carried out according to the clients' nationalities (French, German, American, etc.) and types (central banks, banks, corporates, mid caps – middle capitalisation – and so on) and not, as is the case with trading, according to the nature of the product sold (spot, equities, bonds, convertible bonds, swaps, swaptions, options, exotic options, structured products, etc.) and its pricing currency. It could even be said that salespeople have more comprehensive rights over their assets insofar as their freedom is less curtailed by limitations imposed by risk management. As one trader commented, "there are limitations on risk-taking but no limitations on creating volume". Nonetheless, when counterparty risk was taken into account, particularly following the collapse of Herstatt Bank (1974), Barings Bank (1996) and Enron (2000), it resulted in a limitation on "credit risk" and a reduction in salespersons' capacity to take action on the various elements of a client's portfolio.

When moving from front office positions to support functions such as IT and back office, we find that the characteristics that turned the allocation of work into an allocation of rights become blurred: less availability, less durability, less exclusivity. Hence, the compartmentalisation of domains of activity is far less marked in the fields of computer engineering and R&D than it is for front office professions. The IT engineering team at Saturn Bank usually worked on projects that changed from month to month and sometimes even from week to week. Although some domains are valued more highly and tend to be monopolised by those lucky enough to occupy them (for example, the Monte Carlo simulation methods which enable pricing parameters to be calculated for the most complex products), the fact that projects recur so irregularly prevents the strict compartmentalisation of engineers' domains of activity or the stabilisation of links between engineers and portions of activity. This example shows that IT employees' rights are considerably less comprehensive. There is less overall stability in time and less protection against others employees' incursions. Considering that the actions taken in this support sector are usually ordered by front office, there is also less freedom of action. In some respects, the situation as regards IT lies somewhere between that of front office and back office. Back office and support functions in general are characterised by their very low level of control over the firm's assets. They serve the front office and their role is to carry out the tasks asked of them (settle transactions, draw up the accounts, sign work contracts and fix computers) rather than decide on an action to be taken. Even if back office work is extremely repetitive in many ways (just as front office work is), in the medium term there is major instability as regards the allocation of tasks. Support functions are constantly being reorganised: around once every two or three years at Saturn Bank between 1995 and 2001. In the front office, meanwhile, the names of market activities may change from one reshuffle to the next, but the previous functions continue to exist, and the relationship between the employee and the firm's assets remains stable.

Analysing the opposition between front office and back office (as well as between different positions in the hierarchy) allows us to highlight the unequal nature of the distribution of rights over a firm's assets. The volume of employees' rights differs in intensity (freedom to engage in a large number of actions in a given domain), extension (size of the domain of activity), durability and exclusivity. At one end, the domain of activity has a structure that is close to the property right defined by the French civil code. Holders of that right have what Alchian and Demetz call the "residual claimant right" over the domain of activity, in other words the right to manage the commodity in the absence of a specific clause (Alchian and Demsetz 1972, pp. 781–783; Milgrom and Roberts 1992). The clauses to be specified for permitted actions are too numerous and, as a result, it is not possible to draw up complete contracts. When an employee is allocated a domain of activity, the list of actions to be taken is not fully specified. The employee has a certain amount of freedom to act outside of any instructions given, and to combine actions that are instructed outside of any instructions of combination. At the other end, for example in the upper levels of the back office hierarchy, the proportion of prescribed tasks is far higher. In the case of the pure prescribed action, with the ideal type being the Taylorist mechanical gesture, the allocated domain of activity is reduced to almost nothing.

Variations in modes of attribution

Finally, I will study how the ways through which rights are attributed to employees may impact their strength. The allocation of work, which creates unequal rights over the firm's assets in terms of volume and profitability, is subject to continual monitoring by actors. While the hierarchy does supervise this distribution of rights, we should not consider this discretionary decision in overly hierarchical terms. The distribution process is a negotiation, and sometimes the senior employee responsible for dividing up these assets does not so much allocate as retain the allocation already obtained by powerful subordinates. Indeed, it is often the case, particularly in small firms, that financial operators develop new activities on the fringes of the domain assigned to them. In these cases, they claim to be "developing a business".

These variations in ways of allocating activity, endorsement versus devolution, have an impact on the origin of employees' sense of ownership. When a domain of activity is endorsed, the sense of ownership is much stronger and is based on the overall set of activities that gave rise to it: selecting assets, inventing the method for increasing their value, defending them against external predation and explaining their advantages to executives. In the world of finance, people derive the greatest sense of pride from having developed something "on their own"; in other words, from establishing a client portfolio, securities portfolio or arbitrage system "alone". "Self-made men" who feel they have established their activity by themselves often criticise "heirs" who have inherited pre-existing activities: "I created the sales portfolio specialising in asset swaps out of nothing, because there weren't any [clients]," exclaimed a sales woman enthusiastically. "I don't have enough of a technocratic mind [to work on big structures] . . . And as I chose to work on structures on a more human scale, I bring in my own business," echoes a head of trading room at Pluto Bank. In contrast, those who inherit pre-existing assets that are already fully functioning only develop a sense of ownership over time.

The method by which a right is transferred also influences the relationship between line managers and the assets they concede. When a line manager reallocates firm's assets that she has not conquered herself, she asserts and, above all, represents the firm's eminent property right over those assets and therefore does not develop any special attachment to them. Often, however, particularly more recently in the French financial markets, line managers have the feeling that they have created, established or developed these assets, and they retain a sense of attachment and paternity towards the asset being conceded, which does not dissipate through concession. During the heroic ages of finance, these assets may have come from nothing and been pulled out of their original vacuum. One head of trading room, recounting his early career at Saturn Bank in the late 1980s, remembered that "we had the feeling that we had to occupy the land as if we were conquering the Wild West. You have to mark out the land and cry, 'That's mine!' Today it may be worth nothing but tomorrow it might be worth a fortune, and you have to claim it for yourself". They may also have been hard-won in battles with other departments, a conquest that also gives people a very personal claim over these assets.[14]

Whether conquered or created, or at the very least personalised, those who own these domains of activity have a great sense of attachment to them, which they retain even after the domains have been divided up: "I gave him a share of my clientele" (seller); "I'll give him an area" (trader). In this case, the act of transferral produces far more than just a simultaneous legitimisation of the hierarchical position. It produces a system of expectations towards the individual and the assets being transferred.

The ways and means by which individuals form a relationship with the firm's assets are not established at the outset of the activity. The distribution of rights is unstable and may be reconsidered in order to take advantage of a change in power relations or a reorganisation of the activity. For example, in the trading room it is common to see traders from other desks snooping around their colleagues' domains of activity. They wander over and casually ask questions in order to obtain information about their colleagues' activity. Naturally, some of these harmless, everyday conversations have a social function. However, the employees are also trying to get information on the distribution of implicit property rights and also to gauge the quality of that distribution.

A convertible bonds desk at the Titan brokerage firm had the dual disadvantage of being newly established and losing money at the same time. Traders from neighbouring options desks would hang about nearby to see what was being done. What they were actually doing was challenging the distribution of rights. They believed that the trading of convertible bonds was basically a form of arbitrage with a similar level of volatility to options arbitrage and that it should not have been made independent from their own activity. They were trying to glean information for two reasons: to familiarise themselves with the rights that they were hoping to be allocated; and to identify arguments that would support a change in allocation. If the trading of convertible bonds was working well, they could try to move into that domain or develop a similar business on the fringes of their own main activity. If it was not working well, they could argue that the portfolios should be reallocated to true volatility professionals such as themselves. In this way, some traders succeeded in being allocated major securities portfolios after other traders left during bad years.

There is a whole range of strategies such as this aimed at increasing the volume of employee rights over a firm's assets. The most common of these consists in increasing the intensity with which assets are exploited: either by extending the limits placed on individual risks or increasing the size of the teams, etc. required to do the same activity. Particularly in systems that follow or partly follow a formula, this strategy can bring about an automatic rise in bonuses (even if profitability is slightly lower). In order to justify bonus differences in the labour market, traders from Mars Bank, when discussing their counterparts at Mercury Bank in front of a headhunter ready to judge them on the basis of their different bonuses, were quick to point out that "at Mercury it was all too easy to get such high bonuses with the risk limits they had".

This increase in intensity is often combined with increased extension. Gradually, ranges of new products (e.g. swaptions for a swaps specialist) and types of clients (e.g. Belgian clients for a specialist on Luxembourg) that are related to the main activity may result from new domains of extension or the conquest of new rights. A more original alternative is for portfolios to be built up on the basis of close personal relationships and circumstances, even though the logic behind them does not really follow the nature of the activity. One trader from the Titan brokerage firm thus recalled how actors have an interest, often little-known, in staying with a financial firm from which all the employees are resigning, because client, securities and software portfolios suddenly become available. The urgent need to increase their value demands a major redistribution among those who remain. He described how one colleague, unlike the rest who were developing their value and the value of their shares by testing them on the labour market, had increased his own value by never resigning and taking on part of what was left after his own colleagues had resigned.

Dispossession is the dark underside of this asset accumulation strategy. It takes on a spectacular form when it comes to the Anglo-American style of dismissal. A line manager informs the employee out of the blue. Any financial activity is then forbidden and the dismissed employee has one hour in which to gather her belongings and leave the office, with paid notice of termination. Although I have never met anyone who has experienced this, the procedure is well documented.[15] In France, labour laws provide better protection to employees and dismissal procedures are less abrupt and less common. Nonetheless, when a market is saturated, or a competitor encroaches on the firm's territory, or a series of errors, misfortunes or misappropriations brings losses, a variety of types of dispossession can also be initiated in France, such as dismissal, transferral to the back office or demotion. At Saturn Bank, following the Asian crisis of 1998, some assets suddenly lost value, particularly in the trading of currency and interest rates in the emerging markets. There were redundancies. Some traders called on the General Confederation of Labour (CGT) to defend them. The situation was surprising enough to warrant press coverage.

> According to an HR professional at Saturn Bank, in this wave of change there were clear cases of demotion: one trader, whose portfolio, computer, telephone, projects and clients had been taken away for one year, was left only with his chair and a daily request from his line manager calling on him to resign. The case went to court. The lawyer hired by the HR professional to defend Saturn Bank managed to "slightly" reduce the damages (the trader had claimed 150,000 euros in compensation) by proving that the deprived employee had not sought another job elsewhere during his period of demotion.

***

Before I draw all the conclusions of this initial allocation of rights, I should also explain how the allocation of property rights characterised here differs from that characterised by the neoclassical theory of property rights in the manner of Alchian and Demsetz (Demsetz 1967; Alchian and Demsetz 1972 & 1973). The organisation of financial assets is not necessarily an example of optimum management. Certainly, the allocation of property rights takes into account people's capacity to increase the value of the firm's assets: assets are allocated according to employees' skill level, and the size of the assets allocated is increased according to proven successes, as if the firm were learning to differentiate the value of individuals in a stochastic, belated and veiled manner. However, this capacity for selection should not be overestimated. The skills that bring financial success, particularly in the field of speculative trading, are indeed especially difficult to characterise and select.

Randomness reigns supreme, at least in the neoclassical interpretation of the formation of share prices. A series of successes may be nothing more than a trick played by chance and not an insight into the employee's capacity to increase the value of the assets conceded. At least, this is the interpretation made by trader Taleb, who distances himself from his peers with his iconoclastic views (Taleb 2001). According to him, traders whose positions (and bonuses) increase along with their own success are merely "lucky monkeys" who often delude themselves by believing in their own skill. Even if his conclusion is somewhat nihilistic, based entirely on the efficient markets hypothesis taken to its extreme, and no doubt exaggerated, he highlights the great difficulty in identifying financial competence and attributing property rights on the utilitarian basis of their increased value.

In actual fact, particularly in the early days of derivatives trading rooms, employees were usually hired through personal contacts, even family contacts. The logic used then was not so different from that of Ali Baba when he revealed the secret of the cave to his brother: sharing profit with a close friend or relative (the logic of "take some for yourself"). In order to truly allocate rights in an optimal manner, they should be auctioned off. However, with a few exceptions,[16] jobs are never put up for sale. Rather, they are given. Employees' limited ability to pay, the high level of uncertainty over the profitability of future positions and employees' inability to endure major financial losses are likely to prevent the parties from entering into a sales contract rather than an employment contract. Lastly, I should add that a sales contract involves a formal and material procedure that is completely different from that of a work contract. In the absence of any reorganisation of work, this contractual innovation (sale rather than wage labour) could be recategorised as a work contract by either of the parties.

If the use of strategies is so important for winning and retaining rights over the firm's assets, it is because the distribution of existing assets contains the seeds of distribution for non-existent, virtual assets that will come into being – in short, profit. The distribution of property rights contains the seeds of distribution for the fruits of ownership. However, for all that, in the financial firm this distribution of profit is by no means carried out automatically. It is the product of circumstances, discussion, manipulation, the invocation of justice and power relations. In order to understand the way in which future fruits are attached to present rights, let us first conceive their initial detachment.

Notes

1 "We do not deserve our place in the distribution of native endowments, any more than we deserve our initial starting place in society. That we deserve the superior character that enables us to make the effort to cultivate our abilities is also problematic; for such character depends in good part upon fortunate family and social circumstances in early life for which we can claim no credit" (Rawls 1971, p. 89).

2 The three categories of inequalities described, all of which are arbitrary, are not equivalent. Any modification of inequalities (in whichever direction) within the firm is the firm's responsibility. On the other hand, it would be difficult for it to modify overall social inequality (for example, the structure of human capital). Society as a whole can modify its own inequalities but it has difficulty modifying natural inequalities. It can, however, compensate for them.

3 In one workshop they studied, Bernoux, Motte and Saglio observed an allocation of tasks each time workers began a shift (twice a day). The most senior workers who had

built themselves a reputation almost always managed to be assigned the same tasks each day – "good jobs" that required less effort and were more prestigious in terms of the technical nature of the tasks (Bernoux, Motte and Saglio 1973, pp. 40–44). The authors noted that an older worker on the "best" machine could complete his working day in three hours.

4 Interchangeability and exchange were the rule in Roy's factory, where he regularly moved from "gravy jobs", where the quota had to be met, to "stinkers", where workers slacked off because the rate itself was very hard to obtain.

5 This was the case with maintenance workers in the industrial monopoly (Crozier 1964).

6 It is striking to note that this liberal school of thought encounters the same difficulties as individualist bourgeois thought when required to conceive the collective property of a legal entity. This is one of the reasons for the late introduction of laws on public limited companies in the nineteenth century and for the nationalisation of the clergy's property, and even for the Allarde decree and the Le Chapelier law that abolished guilds (Patault 1989).

7 To avoid all problems of common ownership, Roman law required landowners to leave a strip of uncultivated land around plots (boundaries), and the owners of each house to leave a free space around the walls (*ambitus*) (Patault 1989, p. 153).

8 The very poor results of France Telecom and Vivendi in 2002 led to a sudden rise in these firms' default risk, at least as far as the market was concerned.

9 "Each of the desks has a product or a list of products it quotes. Within a room, the same product can never be quoted by a different trader or by different desks" notes the head of the fixed income room at Neptune Bank.

10 Some of these boundaries are the result of past financial market regulation. In the United States, the Glass–Steagall Act, enacted after the 1929 crash, restricted affiliations between commercial banks handling lending from investment banks handling securities. These regulations were gradually dismantled during the 1980s and 1990s, and abolished altogether under Clinton, meaning that American banks have the potential to be universal banks.

11 The salesperson function (then called "foreign exchange dealer") was introduced in France for the foreign exchange market – the oldest market activity – in the 1970s, following the American "Bankers Trust" model, by Lepetit at the Banque de Suez et de l'Union des Mines (Lepetit 2002). When activities began (as in the case of securities lending in the 1990s), commercial activities and trading were not separate, and only became so when the market was sufficiently mature.

12 When tensions run high within a team, this assistance in managing an area of activity is not even provided. One female seller told me that on one occasion her client called while she was in the toilet and her boss, another woman, informed them, "Oh, I think she's gone away on holiday!"

13 Most financiers' accounts of finance attribute great importance to a mentor who protects the new arrival and initiates her into the techniques and know-how needed to survive in the hostile world of finance. Cf. for example the account provided by Lewis of his learning process as a salesperson: after an early run of bad luck, Alexander takes him under his wing and trains him as a bond salesperson (Lewis 1987, pp. 204–217).

14 Hence, MacKenzie describes the conflict over the devolution of ABS-CDOs portfolios (collateralised debt obligation of mortgage asset-backed securities) between ABS teams and CDO teams. The victory of CDO teams, more legitimate due to their previous involvement in corporate securities, had dramatic consequences. They used correlation of defaults of firms in the same sector as an estimate for the correlation

of defaults of mortgages, a choice that happened to tragically underestimate its true magnitude and to fuel the subprime crisis (MacKenzie 2011).
15 It is described several times by Rozan (1999).
16 Before 1987, public office stockbroking positions were sold off in this way. Similarly, individual floor trader positions on the open outcry markets were put up for sale, at least in secret.

References

Alchian, A and Demsetz, H 1972, 'Production, Information Costs, and Economic Organization', *American Economic Review*, vol. 62, n°5, pp. 777–795.

Alchian, A and Demsetz, H 1973, 'The Property Right Paradigm', *Journal of Economic History*, vol. 33, n°1, pp. 16–27.

Artus, P 1995, *Anomalies sur les marchés financiers*, Economica, Paris.

Bernoux, P, Motte, D and Saglio, J 1973, *Trois ateliers d'OS*, Les Éditions ouvrières, Paris.

Berthoud, G and Busino, G 1981, 'La propriété: entre la nature et la culture', *Revue européenne des sciences sociales*, vol. 19, n°59, pp. 17–54.

Beunza, D and Stark, D 2004, 'Tools of the Trade: The Socio-Technology of Arbitrage in a Wall Street Trading Room', *Industrial and Corporate Change*, vol. 13, n°2, pp. 369–400.

Borges, JL 2000, 'The Lottery in Babylon' in *Fictions*, Penguin Books, London, pp. 51–58.

Bourdieu, P and Passeron, JC 1979, *The Inheritors: French Students and their Relation to Culture*, University of Chicago, Chicago IL.

Bozon M and Lemel, Y 1989, 'Les petits profits du travail salarié. Moments, produits et plaisirs dérobés', *Revue française de sociologie*, vol. 30, n°1, pp. 101–127.

Collins, R 1998, *The Sociology of Philosophies*, Belknap Press of Harvard University Press, Cambridge MA.

Confavreux, J 2002, 'La Bourse et sa vie', in *Surpris par la nuit* (radio broadcast), 15 May 2002, France Culture, Radio France, Paris.

Crozier, M 1964, *The Bureaucratic Phenomenon*, University of Chicago Press, Chicago IL.

Demsetz, H 1967, 'Toward a Theory of Property Rights', *American Economic Review*, vol. 57, n°2, pp. 347–359.

Ewik, P and Silbey, S 1998, *The Common Place of Law: Stories from Everyday Life*, University of Chicago Press, Chicago IL.

Fichte, J 2012, *The Closed Commercial State*, SUNY Press, New York.

Furubotn, E and Pejovich, S 1972, 'Property Rights and Economic Theory: A Survey of Recent Literature', *Journal of Economic Literature*, vol. 10, n°4, pp. 1137–1162.

Gautié, J, Godechot O and Sorignet, PE 2005, 'Arrangement institutionnel et fonctionnement du marché du travail. Le cas de la chasse de tête', *Sociologie du travail*, vol. 47, n°3, pp. 383–404.

Godechot, O 2001, *Les Traders. Essai de sociologie des marchés financiers*, La Découverte, Paris.

Godechot, O 2006, '"Quel est le salaire de marché?" Enquêtes de rémunération et mise en forme du marché du travail dans l'industrie financière', *Genèses*, n°63, pp. 108–127.

Godechot, O, Hassoun, JP and Muniesa, F 2000, 'La volatilité des postes. Professionnels des marchés financiers et informatisation', *Actes de la recherche en sciences sociales*, n°134, pp. 45–55.

Hart, O and Moore, J 1990, 'Property Rights and the Nature of the Firm', *Journal of Political Economy*, vol. 98, n°6, pp. 1119–1158.

Lepetit, JF 2002, *Homme de marché*, Economica, Paris.

Lewis, M 1989, *Liar's Poker*, Hodder and Stoughton, London.

Linhart, R 1981, *The Assembly Line*, University of Massachusetts Press, Amherst MA.

MacKenzie, D 2011, 'The Credit Crisis as a Problem in the Sociology of Knowledge', *American Journal of Sociology*, vol. 116, n°6, pp. 1778–1841.

Marx, K 1990, *Capital. A Critique of Political Economy*, Penguin Books, London.

Milgrom P and Roberts, J 1992, *Economics, Organization and Management*, Prentice-Hall, Englewood Cliffs NJ.

Naville, N 1962, 'Division du travail et répartition des tâches', in *Traité de sociologie du travail*, eds G Friedmann and P Naville, Armand Colin, Paris, pp. 383–385.

Orléan, A 1999, *Le Pouvoir de la finance*, Odile Jacob, Paris.

Patault, AM 1989, *Introduction historique au droit des biens*, PUF, Paris.

Rajan, R and Zingales, L 1998, 'Power in a Theory of the Firm', *Quarterly Journal of Economics*, vol. 133, n°2, pp. 387–432.

Rawls, J 1971, *A Theory of Justice*, Harvard University Press, Cambridge MA.

Roy, D 1952, 'Quota Restriction and Goldbricking in a Machine Shop', *American Journal of Sociology*, vol. 57, n°5, pp. 427–442.

Rozan, JM 1999, *Le Fric*, Michel Lafon, Paris.

Taleb, N 2001, *Fooled by Randomness. The Hidden Role of Chance in the Markets and in Life*, Texere, New York.

Tartarin, R 1982, 'La théorie des droits de propriété: vers un historicisme libéral', in *L'Économie-fiction. Contre les nouveaux économistes*, Maspero, Paris.

4　The sense of ownership of profit

A multitude of imperceptible limits and boundaries divide employees' domains of activity within financial firms. The company's technical task of organising labour is transformed into an operation of allocating property rights. It is out of this constellation of overlapping and incompletely divided productive units that profits emerge. They are sometimes modest, sometimes average, but often substantial.

What status should be given to those fruits that surface? Should they be unilaterally allocated to capital? How should this windfall be shared out? The distribution of bonuses is one area where the financial firm wrestles with this question of division. An intense period of active debate occurs at various levels of the organisation, both individually and collectively, during which a number of distinct logics and criteria overlap such as personal merit, replacement costs, accounting results, labour market activity indicators, past performance by units or transversal equity, etc. Beyond the unstable plurality of this argument-based order, it is the employees who seek to somehow assert their rights over the firm's profit. They try to establish the legitimacy of their claim both in their own eyes and in the eyes of others, as well as the inevitability of a particular distribution. To do so, they must extend themselves within their domain of work, from rights granted over the firm's assets to financial profit. Thus, they seek to extend their existing rights beyond their initial basis and connect them with rights over fruits generated.

The task of this chapter is to analyse more precisely the structure of rights that underpins the strategies used to legitimise claims over profit. To that aim, profit is defined here as a masterless thing over which employees in the financial industry attempt to assert their rights. In order to do so, employees utilise basic methods of appropriation, developing claims based on the assets allocated to them as well as on their place in the order of the production process. Reinterpreting the division of labour in the light of this structural model provides an overview of various rival and unequal work positions within this appropriation process.

Profit as a masterless thing

At the risk of creating a paradox in the eyes of those who consider that profit, by definition, is due to shareholders, I will consider profit in a state of complete detachment: as a masterless thing[1] or *res nullius*. Incidentally, legal doctrine itself is not unanimous in granting the capitalist's right to employees' production. In his PhD thesis "L'appropriation des créations de salarié" ("The appropriation of employee creations"), Di Malta maintains that a work contract is "neither attributive nor translative of property" (Di Malta, 1992, p. 456). When he analyses employees' rights over their creations (i.e. copyright, industrial property rights), he observes that in many instances there is a lack of legal foundation to appropriate employees' creations such as written work, software or patented inventions. Often the employment contract specifies a provision of services and does not transfer the employee's created work to the firm.[2] If, generally speaking, profit is a multifaceted, complex product that is generated both by work and by circumstances, by luck as well as by rules, then to whom should it be attributed? For the firm and employee alike, employment contract is neither attributive nor translative of property rights. One may therefore consider that profit, by nature, has no set purpose and thus theoretically conceive of it in an initial state of complete detachment.

The exoticism of approaching profit as a masterless thing appears less arbitrary when one considers the highly variable pay levels of the different parties involved. Is it not strange that some financial firms are frequently three, four or five times[3] more profitable than companies in other sectors (Krippner 2005; Tomaskovic-Devey and Lin 2011)? Does it not seem odd that the wages of engineers who graduated from the elite *École Polytechnique* or from Stanford MBA are sometimes 10, 20, 50 or even 100 times higher than those of their fellow students who went on to work in other sectors (Oyer 2008)? To which source of productivity should this overpayment be attributed? Does productivity stem from capital? If so, why should capital be so productive in finance and yet so unproductive elsewhere? Or does it come from work? And if this is the case, how does finance magnify the productive force of work to such an extent?

In economic theory, formulating profit as a rent also means attributing it with an indeterminate status. Rent is neither the product of labour productivity nor that of capital. Rather, it is the result of complex mechanisms that limit competition: regulations, property rights, oligopolistic concentration, fixed costs or transaction costs. The concept of "value creation", developed by the Stern Stewart & Co. firm in the early 1980s (Lordon 2000a), expresses this idea of rent. Serving as the foundational principle of many bonus formulas, "created value" is calculated as the remaining value once the normal return on capital (interest and risk premium) and labour remuneration (fixed wages) have been deducted. Nevertheless, as Frédéric Lordon rightly points out, there is no reason why this rent should be pre-allocated to shareholders alone:

Economic value added (EVA), known as shareholder value, constitutes an unfair claim on two counts. First of all, it seeks to guarantee fixed compensation for capitalists while the legitimacy of their income is based solely on their commitment to bear the economic risk involved. Second, it continues to consider the surplus obtained *once guaranteed shareholder income has been paid* – strictly speaking EVA – as the shareholder value, in other words value allocated to shareholders!

(Lordon 2000a, p. 139)

Masterless things, the jurists explain, "are not appropriated but have the potential to be appropriated" (Terré and Simler 1998, p. 14). In the same way, it cannot be said a priori that created value is attributable to either shareholders or employees. It simply exists. Only through the distribution process does it come under the control of different actors. Characterising created value as *res nullius* allows us to focus precisely on the different phases of its appropriation.

The appropriation of a masterless thing will always lead to problems of legitimacy. It is presented as a fait accompli and, as such, can easily turn into a loathsome form of arbitrariness. As Rousseau stated, "The first man, who, after enclosing a piece of ground, took it into his head to say, 'This is mine', and found people simple enough to believe him, was the true founder of civil society" (Rousseau 2009, p. 63). Far from being a mere echo of the mythical golden ages of the origins of humanity, the question of vacancy and the appropriation of goods resurfaces each time new goods have made a sudden appearance, such as collective goods, patents, employee creations (Di Malta 1992), inventions, constructions, and, here, profit. Therefore the question of the acceptability and fairness of the method by which they are appropriated is still of great importance.

This question of the fairness of the original appropriation was both the keystone and the stumbling block for political philosophies, such as libertarianism,[4] which established social order on the basis of ownership and agreement. Which collective agreement should be invoked so as to enable a unilateral, original appropriation? From the far right to the far left, a whole range of answers to this question has been put forward (Vallentyne 1999). Should anyone be able to unilaterally appropriate a vacant property simply by being the first to occupy it, as long as no one else objects (Nozick 1974, p. 865)? Or should rightful appropriation only be allowed under certain conditions, namely when no one else is wronged by appropriation?[5] Should property rights only exist when others specifically grant them that right?[6] Or perhaps property rights should not be granted under any circumstances. In any case, what does first occupation mean exactly and how can it be defined? For instance, Hume used paradoxical examples to point out the arbitrary nature of the demarcation of both "first" and "occupation".[7] These theoretical academic debates may echo the debates and practical procedures mobilised during a bonus payout, in which methods of appropriating profit are materialised.

Let us look at the original act of appropriation made by Rousseau's first peasant owner. Much of its strength comes from the performative utterance (Austin 1962). In the eyes of the first owner as well as that of others, it is the verbal claim that brings about a shift in the status of the property from one of free availability to one of exclusivity.

Saying (or being capable of saying) "this is mine" is the performative act that accompanies the most common forms of appropriation. In the world of finance, it is expressed through the statement "I earned/I brought in this much". Here the grammatical arrangement suggests a causal determination of economic relations (between the "I" and the "earnings") and an affirmation of the legitimate form that the handover of profit should take (in the form of a bonus). Once it has been established, this link between a subject and a result is very difficult to undo. It carries the force of "simple ideas" (Lordon 2000b) and reasserts its self-evident power as soon as the counter-arguments put forward in an interview, conversation or debate digress slightly. A considerable amount of effort and explanation is required in order to gain acknowledgment of the fact that the subject is not necessarily singular – an "I" or a "she" – and that the outcome is not always the calculated result attributed to that individual. A trade unionist from Neptune Bank wrote an article criticising the 10-million-euro bonus paid to the head of the equity derivatives trading room. He put forward an alternative grammatical characterisation of the financial results: "They are the product of *our* work." The fact that it is impossible for so many employees (because of their position in the hierarchy, their involvement in financial activity or their ideology) to be a part of the consensual and inclusive trade unionist "we", further encourages the grip from the singular, exclusive subject. At Neptune Bank, the head of the back office was a rival of the multimillionaire head of trading room and therefore was forced to resign after the latter rose to become head of capital markets. Nonetheless, the back office head still affirmed a grammatical individuation of the result in favour of his rival:

> If the product line formula is validated and the inside figures are validated, which they are, then I've got no reason to dispute that [bonus] amount . . . Not the amount, no! He won it! He deserved it! If he can get the same result with fewer traders than others, then all the more reason.
>
> (Head of back office)

To move away from the substantification offered by the presentation of results, let us carry out the same critique of grammatical categories that Nietzsche made against the premises of classical metaphysics.

> "There is thinking: therefore there is something that thinks": this is the upshot of all Descartes' argumentation. But that means positing as 'true a priori' our belief in the concept of substance – that when there is thought there has to be something "that thinks" is simply a formulation of our grammatical custom that adds a doer to every deed. In short, this is not merely the substantiation of a fact but a logical-metaphysical postulate . . . If one reduces the proposition to "There is thinking, therefore there are thoughts", one has produced a mere tautology.
>
> (Nietzsche 1968, p. 268)

According to the Nietzschean model, one might say, "We produce, therefore there are products." The phrase "there are profits" is the presentation most radically opposed to the statement "I earned this much". It constitutes the presentation in the light of which individuation as a process becomes visible and thereby comprehensible. Becoming familiar with profit by dividing the activity into analytical accounting units, profit centres and cost centres, is most certainly one stage of this subjectivation. In the trading room, profit and the calculation of profit are omnipresent. The profit and loss (P&L) indicators calculated daily (if not in real time) serve as an indicator for evaluating actions that have been taken. When a transaction is concluded, a new P&L is posted. If a share price moves within the portfolio, there is a new P&L. One consequence of this methodological incentive to "think profit" in the trading room (Godechot 2001, p. 183) – which should be understood more as a routine, familiar, automatic awareness of the profit indicator when taking actions than as an intense, obsessive thought process – is that profit becomes an individual person's profit. Accounting, particularly cost accounting, thus serves as a factor of individuation within the financial firm.

It is not enough to merely identify this factor, however. The notion of "this is mine" is no doubt based on the distribution and organisation of accounting recorders. But it is also largely rooted in the organisation of activity, particularly on the allocation of the firm's assets, which supports a plurality of basic forms of profit appropriation.

Basic forms of profit appropriation

Jurists have sometimes invoked the logic of accession, and within it the logic of specification, as a reason for the appropriation of profit by the firm rather than by workers (Di Malta 1992, pp. 139–144). Article 546 of the French Civil Code contains an old saying from Roman law (accessory follows the principal): "Property in a thing, whether moveable or immoveable, confers a right over all that it produces and over all connected to it by accession, whether naturally or artificially." It thereby allocates the fruit (recurrent productions) and the produce (temporary productions – such as the trunks of trees uprooted in a storm) to the proprietor of the property that bears them.

The logic of accession can sometimes seem like common sense. How can ownership of the apple not be conferred on the proprietor of the land on which the apple tree grows? The right of accession also remains deeply puzzling. Ownership goes beyond its initial boundaries to capture all the elements that are devoid of status and which come close to it according to the different methods of proximity (attachment, contiguity, foundation, proliferation, etc.). Moreover, Locke used this right of accession as the basis for the right of property over goods. Property rights, for Locke (1968), came from the combination of self-ownership (a "fundamental" right for him), the particularity of labour (a modifier of nature) and the right of accession.[8] When all of these aspects are considered, the right of accession takes on mysterious characteristics that have often been questioned in the philosophy of law.[9]

Hume rightly recalled that accession is basically a question of "imagination": "Where objects are connected together in the imagination, they are apt to be put on the same footing, and are commonly supposed to be endowed with the same qualities. We readily pass from one to the other, and make no difference in our judgments concerning them; especially if the latter be inferior to the former" (Hume 1963, p. 112). He continues by providing a number of examples that underscore the arbitrariness of the demarcations of the inferior and the superior, the principal and the accessory. An estuary is appropriated by a country as its accessory, he points out, whereas an ocean cannot be appropriated in this way. The imagination, when used in the service of this demarcation, is one of proximity, both in terms of form and matter. Durkheim was another one to be quite struck by the concept of "right of accession". By analysing the concept, he sought to demonstrate the similar nature of property and the sacred thing: "Property is contagious," he explains. "The thing appropriated, like the sacred thing, draws to itself all things that touch it and appropriates them" (Durkheim 1957, p. 147).[10]

Let us now take a closer look at the example of the front office operator. As seen previously, she has implicit (but not official) ownership of a securities portfolio or client portfolio. This portfolio is mixed: one part is inherited, another part is developed independently (establishing her own business), and yet another may have been won from internal rivals within the firm. This property is supported and confirmed by the hierarchy (the firm), which is the guardian of the property right boundaries that lie within it. Over time, the property becomes the operator's right. She has a stable, long-lasting relationship with the assets she manages and is protected against external incursions. She is invested with intentionality and responsibility by virtue of her duty to increase their value, which is measured by an automatic profit counter (P&L for the trader and sales credit for the salesperson). This configuration is very useful when considering the portfolio to be the principal (her principal) and profit to be the accessory (her accessory). This material configuration encourages financial operators to believe that the profit generated by *their* portfolio is indeed *their profit.* "I worked for three days and paid back my employer," said one trader who was incensed by the firm's encroachment on *his* profit. Here the firm's secondary role as the provider of capital is acknowledged, but it is not seen as needing to be compensated beyond this specific function. Anything produced beyond compensation to the firm for its capital is seen by the employee as the substantial residue of his portfolio and property.

This conception can be seen in even tiny details. For instance, on the securities lending and borrowing desk described in *Les Traders*, when one of the traders takes a few days' holiday she entrusts her Spanish securities portfolio to her colleague. He then manages someone else's portfolio "with due diligence". From answering the telephone to concluding transactions, he does everything necessary to increase the portfolio's value. If major changes need to be made to the structure of a transaction, he calls his colleague at home to ask for permission. The result of this activity carried out in her absence is nonetheless accounted for on her portfolio and she may be given credit for it. Since her portfolio generates the profit, it is considered to be her profit, even *in absentia*. Except in the case of portfolios that are jointly owned (for instance in the case of small desks with two or three workers), help given to colleagues results in profit being allocated to the holder of the portfolio, and not the person who provided assistance. There may well be discussions over the legitimacy of such a division, but these mostly arise when a loss must be jointly borne.

However, in most instances, when operators support each other, they respect the structure of property rights and the allocation of profit to the owner. So when Pluto Bank established individual automatic bonus formulas for traders – an operation that could be interpreted as a stabilising and strengthening of property rights over assets – it brought about a greater sense of calm and increased collaboration and support between traders. As their head of trading room explained, "They're highly specialised. They're not in competition with one another and so they have an objective interest in talking to one another, and they do talk." In other words their property rights did not overlap and they no longer competed to influence their manager (Milgrom and Roberts 1988); and, as a result, they were able to help each other just as property owners do when managing goods. Although there was nothing in the pay structure to incentivise them, there was also nothing to disincentivise them from providing free assistance.[11]

The accounting department at Pluto Bank provides an example of a structure that pushed the division of assets the furthest, or at least to the extent that the internal structure of rights resembled Roman law. The division of labour in the bank was very simple. There were no salespeople or analysts to market products to clients. Traded products were very common; on the one hand, this allowed the back office to be streamlined and, on the other hand, it meant that there was no need to hire expensive teams of experts in maths and IT in order to develop pricing models. Portfolios were divided up between traders according to the principle of complete division, allowing duplication and overlapping claims to be avoided. The profit appropriated by portfolios and traders was established by a rate that was included in their contracts. Nevertheless, the example given here of Pluto Bank, a small organisation, shows a limited case where profit was viewed unequivocally as belonging to the portfolio from which it emerged.

Primacy and appropriation

In large organisations where the division of labour is more complex and intense, the firm's assets are subject to simultaneous ownership.[12] For instance, when financial profit is the fruit of a client portfolio that is co-managed by salespeople and financial analysts, a securities portfolio managed by traders, and a machines and software portfolio administered by IT workers, it is not easy to allocate financial profit simply on the basis of the right of accession based on controlled assets. Beyond the connections that exist between the plurality of allocated assets and recorded profit, more basic methods of appropriation are used that usually depend on employees' engagement in the world of assets.

Let us now return to Rousseau and the foundations of his analysis of property. In his account, certain aspects of property stand out: the arbitrary dimension of appropriation, its performative nature ("this is mine"), and its rooting in collective belief ("people simple enough to believe him"). However, the notion of enclosure also highlights the importance of the initial proprietor's engagement in the activity. When that initial engagement takes place, several elements are brought together in a single individual and a single action.

In a financial firm, these components can be identified as follows: the idea of one's own territory, the desire to make it one's own, labour (developing the territory, even if only through its enclosure) and the organisation of exclusion (enclosure, once again). These different methods are present and implemented during the appropriation process. Of course, there are many ways of being first, and this ambiguity can give rise to numerous conflicts between individuals who invoke different forms of primacy. For example, should the first vision or the first contact be seen as most effective? I will now discuss three ways of being first in finance: first will, first activity (in terms of labour) and the first idea.

First will

Both the philosophical tradition and the liberal legal tradition consider will to have a decisive role in the act of appropriation. Kant believed original acquisition to be the actualisation of a unilateral will over an external object.[13] Similarly, in order to characterise the fact of possession (from which ownership can arise when appropriation takes place), the German jurist Savigny made *animus* (the intention to act as the possessor) rather than *corpus* (the exercising of prerogatives) "the decisive and sovereign element that establishes possession" (Terré and Simler 1998, p. 121). In finance, the will to take control of profit is also a decisive element. Will here has a power of accession: when financial profit has been isolated and that isolation is intended, the voluntarist way of thinking quickly establishes profit as the product of the realisation of the will, disregarding all other circumstances. The legal status of profit is then modified by the interference of will. Lewis describes in lyrical terms the feeling of excitement produced by this use of will in the appropriation of profit:

> There is a magic moment, during which a man has surrendered a treasure, and during which the man who is about to receive it has not yet done so. An alert bond trader will make that moment his own, possessing the treasure for a magic microsecond, taking a little of it, passing it on.
>
> (Lewis 1989, p. 38)

One consequence of the right of accession of the will is the contrast in attitudes of financial operators and, even more broadly, of other economic actors, when faced with profit and loss. There is a tendency in such situations to appropriate profit and detach oneself from loss. Performance is attributed to personal qualities, while failures are put down to external circumstances: unhappiness, a bad economic situation or the mistakes and malevolence of others. One head of a trading team at a brokerage firm recounted the following:

I usually say, jokingly, that with salespeople if the idea they've sold to the client is a good idea, then its theirs; if it's a bad idea, it's the analyst's; if the order is well executed, then they managed it properly but if it's badly executed then the stupid trader messed up. They're never to blame . . . You sometimes hear, "I was really careful with your order, you see, we've got a good average price" . . . Or, "Yeah, I know, the trader didn't follow through, what can you do?" . . . I look at him and say, "Are you going to stop your bullshit?" Sometimes, in a room, you almost come to blows. Because you have to be strong to understand certain things.

This asymmetry is sometimes seen as an opportunistic strategy in the service of individual interest. However, it also stems from considerations of the legitimacy of workers' engagement in the activity.[14]

People want profit. They do not want loss. Loss, even if it happens within one's own area of responsibility, is not wanted for itself. It is always the fault of circumstances or bad luck. Profit, on the other hand, even if it is the result of sheer luck, becomes the operator's profit as soon as it is wanted (the operator at least wanted to try her luck). It is possible to identify a very common attitude in finance and, more broadly, in economic life: "I am responsible for profit because I wanted it/I am not responsible for loss because I did not want it." Before the court of economic life, people plead voluntary profit and involuntary loss. Consequently, one can understand why those same actors may request different distributions of profit and loss.

First action

The fact that the development of the individual in the world of assets takes place more through labour, action and the transformation of the world, than through will – whose localisation and final capacity always remains arguable – forms the core of Locke's jusnaturalist philosophy (Locke 1968). This idea can also be found in many other philosophers and jurists of the modern age (Berthoud and Busino 1981, p. 22), even extending, albeit in a transformed state, into the social-ist concepts of the nineteenth century, including those of Marx and Proudhon. In the world of finance, labour is not a dominant value. As one gets closer to the front office, a logic based on results becomes an increasingly dominant one where profit is seen more as the fruit of portfolios and will than that of labour.

Labour is invoked more on the fringes of the financial world. It is often com-municated to the outside world that working hours are not counted. At the same time, some junior employees daydream about their seniors' exorbitant bonuses. When asked to justify their relatively modest pay and incomplete success, some back office staff invoked the "crazy pace" of the trading room, difficult working conditions (stress) and extra hours that exceed the legal limits. The logic here is "you reap what you sow", a phrase that one young risk controller who recently graduated from ENSAE (a top French engineering school) exclaimed emphati-cally when I showed him sums of money that went beyond any amount he had ever dreamed of receiving. By actively reaffirming the neoclassical principle of the absence of rents or arbitrage opportunities, he was able to provide a better justification for his choice of career. After a few more years in risk control where he earned small bonuses, he was convinced he would move into more lucrative trading, and finally "reap" such benefits.

Nevertheless, the fact that the rhetoric of labour is more present on the fringes of the financial world than in its core does not mean that labour – which is measured more in terms of its quality rather than its temporal quantity – has no effect on people's sense of ownership of profit. When labour is combined with a situation in which profit may be subject to the will to appropriate it, feelings of ownership are particularly strong. And when labour is no longer apparent, appropriation by will alone may be perceived as illegitimate. Thus, capital markets managers and heads of trading room are harshly criticised when their bonuses are divulged. People consider them to have withdrawn from the market and believe that no obvious engagement in market transactions can support this appropriation of profit. One outraged trade unionist and head of a trading team said the following about the 17 million euros received by the two heads of trading room at Neptune Bank: "The product was not generated by them [the heads], but by their teams."

This kind of response is not limited to trade unionists quick to measure the fairness of a distribution by the quantity of labour that has gone into it. "Not justified in relation to the personal contribution of the recipients," exclaimed one trader in the questionnaire handed out. "They don't shock me if they are the real result of a value added and of profits generated for the bank, but they are shocking if the amounts are taken from teams," echoed another trader. At Saturn Bank in the year 2000, the head of the R&D team estimated the bonuses of the "G8" (the eight managers of the trading room) at between 1.5 and 3 million euros. Even if these sums remained a secret, he considered them to have been usurped. Not only had the managers withdrawn from market activity but they were also accused of doing nothing more than exploiting old financial ideas to death without updating them. Heads of desk at other institutions such as Mars Bank denounced the separation between trading room managers and lower-level financial operators that was rife at Saturn Bank. One said, "There's a caste system at Saturn." His colleague went further, "The caste system isn't productive anymore. The producers are mistreated. The equivalent of the G8 at Mars [i.e. themselves] has stayed close to production." In fact, heads of desk and trading room often justify receiving bonuses by arguing that their portfolio and work activity are productive enough to finance them:

A frequent criticism made of bosses at Saturn is that "they exploit others".

That's true, I agree, replied the head of the fixed income room at Neptune Bank. I've always made a habit of taking positions and making a profit, and of paying myself a good wage. But I never exploited anyone. I always brought in far more than I cost.

While labour, as can be seen in the quote above, is a powerful appropriator when coupled with first will, its effectiveness as a claim is lessened in the service of an external will. Traders will sometimes shed a sympathetic tear over the "relentless" work of back office staff and IT services.[15] Generally speaking, however, it is believed that "they bear no responsibility for profit" in the absence of will or the freedom to make decisions. In order to defend their bonuses, they make a case for the overlooked intentionality that indeed accompanies their work. One middle office employee, complaining about the modest bonus she received in comparison with those of the front office staff she helped, alluded to the fact that the middle office "got lumbered with all the front office's mistakes" and that she had "corrected orders that you couldn't make head or tail of". Her argument was made stronger by the fact that she also occasionally saved profit (intentionally), rather than just consciously allowing it to emerge, by carrying out the daily work (ordered by the intentionality of the front office) of confirming and accounting for transactions.

First idea

The protection of intellectual property rights through government regulations of patents, copyright, designs and trademarks, is quite new. The first signs of it appeared at the start of the modern age, and their rationalisations, in the form of major laws that organised them, generally date back to the end of the eighteenth century (David 1998). Intellectual property rights remain a heterogeneous set of claims defined by arbitrary limits. For instance, the limits between an idea – which is generally not protected – and an invention on the one hand, and an idea and a written work on the other hand, are both tenuous and unstable. Indeed, intellectual property seems stubbornly resistant to a jusnaturalist foundation and today remains hotly disputed. Unsurprisingly, these rights are still ambiguous for employees when they take part in a creative initiative (Di Malta 1992).[16]

In so far as finance only rarely recognises copyright and patents in positive law, it may seem strange to invoke property rights when describing employees' methods of appropriating profit in finance. While they do have some effectiveness, it is mainly in the area of software[17] and, to a lesser extent, financial analysis. But generally speaking, positive law poorly protects financial products, financial concepts and financial formulas.[18] Peter Bernstein recounts how six months after Black and Scholes published their article on options pricing, Texas Instruments was selling calculators that could find the Black–Scholes value (Bernstein 1993, p. 230). Yet even though this formula had revolutionised the derivatives industry over the previous 30 years (MacKenzie and Millo 2003; MacKenzie 2006), the two economists earned nothing from the technical marketing of their ideas.

> This lack of any protective legal framework for financial innovation was in fact strongly criticised by a former head of the options department. He believed that during his time at Saturn Bank he was systematically robbed

of the products that resulted from his innovative inventions by "arbitragers" who borrowed his ideas: the guaranteed fund products he claims to have created were bandied about by his rivals who "weakened" the concept. In 2002, while head of a small hedge fund, he thought he had developed a new method for very short-term speculation that combined charts, statistics and options. He sought a solution (with no success) to protect his method from rivals. Several of those I spoke to in finance were aware of the project as a whole, but generally they doubted the validity of his new idea and saw it more as an attempt by the former head of the options department to return to the forefront of French finance.

If finance has shown some respect for intellectual property rights in practice, it is probably due to its close relationship with the scientific field and its mode of operating (Bourdieu 1999 & 2004), at least in the area of financial engineering. One Proxima trader thought of his statistical trading as "an everyday competition" and as "a PhD as well": "It's the markets as a whole that validate what I do." One quant at Universal Company wanted a portfolio of operations to manage, not to "find the right formula for making money" but rather to "make money for proving the formula is right".

The first idea, when disassociated from first will, is not a very solid basis for appropriation. In the impartial world of science, it is important to develop an idea for its own sake and not for its by-products (such as the financial profit that would result from it). Moral rights, starting with name-giving, matter more than property rights. Nevertheless, the first idea is appropriative in the sense that any appropriation resulting from the first idea by an individual other that its author may appear usurpatory. This could be summarised thus: "I don't chase profit with my ideas, but I don't want anyone to benefit from them in my place." In the field of financial engineering, one of the challenges of this struggle is also gaining access to the "monopoly of scientific authority". However, the scientific value of a new financial idea – which has the potential to confer scientific authority – has the particularity of being tested and measured by the profit it generates in firms. The appropriative link between the idea and its realisation therefore runs deeper than a mere attribution by default in order to prevent any alternative attribution.

However, promoters of new ideas may face numerous obstacles before successfully appropriating profit. In particular, there may be doubts about the *effectiveness* of an idea, its *ownership* and its *originality*. For instance, a quant might offer a great idea about conducting arbitrage, but financial operators may be suspicious of arbitrages that look too good on paper. For this reason, when implementing an idea, the operator must face the realities of the market, such as the sufficiency of cash flow or the level of transaction costs. In the common practice of market transactions, the initial idea (i.e. the mathematical demarcation of an arbitrage, the pricing formula) often seems less important than the operator's desire to defend her profit against opposing forces. Moreover, the effectiveness of the idea may be contested over time. Trading rooms have themselves taken internal measures to recognise the strength of an idea over a limited period, whose definition is arbitrary:

How did you go about paying the engineering team?

We set up a sales credit system for the engineering team. We had double sales credit. For sophisticated products designed by the engineering team, the products followed the same system for the first six months of their lifetime (we carried out the first listing of a product): sales credit for the salesperson and a result in the trader's P&L, but the amount of allocated sales credit was also allocated to the engineering desk as a purely analytical measure. Exactly the same amount as for salespeople. We doubled the sales credit.

Only for the first six months?

Yes, because after that the product was considered to have fallen in line with our trading standards and to have no further value added to the package. The product developer conceives the product and helps to sell it. The product has to be explained to the salesperson and the trader. They are taken to meet the client. Then of course it's over. The product becomes commonplace in the market. It's only to be expected that it has a relatively short lifetime. Some people only give it three months.

(Head of fixed income trading, Neptune Bank)

It is often said that an idea, in its immaterial state, can be reproduced ad infinitum at very little financial cost. On the other hand, it is sometimes forgotten that intellectual innovation is the product of an interactive relational structure (Collins 1998) that fosters an unstable foundation for rights: pirating on the one hand and simultaneous ownership on the other. Finance is certainly no exception, and people are constantly putting forward ideas that are not their own,[19] or disputing the originality of their colleagues' ideas: "He has no ideas, all he does is implement [academic] papers" said one quant about the head of quants for fixed income trading at Saturn Bank. "He tried to steal my ideas," added a junior quant who had been reprimanded for not sharing a creation he had developed with traders in the room.

Therefore, for all these reasons, appropriation based on conception alone is certainly not the most powerful modus operandi.

Positions in the organisation of labour and appropriation of profit

The four methods of appropriating profit identified here (based on ideas, action, will or assets) are not equally open to every employee. Rather the type of profit claim an employee can invoke is fundamentally dependent on their position in the production process and in the organisation of labour. As I have shown, the amount and structure of assets allocated to employees differ greatly according to whether they work in the front or back office. The chance of implementing a first will, a first idea or a first project depends on one's position in the production process. Just as it is easier for a sailor perched on the maintop of a boat to discover new lands than it is for an oarsman in the hold, front office operators are given most of the responsibility for concluding transactions and are therefore in a position to invoke first will more easily than back office workers who are in charge of settling, delivering and recording transactions.

As a first approach, I will establish a connection between the different positions in the division of labour and the different categories used in law when analysing ownership. Traders and salespeople are in a position to hold the *useful ownership* (i.e. the *dominion utile* of the feudal system) of their jobs, portfolios (securities or clients) and software. This position is particularly vital in that it is the structural place where the first will to appropriate profit is formed. However, traders and salespeople are not the only ones who can lay claim to the fruits.

Heads of team, heads of desk and sales managers are the ones in a position to hold the *eminent ownership* of the allocated domain of activity. They can allocate or withdraw portfolios, clients, jobs and, to a certain extent, hire and fire. In short, they have the authority to reallocate the rights that have been conferred on their team members. However, this transfer of utility is never complete, and the manager retains a kind of *droit de suite* over the asset transferred, or rather conceded.

Apart from the claims made by holders of *useful ownership* and *eminent ownership*, two other categories of employees also battle it out in the race to appropriate profit, albeit with less of an advantage. The third category, *authors and inventors* – represented by financial engineers, IT specialists and, to a lesser extent, financial analysts – hold positions in which immaterial assets such as mathematical formulas, analyses, ideas, algorithms, and software are developed and accumulated. When it comes to these immaterial assets, these actors are in a position to hold intellectual property rights. Finally, the last category of this analysis, those engaged in the *lease of work*, enables a characterisation of the relation to profit of employees (like support function employees) who typically execute orders given by the front office. Instead of being allocated with domains of activity (and therefore property rights over the firm's assets), these employees are ordered to carry out prescribed actions. As a result, not only are they endowed with fewer property rights over the firm's assets but since their position is structurally lower with regard to the uncovering of profit in the markets, they also find it more difficult to make any claims over profit.

Useful ownership of financial assets

Financial operators, especially traders, are in a highly favourable working situation that makes them obvious candidates to receive profit. Admittedly, these workers do not have full and complete ownership of the assets they manage. In positive law, profits belong to the firm as a legal entity, and in practice their ownership depends on continual confirmation of the hierarchy that underpins it. Full transferability, or the capacity to abuse, is without doubt the characteristic of property law that financial operators find most lacking. (Although it should be noted they can acquire part of this right by rising through the hierarchy and becoming heads of desk.) However, financial operators use their job and portfolio, or, more specifically, they have right of "use" over assets, and this *useful ownership* places them at the forefront in the appropriation process by making them candidates for profit.

Financial operators are positioned right on the maintop of the financial organisation, from where they can see and seize profit. They may consider profit to be theirs, not only because profit has grown from the assets for which they are responsible, but also because in their daily work they have conceived a first idea, they have had the first will to realise that idea, to enter the market and, through the first action, to seize profit.

During the so-called golden age of the 1980s, this model worked well, and often exclusively, for traders. Of course, 30 years ago bonuses were typically lower (and still in their infancy in France). But at this moment traders also had far more independence within the organisational hierarchy because the division of labour under which they operated was very weak. Generally speaking traders were in charge of financial engineering (pricing models), product marketing and financial analysis, among other things. They were not required to share profits with other petitioners. However, traders' collaborators, whether shareholders or the back office, were not generally viewed as true candidates for profit. Rather they were seen as collaborators paid for the value they added (labour, capital) and not for the value of what resulted from their contribution.

This earlier method of dividing profit follows the legal logic of specification[20] stating that when a craftsman makes something with primary materials belonging to the owner, the product then belongs to that owner, who has an obligation only to compensate the craftsperson for her labour. Under a trader's "supervision", an assistant trader or back office administrator would calculate a statement of transactions and arrange settlement and delivery. Although these employees were indispensable, they were not seen as needing to be compensated above what their work was worth based on the value set by the labour market. According to the same logic of specification,[21] independent traders, considering their activity to be the principal, would only pay capital at its original cost. In fact, some star traders working independently, particularly in the 1980s when the division of labour was far more fragile, developed original legal structures and minor partnerships in which their share in the profits was contractualised:

> After being employed as a trader at Indosuez, Rozan entered into contracts that were increasingly atypical: he was engaged in a written profit-sharing scheme at Thomson Finance then established a limited liability company, hosted by the BGP bank, where he traded on Soros funds (Rozan 1999). This star trader then became a kind of entrepreneur of the self both in practice and in the legal form guaranteed by positive law.
>
> Jean-François Lepetit recounts a similar episode during the same period: "[Our team of five traders trading notional options on the Matif] led this

contract and brought in 10 million euros of extra profit to the trading room . . . During this period, Jean-Philippe Frignet, having left Indosuez and Chicago, returned to Paris and was developing derivatives at BGP, a subsidiary of Crédit Agricole d'Île de France . . . Defying the moral obligation under which his own boss had placed him not to poach from the Indosuez teams he knew better than anyone, he came to see me one day with the news that he had just hired our entire notional options team [which generated an annual revenue of 10 million euros]. He took pains to explain that his project was considerably more tempting for traders. And for good reason, since Crédit Agricole had allowed him to create a specialised subsidiary whose operators would have rights over a large share of the capital and the results, 50% if I remember correctly . . . Indosuez never managed to get the same results in this derivatives niche" (Lepetit 2002).

In the late 1990s, the early days of hedge funds gave rise to similar prerogatives. A number of traders (and salespeople) managed to make this utopia of financial autonomy a reality and to perfect the exclusivity of rights over the financial assets they managed, particularly through indexing bonuses (around 20%) to profits, to which were added profits they made as fund partners. Nevertheless, even within hedge funds, a division of labour and assets developed as soon as they grew in size. Differentiated functions then became the underlying for that same profit. There was no fundamental difference between the social structure of a large hedge fund and that of the capital markets department of a major bank. Furthermore, in both a large hedge fund and a bank, financial operators no longer had exclusive rights over assets, will, ideas and work. There was competition from other rivals.

Eminent property right

Heads of trading room have to divide up a domain of activity of which they have had *useful ownership* in some capacity or another. That domain is not so much the firm's property, which they must manage by delegation, as their own *eminent* property. Coining the delegation of assets from a head of trading team to a trader as a phenomenon of "eminent property" makes it possible to understand its true nature.

From this perspective, managers are similar to feudal lords. When their own powers are no longer sufficient to develop their territory, instead of granting tenure to colonists, the managers assign a portfolio or job to an employee: either by making a new hire (after all they hold a large share of the firm's hiring power) or by promoting someone already working at the firm (often an assistant trader, back office administrator or research engineer). This transfer works in an ambiguous way. It is more of a concession than a cession, and licensors still retain rights over licensees, as was the case with the feudal *droit de suite*. First of all, the manager, like the feudal lord, retains the prerogative to take the asset back and reallocate it. Even more importantly, the profit that arises from licensees remains "theirs".

This is not only because they have properly managed their employee portfolio by hiring the "right" people and "managing" them correctly, or because those right people have enhanced the value of an asset that was initially their manager's "property" and thus retains part of her personality, but also because managers may still claim some of the primacy in terms of will, ideas or work. As such, the employees can be made the mere executors of the managers' will, a mere specification of their ideas and nothing more than a replication of their past labour.

> The head of equity derivatives trading at Mars Bank, although a fierce critic of the "wall" that divided "management and production" at Saturn Bank, which he claimed was "run by people who quit trading a long time ago", also stopped trading in 2002 and began managing a team of 25 people. He had "idle time", got bored, had "a lot of management work" and had "more time to chat to everyone during the day". "It's a different job," he said, one that he didn't "dislike". In 2001, he earned 3.8 million euros and 5 million euros in 2000. In 2001, his best trader earned 1 million euros. He explained the reasons for this difference.

> *How can you explain the fact that there is such a big gap between your salary level and that of your best staff?*

> Because the best trader last year was me.

> *Because you had a portfolio?*

> I had a portfolio with no cash flow. I'm exaggerating. I've no idea who the best trader is. I'm always the one who decides the initial strategy. What I need are guys who really know how to do what I ask them.

> *Do you intervene a lot?*

> Not physically, in the actual position . . . I manage the room's overall position. I say to them, "Do this, this and this!" Not Peugeot or Renault; buy volatility or whatever, sell it for a massive amount in two years, for so many millions of euros. It's true that I could physically do it. It's like the guy who designs a house and then builds it. But I've no idea who's more important.

> *They execute . . . ?*

> No. They have to be sharp to execute properly. Of course, they have a certain amount of independence . . . But, the strategies are designed by us, by the management, by me . . . Without us, most of them wouldn't be able to earn much money. They're not researchers or developers. They need a system. That's obvious.

This example, as recounted by a head of trading, reveals the ambiguity of rights granted over assets. What traders believe they govern has more ancient and general origins. This hysteresis effect in the process of appropriation confers an especially large share of power on a particular category of employees that I will call *internal entrepreneurs*. These individuals began working in the various niches of finance in France during the late 1980s and early 1990s, when trading was still in its infancy. Traders who worked during this time all speak of the extremely "home-made" nature of the activity in its early days.

> "When we were developing activities, we were everything at once. First IT specialists, then traders, then salespeople, then marketers – we did a bit of everything. At the end of the day I wasn't anything in particular, except for an activity developer," said the head of equity derivatives, who joined Saturn Bank in 1989. At that time, particularly at Saturn Bank with its highly industrial strategy, "The idea was . . . to duplicate, replicate [industrial processes that had been tried and tested in currency trading], take over the field and expand horizontally as quickly as possible, with a certain amount of disorder but without compromising on quality or control."
>
> "The tactic or development plan used in this options sector was always the same, in other words to take over the domain in underlying assets and trading. We approved models and arbitrated. We generated a lot of volume and tried out the mechanics. It was all tested by the back office. When things were more or less finalised, we put the salespeople in place. This was the system that underpinned our development . . . We did a fair amount of hiring, and within six months we were sending people to New York. In other words, in the American market we needed an index trader, an equity trader, an arbitrager, a convertible trader, etc. And then later on we had Latin America, Japan, Hong Kong, Singapore – we spread everywhere."
>
> This head of trading room was also aware that he had been "lucky to come in at the right time and catch the train just as it was leaving": "I surfed the wave and it swelled right beneath me."
>
> At the beginning, he traded long-term warrants but gradually took charge of developing equity derivatives markets. He took advantage of the departure of his boss – who had been head of the options department and the true founder of derivatives activity at Saturn Bank – and the reorganisation of the options division, in which options were divided up according to their groups of underlying assets, becoming head of the equity derivatives room in the mid-1990s. He oversaw major investment in the early 1990s, hiring new staff at a steady rate and creating a whole range of derivatives products. Following the expansion of derivatives-related activities and the take off of the equity markets, the income generated by his room rose rapidly between 1996 and 2000, and it is presumed that his bonus must have done the same. I have heard rumours of a 5-million-euro bonus for 1998, which probably doubled in 2000.

There are many epic sagas of this kind. Employees I have met or heard of who took advantage of the year 2000 and earned a bonus of more than 5 million euros on the Paris market are generally individuals who joined banking between

1988 and 1994, creating departments where almost nothing previously existed and everything had to be created from scratch. They were often people who organised financial production individually and then delegated, and rose through the ranks. Around that original core of financial activity, they became heads of team and heads of trading room. Sometimes they might have invented functions and organisational methods along the way, but nearly always they took advantage of the rapid increase in volume in the financial markets.

Although they remained employees, these creators of activities bore a resemblance to entrepreneurs, but inside the firm. Their success was the living proof that capital alone generated nothing. Before the *internal entrepreneurs* came along "there was nothing" and they can trace the start of that "something" back, chronologically at least, to their own presence. Under the entrepreneurs' supervision, the assets sphere mushroomed from a small number of original assets to "incredible factories".[22] These employees can therefore vigorously defend their role in creating those plants. Once the activity was fully developed and these early leaders were in command of these factories, they earned the dividends of their activity: the profit from past investments made under their supervision.

Authors and inventors

Thanks to the increased division of labour in the 1990s, new functions were established in finance in order to produce ideas or technical processes that would enlighten traders in their decision-making (financial engineers, R&D engineers, quants), to help salespeople to develop marketing strategies that would convince clients to enter into transactions (sell-side financial analysts, strategists, chartists, economists, etc.), and to provide a basis for portfolio managers' decisions (buy-side financial analysts, strategists, etc.). While very different in terms of recruitment and assignments, these professions share a similar positioning with regards to market decision-making, delimitation and the seizing of profit. They provide intellectual tools like predictions, reports or analyses; or technical tools such as pricing software, algorithms and new product development that are made available to financial operators, while avoiding forcing operators to use them or conform to a standard application. As a result, there may be some ambiguity as to the final role of these ideas in the emergence of profit. Do financial operators merely press "'shift F9' like an oaf", as willed by a R&D engineer as a way of stripping them of their powers – starting with their bonus – or do they have to create their own ideas, which, in the end, owe little to the ready-made concepts provided? Such traders claim to redo all forecasting themselves without using the dividends or results forecasts made by financial analysts. They argue that this information amounts to little more than "marketing and window-dressing for the clients" and therefore is inadequate when it comes to real forecasting. Yet the vagueness that surrounds the origin of ideas does nothing to benefit the *authors and inventors* asserting their rights over profit.

What is more, even when an idea is their own, the appropriation of profit solely on the basis of the first idea is a delicate matter:

A quant told us that at Saturn Bank two other quants had developed a software program that carried out arbitrage between different assets of a single economic sector. It exploited statistical correlations between prices in order to predict the relative behaviour of a stock in relation to its sector. The software they developed carried out market transactions without requiring human intervention. This team of quants worked for a trader with their experimental machine. However, apparently the revenue generated fed the trader's P&L (and therefore his bonus) but not their own bonuses. My informer was extremely shocked by this situation and saw it as confirmation of the usurpatory practices of traders, who are unable to change their view that the firm is divided into profit centres (them) and cost centres (the rest).

Naturally, I do not have all the elements needed to assess this situation. It may be an example of entirely opportunistic appropriation. However, I could also put forward the more interesting hypothesis that the trader saw himself as the owner of profit, even in this case. The trader may have gone to the quants to explain the arbitrage ideas he had in mind and wanted them to develop; he may even have lacked a precise idea of what he wanted but thought the quants may have their own ideas. In this scenario, therefore, the trader would have believed he was allocating quants with prescribed actions ("make me a software program that deals by itself") rather than assets ("here's a portfolio, you're free to find a way to enhance it"). He would then have been the owner of not just the raw materials of this arbitrage – the securities portfolio on which the software operated – but also the arbitrage idea and therefore the *animus*, or the will to be the owner of the fruits in question. In this version of the situation, the quants did not contribute any new assets, simply doing a particular job that had to be compensated as such.

Having the organisational capacity to desire profit is a way of avoiding a situation in which the profit generated from the idea is stolen and falls into the hands of the person who implements the idea. The aforementioned trader at Proxima Bank – who operated in a different organisational context from that described by the quant from Saturn Bank – developed statistical models that detected correlations and enabled a profit to be made. He could quite easily have developed an automatic machine, he claimed, but preferred to have a human execute the model's suggestions, believing this would result in higher quality. Thanks to the increased activity level on his desk, he also recruited two buy-side traders who executed transactions. However, they remained mere subordinates, and in this case the trader retained first will over the profit.

Although somewhat lower in relation to market operators, the position held by *authors and inventors* seems to have strengthened over the last few years. The pay levels of financial engineers, and particularly those of financial analysts, have soared. In the case of analysts, it is interesting to note that the rise in pay levels[23] has coincided with a merging of their functions with those of the front office. The transformation of asset management and the organisation of an industrial management process (Kleiner 2000) has indirectly led to changes in sellside analysts' influence in brokerage houses. In the client management departments of asset management firms portfolio managers now have substantial support from buy-side experts. Along strategists who develop sectorial knowledge and buy-side traders who execute orders on the market, buy-side analysts specialise in identifying firms that will over-perform or underperform. Partially as a result, portfolio managers no longer choose the brokers they will entrust with executing orders. Management firms delegate their transactions to brokerage firms according to their ranking. Evaluations of the quality of advice that brokerage firms provide to management firms – both to portfolio managers and to buy-side analysts – now play an important role in the classification of the brokerage firm and the brokerage flow that is received.

This transformation has resulted in a clear increase in sell-side analysts' share of commercial activity. Analysts today spend more time "selling" their ideas (or rather showcasing them) than producing them. Commercial activity now accounts for two-thirds of the daily activity of a senior analyst.

> A member of the board of directors of a brokerage firm, who had worked for many years as the head of a team of analysts, explained the new commercial position of analysts: "We use an important go-between, which are the salespeople. The problem with having these go-betweens is that they consume part of the value added. Salespeople are specialised in 200–400 securities. They have to sell foreign firms of which they have little knowledge. They only retain the basics. If they are dealing with a generalist, then they are on an equal footing, but if they are dealing with a specialist (oil, banking, etc.) then they are at a disadvantage. In this case, they should avoid being the ones to sell their ideas. They can keep abreast of events. But analysts must now play a direct part in marketing." One consequence of this direct role is that analysts telephone all "their" clients once a month. They send them reports as well as a daily electronic newsletter detailing the current economic situation in their sector. They often travel for meetings with buy-side analysts and portfolio managers.
>
> Like most analysts, this former head of analysis was fairly sceptical about the role of salespeople in brokerage firms: "The problem in our profession is ultimately the role of salespeople." "Salespeople are a bit like people standing guard on the door," echoed the head of analysis at Saturn Bank. And yet, even when threatened with extinction and denigration, in this brokerage firm and at Saturn Bank alike senior salespeople are paid more than analysts.

Although the situation continues to change, at least in France[24] analysts are no longer simply producers of ideas. Rather they have joined the ranks of those possessing the will to make a profit by seeking out clients and getting them to agree with their ideas. This makes analysts far more likely to believe that profit rightly belongs to them. Increasingly they have come to believe that their actions generate brokerage flows and, better still, major securities transactions like tender offers.[25]

Lease of work

The role of support function employees (back and middle office, accounting, HR, IT) is to serve the front office and execute their orders. This is true even for those in senior positions. Therefore, despite the diversity of the activities of support function employees, they play a secondary role in the production process. They do not carry out the first labour that generates profit. Admittedly, some support staff – much like trade unionists – believe that it is labour as a whole that creates profit and therefore precedence should not be established according to the arbitrary order of the production process. However, this collectivist vision quickly wanes as soon as employees try to define the limits of the group that generated the profit, particularly in environments such as these where employees are unionised at low levels. Questions about distribution quickly emerge: Should it be limited to the capital markets bank or should it also include the retail bank as a whole? Perhaps the cleaning company staff creating a more pleasant working environment for financial operators – and therefore enabling greater efficiency – should also receive part of the profits?

The symbolic boundary between profit centres and cost centres has certainly had an impact, and support staff – particularly those in jobs like the back office, accounting or HR that are valued the least – usually believe that they did not create profit and therefore have no claim over it. The bonus logic is often challenged in these jobs, and even when it is accepted, a bonus means something other than a realisation of the appropriation of profit.

> Yes, they did [believe that support functions shouldn't receive bonuses]. At the beginning they supported this idea. I explained that they might be right in intellectual terms but that, in such cases, we'd have no one left to do the work, and that we'd have to withdraw from the market.
>
> (Head of back office)

Back office employees see themselves, and are seen by others, as workers who provide services; they must be compensated accordingly, but they do not need to participate in the sharing-out of profit. Consequently, any bonus they receive is viewed more as an increase in their basic wage than a realisation of rights over profit.

Although this situation is generally unfavourable, it has the advantage of allowing office support staff to distance themselves from loss. After all, if they do not associate themselves with profit when profit exists – and if the bonus–salary coupling is never anything but a payment of their services in line with their value – then they must receive a bonus even when profit does not exist. At Saturn Bank, the support staff that served the fixed income and foreign exchange trading rooms deplored the fact that they were paid paltry bonuses following poor results achieved by their front office. By contrast the support workers serving the highly profitable equity derivatives trading room were quite happy to receive higher payouts.

***

This chapter has examined the creation of a belief in the legitimacy of bonus distribution. The basis for that legitimacy can be found not so much in discourses (even if these do contribute) as in the effects of evidence produced by the day-to-day running of the firm.

Let us pick up the thread of the chapter's reasoning. Prior to bonus distribution, there is a continual division of activity, a division whose technical dimension conceals the social dimension. The stability, protection and exclusivity of the productive assets (e.g. portfolios, clients, machines, software) conceded to employees turn them into virtual property rights. They gradually become the basis for an extension of the employees' intentions and physical presence in their working environment. Through these assets, the accounting department connects the profit with its practical owner. Employees can make use of the basic logics of profit appropriation. Assigning the fruits of the assets to the owner of the asset, or what I call the logic of specification, comes first. If this is not sufficient, the logics of primacy, first will, first idea and first action are invoked.

Access to these basic means of appropriating profit depends on the employee's position in the organisation of labour (see Table 4.1). Heads of desk and heads of trading room – since they hold *eminence ownership* of the assets they concede – are in a particularly strong position, as are financial operators, who hold *useful ownership* of the conceded assets. Inventors have more difficulty asserting the logic of the first idea. Support staff, who *lease their work*, are often at the greatest disadvantage since their action remains secondary in the overall structure. The distribution of the symbolic capacity to appropriate profit is therefore very unequal. It reflects the fact that there is ongoing inequality in the division of the activity.

What may have initially seemed like a detour has given us a better understanding of what stirs individuals into action and what makes them feel they are the legitimate owners of profit. This belief gives rise to employee claims, aggressiveness, resentment or satisfaction. The idea that employees should receive the

Table 4.1 Positions in the division of labour and basic methods of appropriating profit

Access based on → *Position in the division of labour* ↓	*Holding of company assets*	*First will*	*First actions*	*First ideas*
Heads of desk, particularly heads of trading room (*internal entrepreneurs*) have the *eminent ownership* of the assets of their room or desk	++	++	0	+
Front office operators, traders, salespeople, have the *useful ownership* of the portfolios they manage	+	+	++	+
Financial engineers, quants, financial analysts are in a position to become *authors and inventors*	0	0	0	++
Assistant traders, back and middle office administrators *lease* their *work*: they execute prescribed orders	–	–	+	–

share owed to them by right has become established among all employees, not only among those who carry out the distribution and those who benefit most from distribution but also those who benefit least. The symbolic appropriation of profit is therefore a prerequisite for its actual appropriation.

Nevertheless, the belief that there is an obvious owner of profit is not the sole factor that determines the final distribution. I have shown how complex rights overlap and interweave. They do not necessarily lead to a unilateral method of granting ownership of profit, and there continue to be areas of tension and friction. The belief in the legitimacy of the distribution method does not always establish itself so easily. What is the basis for distribution when the belief in a legitimate allocation is not enough to determine the outcome? The next chapter will help to answer this question.

Notes

1 Traditionally, in property law a distinction is made between *res nullius*, "masterless things", things that have no owner to start off with (game, etc.) and *res derelictae*, things abandoned voluntarily (Terré and Simler 1998).

2 He concludes that work contracts should include the voluntary transfer of employees' rights over their creations to the firm. (Di Malta 1992, p. 462).

3 The return on equity from the activities of the Société Générale corporate and investment bank in 2005 was 44% (well above the standard "15% demanded by the markets"). For equities activities alone, this reached as high as 183%.

4 These movements for the most part resulted from discussion centring on the work of Nozick (1974). According to the theory of libertarian justice, a distribution of goods that arises from fair transfers (i.e. agreed by both parties) is considered fair. It is also necessary to demonstrate the fairness of the original appropriation.

5 This is Nozick's "Lockean proviso" (Nozick 1974, p. 178).

6 According to Peter Vallentyne, this is the position taken by "Georgian libertarians" (Vallentyne 1999).

7 "Two Grecian colonies, leaving their native country, in search of new feats, were informed that a city near them was deserted by its inhabitants. To know the truth of this report, they dispatched at once two messengers, one from each colony; who finding on their approach, that their information was true, begun a race together with an intention to take possession of the city, each of them for his countrymen. One of these messengers, finding that he was not an equal match for the other, launched his spear at the gates of the city, and was so fortunate as to fix it there before the arrival of his companion. This produced a dispute betwixt the two colonies, which of them was the proprietor of the empty city and this dispute still subsists among philosophers" (Hume 2003, p. 361).

8 The fact that Locke's reasoning rests largely on accession was highlighted by Hume (2003, p. 108). Nozick, who nonetheless accepts the majority of Locke's demonstration, refutes his materialist and ultimately antiliberal limitation of property to the mere capacity for labour. He also mocks the right of accession as the weak link in that demonstration: "If I own a can of tomato juice and spill it in the sea so that its molecules (made radioactive, so I can check this) mingle evenly throughout the sea, do I thereby come to own the sea, or have I foolishly dissipated my tomato juice?" (Nozick 1974, p. 175).

9 In his overview of property right, Dagognet (1992) contemplates the sexual and uterine dimensions of the imaginary world of accession. He remarks that the "fruit comes after the womb": the calf belongs to the owner of the cow and not to that of the bull. The same is true of slavery in Roman law.

10 He subsequently adds, "The idea [of the 'right of accession'] may be expressed in this way: any thing to which another of less importance is added (*accedit*) communicates to it its own status in law" (Durkheim 1957, p. 147).

11 If competition initially disappeared, it was only because the distribution of property rights over the firm's assets was stable and accepted (and avoided any overlapping). However, this would not have prevented rivalry and conflict from resurfacing when changes were made to the rights allocated to individual employees.

12 On the concept of simultaneous property in customary law, cf. Patault (1988, Chapters 2 and 3).

13 "That is mine which I bring under my *control* . . . ; which, as an object of my choice, is something that I have the capacity to use . . . ; and which, finally, I *will* to be mine" (Kant 1996, p. 411). The protection of the appropriated goods and the enhancement of their value through labour are merely signs of this realisation of the arbitrary.

14 Moreover, it can sometimes be seen in certain economic experiments in which individuals have to decide on the fairness of a distribution not for themselves but for others (Schokkaert 1999).

15 The emotional account given by Rozan (1999, p. 282) on this subject when he leaves Indosuez is particularly significant: "What hurt me the most was that yet again all the cream went to the same people and all the bitterness was left for those who deserved the most. I've seen the relentless work done by Sue, the Chinese girls and the whole back office team. I've eaten enough chop-suey among the tickets and laughed with them over the seventeenth completely made-up tool kit report of the evening, which meant that they would get home at midnight, and I fought to get the bank to pay begrudgingly for their taxi home, knowing they were living on 12,000 dollars a year before tax, and that it wasn't enough to pay for the night classes they often missed because of me and which were their only lifeline! . . . Sue, her friends, the secretaries, the French expats in the IT department, the whole of the back office, all those people who worked like dogs for us and for so little, so badly paid compared to us, we owe our position to them and they'll get no credit for our success. . . . Unfair? Of course it's unfair. But who cared about that on Wall Street in 1986?"

16 Employees retain their rights (moral and property) over literary and artistic creations. However, they have no rights over software. The situation is more complex when it comes to patents. Inventions made during assignments are the employer's property. The law distinguishes two types of invention among those made outside of assignments: those that are attributable to the employer and those that are not. While the latter are the property of the employee, the former must be transferred to the employer. However, the employer is required to allocate extra pay for the employee, as is the case with inventions made during assignments.

17 In his work on the Paris stock exchange, Fabian Muniesa (2005) retraces the multiple transactions to which listing algorithms have been subject. Paris bought the CATS transaction software from the Toronto stock market in 1986. It was modified and sold back to Toronto as the NSC system in 1997.

18 We should note that the financial concept of EVA was patented by the firm Stern and Stewart in the early 1980s (Lordon 2000a). Nevertheless, it could be said that the patent deals less with the formula itself, which is relatively mundane and closely related to

Tobin's "q" calculus, than with the highly complex method of financial recalculation of balance sheets used for re-evaluating profit and capital consumed.

19 "Innovation doesn't exist, but exact copies do. If you want to innovate, you just identify what's being done somewhere else and adapt it to your own market. . . . At the time everyone thought I was this great innovator [for introducing client forex traders]. In fact, I didn't invent a thing. Client forex trading is just American sales . . . " recounted a director general ironically.

20 Cf. art. 570 of the French Civil Code.

21 One might think that specification favours the legal owner alone (the principal). In fact, everything depends on the initial demarcation of the principal and the accessory: "The right of accession, when it concerns two moveable things belonging to two different owners, is entirely subject to the principles of natural equity" states article 565 of the French Civil Code. Article 570 favours the legal owner but is in fact then tempered by article 571: "If, however, the labour were so significant that it greatly exceeds the value of the material used, the work will then be deemed the principal part and the worker will have the right to retain the thing produced, by reimbursing the owner the value of the material, appraised at the date of reimbursement."

22 As described by a vexed head of trading room at Pluto Bank, who stated, "and so what I've noticed is that people who earn a fortune in our profession are those who work in large banks, because they have a much broader trading base. When you work in a medium-sized bank, you earn far less".

23 Sauviat gives an insight into the heights reached by some analysts in the United States (Sauviat 2003).

24 Analysts' salaries on the Paris market rarely exceeded 300,000 euros in the period from 2000 to 2010.

25 The fact that the commercial activity that analysts engage in with firms can give rise to highly lucrative securities transactions (M&A, public offerings, etc.) has led financial firms to pay bonuses to some star analysts who are considered most likely to generate the highest brokerage flows, particularly in the so-called "new technologies" sector, which expanded rapidly between 1995 and 2000. The respective annual incomes of Henry Blodget, Jack Grubman and Mary Meeker, three ICT stars, rose to 12, 20 and 19 million dollars at the end of the 1990s (Sauviat 2003). In the economic downturn, analysts were accused of distorting their analyses with the sole aim of making public offerings.

References

Austin, J 1962, *How to Do Things with Words*, Clarendon Press, Oxford.

Bernstein, P 1993, *Capital Ideas: The Improbable Origins of Modern Wall Street*, Simon and Schuster, New York.

Berthoud, G and Busino, G 1981, 'La propriété: entre la nature et la culture', *Revue européenne des sciences sociales*, vol. 19, n°59, pp. 17–54.

Bourdieu, P 1999, 'The Specificity of the Scientific Field' in *The Science Studies Reader*, ed. M Biagioli, Routledge, New York, pp. 31–50.

Bourdieu, P 2004, *Science of Science and Reflexivity*, Polity, Cambridge UK.

Collins, R 1998, *The Sociology of Philosophies*, Belknap Press of Harvard University Press, Cambridge MA.

Dagognet, F 1992. *Philosophie de la propriété. L'avoir*, PUF, Paris.

David, P 1998, 'Le compromis du système d'organisation de la production intellectuelle', *Réseaux*, n° 88/89, pp. 25–63.

Di Malta, PY 1992, *L'appropriation des créations de salarié*, doctoral thesis submitted to the University of Montpellier, Montpellier.

Durkheim, E 1957, *Professional Ethics and Civic Morals*, The Free Press, New York.

Godechot, O 2001, *Les Traders. Essai de sociologie des marchés financiers*, La Découverte, Paris.

Hume, D 2003, *A Treatise of Human Nature*, Dover Publications, Mineola, New York.

Kant, I 1996, *Practical Philosophy*, Cambridge University Press, Cambridge UK.

Kleiner, T 2000, 'D'un artisanat à une industrie: la transformation de l'industrie française de la gestion d'actifs par l'intégration de routines professionnelles depuis le système anglo-saxon', conference presentation delivered at the 'Journées d'études sociales de la finance', 21 April, École des Mines, Paris.

Krippner, G 2005, 'The Financialization of the American Economy', *Socio-Economic Review*, vol. 3, n°2, pp. 173–208.

Lepetit, JF 2002, *Homme de marché*, Economica, Paris.

Lewis, M 1989, *Liar's Poker*, Hodder and Stoughton, London.

Locke J 1968, *Two Treatises of Government*, Cambridge University Press, Cambridge UK.

Lordon, F 2000a, 'La "création de valeur" comme rhétorique et comme pratique. Généalogie et sociologie de la valeur actionariale', *Année de la régulation*, vol. 4, La Découverte, pp. 117–170.

Lordon, F 2000b, 'La force des idées simples. Misère épistémique des comportements économiques', *Politix*, vol. 13, n°52, pp. 183–210.

MacKenzie, D 2006, *An Engine, Not a Camera: How Financial Models Shape Markets*, MIT Press Books, Cambridge MA.

MacKenzie, D and Millo, Y 2003, 'Constructing a Market, Performing Theory: The Historical Sociology of a Financial Derivatives Exchange', *American Journal of Sociology*, vol. 109, n°1, pp. 107–145.

Milgrom, P and Roberts, J 1988, 'An Economic Approach to Influence Activities in Organizations', *American Journal of Sociology*, vol. 94, Supplement, pp. S154–S179.

Muniesa, F 2005, 'Contenir le marché: la transition de la criée à la cotation électronique à la Bourse de Paris', *Sociologie du travail*, vol. 47, n°4, pp. 485–501.

Nietzsche, F 1968, *The Will to Power*, Vintage, New York.

Nozick, R 1974, *Anarchy, State and Utopia*, Basic Books, New York.

Oyer, P 2008, 'The Making of an Investment Banker: Stock Market Shocks, Career Choice, and Lifetime Income', *The Journal of Finance*, vol. 63, n°6, pp. 2601–2628.

Patault, AM 1989, *Introduction historique au droit des biens*, PUF, Paris.

Rousseau, JJ 2009, *Discourse on Inequality*, The Floating Press, Auckland.

Rozan, JM 1999, *Le Fric*, Michel Lafon, Paris.

Sauviat, C 2003, 'Deux professions dans la tourmente. L'audit et l'analyse financière', *Actes de la recherche en sciences sociales*, n°146–147, pp. 21–40.

Schokkaert, E 1999, 'M. Tout-le-monde est "post-welfariste". Opinions sur la justice redistributive', *Revue économique*, vol. 50, n°4, pp. 811–831.

Terré, F and Simler, P 1998, *Droit civil. Les biens*, Dalloz, Paris.

Tomaskovic-Devey, D and Lin, KH 2011, 'Income Dynamics, Economic Rents, and the Financialization of the US Economy', *American Sociological Review*, vol. 76, n°4, pp. 538–559.

Vallentyne, P 1999, 'Le libertarisme de gauche et la justice', *Revue économique*, vol. 50, n°4, July pp. 859–878.

5   Assets and power

In the previous chapter, I established the first elements required for a "grammar" of appropriation.[1] I highlighted the social and organisational arrangements through which employees can consider themselves to be the owners of profit, be recognised as such and thus demand their share. However, this grammar alone does not enable an understanding of the effective forms of appropriation. It makes an undeniable contribution to our understanding of the rivalries and issues at stake in the bonus distribution process. The plurality of methods of appropriation show that there is nothing natural, unavoidable or uniform about appropriation. Nevertheless, I cannot stop at this pluralist, indeed relativist conclusion; rather, I must tackle the question of why one method of appropriation may dominate the others.

For this, the regime of appropriation has the advantage of being related to the social structure, unlike the regime of justification established by Boltanski and Thévenot (2006, p. 98).[2] These two authors maintain that the regime of justification is a regime of action within which it is very easy to move around and shift from one "polity" to another, as the "polities" are open equally to all actors. Moreover, it is sometimes seen as an "irenic" regime of action that misjudges power relations.[3] The regime of appropriation, on the other hand, takes the social structure (organisational division) as its point of departure, establishes stable, long-term positions – positions taken by actors and not agents – before returning to the social structure (identifying relations of appropriation and expropriation, in other words a division of income). It can therefore be linked more easily to a determinist issue, like that of the social conditions under which one method of appropriation is dominant over another.

The grammar of appropriation lays down the framework that enables a sense of ownership of profit to emerge. It allows us to understand what it is that stirs individuals into action when others have taken what they thought was theirs. It provides an understanding of a successful bonus distribution, in which people's rights to profit do not overlap. But how are tensions resolved when they do overlap? The world of finance is also an environment in which certain forms of opportunism are generally tolerated (Abolafia 1996, Chap. 8), particularly opportunism with regard to bonuses. Thus, it is often the case that operators do not really believe profit belongs to them and is for them, yet they find themselves in a context (budget discussions, negotiations with their boss, proving their worth to the group, and so forth) in which they still seek to make that profit their own.[4] Market operators are prone to speak of "power grabs" and "nuisance potential" when identifying these opportunistic ways of appropriating profit that are not based on a distribution of assets that gives their holder legitimate ownership. The purpose of this chapter is to show that power can nevertheless be conceived on conceptual bases similar to those that allowed us to establish legitimate methods of appropriation. I shall endeavour to show how ownership, which in this case means ownership of assets, may be considered a source of power.

Based on a critical interpretation of the work of Williamson, I shall show that certain characteristics of ownership, such as its redeployability and scarcity, are likely to give it a constraining power over others. These concepts will enable an understanding of the imbalances present in the internal exchange relations between traders and salespeople on the one hand, and between inventors (quants, analysts, R&D engineers) and financial operators on the other hand.

Redeployable assets and power

Analysing ownership is the key for understanding power and domination. When reaching its full implications, it entails a relational analysis. Property right is not simply a question of the bearer having the freedom to use a thing; it also requires others to respect their own exclusion. Property is a means of organising competition between actors (by allocating monopolies) and a constraining structure. However, the constraints imposed by an asset are not limited to an obligation of non-use. In some arrangements, holding certain types of assets may lead to more general forms of dependence: an individual obeys another who holds vital resources.

Asset specificity and hold-up in Williamson's theory

The concept of asset specificity put forward by Williamson is especially useful for understanding power in economic life based on an analysis of ownership (Williamson 1985). Williamson defines asset specificity as follows:

> A characteristic of a specialized investment, whereby it cannot be redeployed to alternative uses or by alternative users except at a loss of productive value. Asset specificity can take several forms, of which human, physical, site, and dedicated assets are the most common. Specific assets give rise to *bilateral dependency*, which complicates contractual relations. Accordingly, such investments would never be made except as these contribute to prospective reductions in production costs or additions to revenue.
>
> (Williamson 1994)

A specific asset is one whose value depends on the collaboration of other actors and which is likely to lose some of its value if that collaboration breaks down.

Ownership of a specific asset (in so far as it depends on another asset held by others) puts the asset holder in a weak, dependent position in relation to the individuals with whom she is exchanging. The value of her asset is preserved only if the exchange relation in which that asset assumes value is perpetuated. The holder is therefore dependent on the other party and risks falling victim to *post-contractual* opportunism – she may be the target of a "hold-up" situation (Malcomson 1997),[5] in which the other party may threaten to end the relationship, leaving her with the burden of a devalued asset. The other party can demand a renegotiation of the contract under terms of trade that are not favourable to the asset holder[6].

Williamson has used the theory of specific assets to explain vertical integration. Upstream independent suppliers could not fully commit to providing goods and services produced thanks to specific assets – such as a mould used to manufacture a precise part – because they would fear a hold-up situation and a highly unfavourable renegotiation of the terms of trade. These risks explain the advantages of both vertical integration and the transformation of the market relation into a hierarchical relation. Indeed, internalising a specific asset may seem like an effective means of preventing opportunistic behaviour. This is apparent when a single owner owns and exploits both the specific asset and the other assets to which it is specific. This solution is less effective when the legal owner cannot be the sole operator and must organise a technical and social division of labour (which generally follows the structure of the assets).

There are a number of arguments to support the idea that a hierarchical solution would prevent certain actors from opportunistically exploiting the low redeployability of some assets. Business relations are more permanent and more difficult to break off than market relations. The unified property of the firm – a legal entity – is guaranteed by law and prevents employees in charge of the most redeployable assets from taking advantage of them, namely by redeploying them elsewhere. Finally, the hierarchical functioning of the organisation could compel or motivate its employees to adopt a cooperative form of behaviour and prevent them from exploiting the asymmetrical redeployability of assets: "since the aggressive pursuit of individual interest redounds to the disadvantage of the system, and as present and prospective compensation (including promotions) can be easily varied by the general office to reflect non-cooperation, simple requests to adopt a cooperative mode are apt to be heeded," states Williamson (1975, p. 29). Williamson and the school of transaction costs have thus maintained that the organisational and contractual form (market, special contracts, hierarchy) is an effective means of arbitrating between specificity costs (specificity is less costly within the organisation) and incentive costs (incentive is less costly in the market).

The overall assertion of this theory is debatable (Gabrié and Jacquier 1994). Williamson believes any organisational arrangement to be an effective response to transaction costs; in short, that the size and form of the organisation can be explained simply by examining transaction costs. Some critics have concluded that "all is for the best in the best of all possible organisational worlds"

(Gabrié and Jacquier 1994, p. 125). Because they are aware that opportunism exists, agents choose the optimal institutional arrangements that enable them to eliminate it. In the end, there is no reason for opportunism to occur because every measure has been taken to prevent it. Contrary to his claim for realism, Williamson returns to a common – and unsatisfactory – method in economics, consisting of simultaneously characterising a problem and finding a rational solution (in this case, signing a long-term contract that cannot be renegotiated) that ultimately makes it disappear.

Furthermore, it is inconsistent with the theoretical framework he adopts, which has three central hypotheses: bounded rationality, opportunism and uncertainty (Williamson 1985, Chapter 2). The fact that rationality is bounded prevents agents from drawing up full contracts that would enable them to avoid situations of opportunism, and forces them to make constraining institutional arrangements such as hierarchies (Williamson 1985, p. 89). Agents therefore have a split calculating capacity: limited in the short term and unlimited in the long term, to the point that they are able, like Ulysses facing the sirens, to take into account their short-term limitations.

While he calls on bounded rationality in order to rule out a solution through contractualisation, Williamson's conception of economic behaviour is surprisingly close to that of neoclassical economics. He uses concrete examples to refute any use of notions such as trust or belief, and considers that the only relevant dimension of social behaviour is calculativeness, or the calculation of the costs and profits of an action in an uncertain context (Williamson 1993). He holds that individuals have an equal capacity to calculate and, above all, to be opportunistic.

However, the level of opportunism is not a universal constant or even an individual psychological parameter (Granovetter 1985 & 1995; Abolafia 1996).[7] Abolafia compares three markets – bond, futures and the New York Stock Exchange – and highlights a cycle of opportunism in the financial markets: the blatant opportunism of some (for example outsiders such as Michael Milken, who threatened the stability of corporate America through his leveraged buy-out policy) creates pressure to introduce restrictions on market transactions. The establishment of such restrictions creates a new level of tolerable opportunism. The pressure to introduce restrictions abates, the restrictions are relaxed and new forms of opportunistic behaviour emerge (Abolafia 1996, p. 179). The opportunism displayed by actors is not constant, therefore. It depends on the organisation of the social structure and the rules of tolerable and reprehensible opportunism. As a result, it is not always entirely possible to measure. When it occurs in unusual forms, it always comes as a surprise before finally becoming partially integrated in the new institutional arrangements.

Williamson sometimes calls on an evolutionist argument: through the learning process, agents grasp which institutional arrangements allow appropriation through a hold-up and which are more robust. However, when he looks more closely at specific cases, Williamson considers evolution to have already taken place and the learning process to be complete, which partly contradicts the hypothesis of uncertainty. If the economic world is unpredictable, then its agents are in a perpetual state of learning and readjustment, precisely because the conditions that create an effective institutional arrangement later disappear and change. Therefore, in a changing world, particularly one of rapid change, the situations of relational dependence produced by high asset specificity are common and that, unless the economic context stabilises, there is no reason to think that these situations will cease to occur. To be sure, in one or the other of these situations, some arrangements may occasionally limit a particular dependence, but such arrangements may, in turn, lead to other dependences, or else the shift in economic conditions may quickly eliminate the need for organisational change.

Furthermore, there is no guarantee that institutional arrangements are always capable of preventing opportunistic behaviour. As Malcomson points out, the contract chosen does not necessarily reduce transaction costs. It can only do so when it can be applied "by going to court if necessary" (Malcomson 1997, p. 1917). Therefore, in some cases contracts may be considered null and void because they are against the law, such as those involving slavery. Or else the contract may be obscure, unverifiable, incomplete or too time-consuming and costly to defend in court (Malcomson 1997, p. 1917). What is more, empirical research shows that the institutional arrangements conceived to overcome opportunism are not as encouraging as expected. Eccles and White demonstrate that when the multidivisional firm has to price transfers between centres, the question of the asset specificity differential inevitably applies (Eccles and White 1988). This question is by no means simple, and whatever the pricing method used, be it the full costing method or the marked-to-market costing method, there are still numerous potential conflicts. This risk of conflict is all the greater given that the compensation of the directors of these centres depends on the accounting results of their department. If there is an over-marketisation of internal economic relations, under the pretext of providing more effective incentives, then it may lead to a strengthening of internal transaction costs and, ultimately, a less efficient productive structure.

Redeployability, scarcity and power

Without going any further into the optimality of institutional responses to transaction costs, from the critique of Williamson's theory let us primarily retain the idea that ownership of specific assets is a common occurrence and that it produces a situation of weakness and dependence in exchange relations.

We need to avoid a common error of interpretation: the specificity of an asset is not directly related to its scarcity. The term *specific asset* may cause confusion if we do not take care to establish to what the specificity actually applies. Specificity does not apply so much to the person who holds the asset – having a monopoly over a scarce commodity is more likely to strengthen her than weaken her – as to the relation between the asset holder and other economic actors who are needed to enhance the asset's value. It is the productive relation that is specific (and scarce) and which can make one of the parties vulnerable to a breakdown in the collaboration. Specificity is the inability to circumvent or redeploy a productive relation. Its opposite, "redeployability", can be therefore seen as major source of power.

Moreover, the power that comes with redeployability and that which comes with a monopoly over scarce resources may be combined. In such cases, holding scarce and redeployable assets gives the holder a great deal of power over others, who will be forced to go through that individual in order to access those scarce assets.[8] On the other hand, holding specific and common assets maintains their holders in a state of relational dependence on the one with whom they use the asset to carry out exchanges. This individual will gain an advantage over them by brandishing the threat of ending the relationship.

Redeployable and scarce assets enable an opportune, indeed opportunistic, appropriation of profit that sometimes goes far beyond the profit to which their holder feels legitimately entitled during the production process. This does not necessarily mean it is immoral to exploit the advantage that comes from having a monopoly over an asset or from the redeployability of that asset. Such exploitation can always be justified in a context in which certain forms of opportunism are given greater value (the art of negotiation, a good sense of timing, etc.). The advantage that comes with redeployability or a monopoly can be seen as a form of power (particularly when one is forced to concede to the transaction conditions that are imposed) but also as an evanescent power (similar to Marxist exploitation): the transaction remains a free agreement between free parties.

In contrast with economic literature that generally conceives the "hold-up problem" in the context of the employer–employee relationship,[9] I will show that the phenomenon also exists between different categories of employees within the financial organisation, and that institutional prevention measures are not always implemented or available. I will consider two cases: the relations between traders and salespeople on the one hand, as an example of the shifting exploitation of redeployability differentials, and the relations between R&D teams and trading teams on the other hand, as an example of the power that derives from having a monopoly.

Salespeople, traders and redeployability of assets

All actors in the financial markets repeatedly highlight the structural conflict of interests between traders and salespeople in the trading room. Traders and salespeople compete with one another to establish what share of the profit from a transaction will be allocated to each of the two parties.[10] Even if this situation occurs less often than the conflicts between members of the front office and back office, it is more visible partly due to its intensity and its relative symmetry: it sets two employees of the same rank against one another (unlike the front/back office conflict which is often only perceived as such by the back office). As one trader from Neptune Bank recounted, "It's a bad situation! We give a price and they add a margin on it! Their aim is for us to set the tightest prices possible to widen their spread as much as they can. Whatever we don't make, they make themselves.

So everything depends on the balance of power between sales and trading." While the trader saw this as the salesperson's greed, a salesperson recalled the imperative of commercial constraints:

> But as a salesperson you're always between the two. You're between the trader, who's never happy, and the client who always has to be satisfied in terms of speed and spread. Because you want things to work. You're graded on your volume but you're also keen for the trader to make money and for the client to do business. There are a lot of obstacles to keeping everyone happy without losing any money.

In addition, there is a whole series of social oppositions that intensify and nuance the clash of pricing interests. In comparison, a relatively high proportion of salespeople are women (30% at Jupiter Bank in 1999) whereas traders are almost exclusively male (90% at the same bank in the same year). Salespeople are usually business school graduates, while traders come from engineering schools. At Jupiter Bank, 40% of the 117 salespeople were business school graduates and 11% were engineering school graduates, as opposed to 22% and 42% respectively for the 164 traders. The structural opposition between the "maths geeks" and the "business guys" in preparatory classes and then in the elite *grandes écoles* is rekindled in the trading rooms, particularly at Saturn Bank with its highly elitist recruitment process. On top of this there is a psychological characterisation: the salespeople are considered superficial, frivolous, extrovert, even hysterical, whereas traders are chauvinist, obsessive, introverted and neurotic.

Despite this, the economic opposition between salespeople and traders is somewhat evanescent. Those at the top of the hierarchy, heads of trading room or even higher, know it, relativise it and deny it, as though trying to defuse a conflict for which they do not want to be held accountable. The transaction price between salespeople and traders is a "market price". It is a voluntary agreement between willing parties. What type of power could be to blame in this context of free negotiation? A perspective based on the redeployability of assets will make it possible to conceive power relations in a context of free negotiation.

Let us summarise the terms of exchange as observed in the majority of derivatives trading rooms. Traders are specialised in one or several complex products (warrants, exotic options, structured products, convertible bonds) that can be developed and backed up by one or several simple products (the underlying assets). The portfolio's expansion is primarily defined by the nature of the products, themselves delimited on a sectorial and geographical basis, by groups of countries or by currency. Salespeople, meanwhile, are specialised in a client base that is defined on a geographic, economic and sectorial basis. This client base is potentially multi-product.

The impact of this organisation is significant. When carrying out transactions with clients, traders are in contact with several salespeople, and the salespeople are in contact with several traders. The transaction is carried out as follows: the salesperson identifies potential clients in order to persuade them, depending on their risk exposure, financial profile or even economic situation, to buy a particular type of derivative product. When the client seems to have committed to a transaction, the salesperson requests a price from the trader responsible for the product, who usually provides both the ask price and the bid price (the spread). The salesperson usually has the freedom to add a sales margin on either side of the trader's spread according to the client's degree of non-sophistication and the low level of competition on the market: it is often said that in a competitive market such as foreign exchange products, it is impossible to do so for a very sophisticated client (large management firms or other banks, for example). If the transaction is concluded, it results in an internal sharing of the profit between the salesperson and the trader, and this sharing can be organised in a variety of ways (I will go into further detail on these later on).

Not all interaction between the client, the salesperson and the trader necessarily results in a transaction. On the contrary, it is common for a client in over-the-counter markets to telephone several different salespeople to request prices. In between two transactions with a client via the salesperson, the trader does not adopt a "wait and see" approach; instead, she must carry out a multitude of transactions in order to optimise her portfolio. In the case of options, every time the price of the underlying security changes, in order to avoid any exposure to the price risk she must reassess the number of underlying securities in her portfolio ("delta-neutral" trading according to the Black–Scholes formula) and also predict changes in volatility or protect herself by buying other options. At this point, traders will make other transactions directly "on the market" without going through the sales team. They have direct access through the electronic interface (for electronic exchanges) or by telephone (for over-the-counter markets) or, if need be, through brokers. If "their" product is liquid enough – which may not be the case for very sophisticated, "tailor-made" options which the traders are the only ones to offer on the market – depending on their strategy and forecasts the traders will make transactions with fellow traders trading the same products in another bank.[11] Traders are therefore relatively specialised, but they retain control over access to the market, which is understood as the limited group of peers trading the product in question. They can always threaten to redeploy themselves exclusively in that market if transactions with the salespeople do not seem profitable. However, they must go through the salespeople in order to access less professional clients, who are precisely those on whom it is possible to take a significant margin.

Hidden power in internal transactions

Some of the terms (price, quantity, etc.) of the relations between traders and salespeople are freely negotiated, while some are subject to constraints. Their relations are necessary in the sense that the salesperson cannot quote a price to a client or engage in a transaction without the trader's support, just as the trader cannot sell a product to a non-professional client without the appointed salesperson's mediation. One salesperson from Neptune Bank recalled that the "salesperson is unavoidable", that "the client doesn't talk to the trader" and the trader should not speak to the client. He admitted that he would sometimes "have liked to ask prices in other banks, but I couldn't" (except for currencies not traded by his bank). The style of organisation used in trading rooms means that traders and salespeople are in a position to develop two types of complementary assets: clients on the one hand and securities on the other. This situation allows the party with the more redeployable asset of the two to capture the profit. However, it is not too easy to determine which of the two parties has an advantage over the other. Each of them can show that balance of power is in the other's favour and that the other party has burdened her own activity with usurpatory constraints. One trader at Neptune Bank stated:

> Yes [our relations are necessary], with a balance of power to the trader's advantage. You have to be accommodating. If the trader quotes a shit price, you get told off by the client. The client will say, "What kind of shit price is that? Do you really think I'm going to trade with a spread of five beeps?" So you go and see your trader and you say: "This is a shit price!" He says: "Yeah, it's like that because . . . blah-blah-blah." So you're always riding on top of the wave. A trader from the same bank and same department, however, considered the "general balance of power" to be "unfavourable to traders" because "it's not a capital markets bank" and "trading is dirty work!"

This contradictory allocation of bargaining power by each of the two parties to the other party should not cause the idea of bargaining power to be abandoned altogether. While it may be true that bargaining power depends largely on the trading room's past activity, management (former salespeople or former traders), strategy, product and client positioning, capital base and even the economic situation, it is also true that it depends largely on the position of the individual within this group, in other words her seniority, career path and the firm's assets that have been allocated to her. To show the simultaneous diversity of the balance of power between traders and salespeople, I present an outline of the potential relations between representatives of these two groups (Figure 5.1). This is only an outline; it does not show real transaction relations as depicted in Baker's highly informative graphs of the structure of transactions on an open outcry market (Baker 1984a & 1984b).

Figure 5.1 allows the concept of redeployability to be represented as a relational structure. Redeployability is indeed one of the mechanisms at work in reticular phenomena. It can be found in a related form in Ronald Burt's notion of "structural holes". He explains that a person who has structural holes in her network, in other words contacts who are not connected through her, has two advantages: "information benefits" (non-redundant information) and "control benefits", which means having the potential to adopt a *tertius gaudens* strategy and being capable of playing contacts "against one another" (Burt 1992, p. 30). To further clarify his argument, two people in contact with each other are in a situation of complementarity in which they can both exploit the profits of a shared

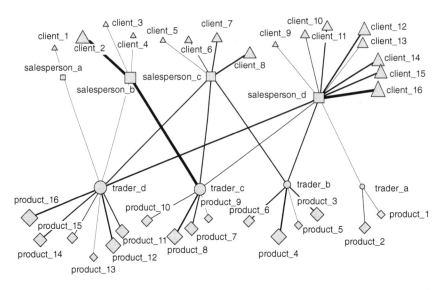

Figure 5.1 Transaction relations between traders and salespeople in a trading room

asset – the relationship. However, the level of redeployability of this asset is not necessarily equivalent on either side. An individual with a large, diverse network of contacts will suffer less damage if the relationship breaks off than an individual with a small, concentrated network. Therefore, if the former is in contact with the latter, the former can threaten to break off the relationship and appropriate the benefits of its continuation. Even if there is no such threat, the latter is so fearful of a breakdown in the relationship that she may willingly concede most of the benefits to the former.

In this figure, Salesperson *a* is a small salesperson who has just one small client, who in turn buys one of the products being traded by a big trader (Trader *d*). For big Trader *d*, a breakdown in the relationship will be of little consequence. On the other hand, it could prove disastrous for Salesperson *a*. It is highly likely that Trader *d* will request (or even if she does not) that small Salesperson *a* accept terms of exchange that are considerably more favour-able to Trader *d* than, for example, big Salesperson *d*, whether in terms of the price (and margin for the trader), the quantity of information passed on, or the degree to which the client's request conforms to the interests of the trader's portfolio. Similarly, small Trader *a* will be in a highly unfavourable position to impose any terms of exchange on big Salesperson *d*. In order to develop her business, she relies on sales transactions initiated by big Salesperson *d*, whereas the latter relies little on the former's access to the market.[12]

These differentials in the power that certain traders wield over certain sales-people, and vice versa, are a simplified cross-section. In order to properly understand them, they must be resituated in a complex temporal dynamic. The unfavourable position of small Trader *a* or small Salesperson *a* is not a vital or permanent characteristic. It depends on the economic situation and the assets they have been allocated by the firm. It often corresponds to an early phase in their career in finance, when the portfolio they are allocated (clients, products) is small and of little importance. Their survival in the world of finance, a series of favourable economic conditions and their increasing skill brings them more assets and boosts their chances of playing strategically against others.[13] When traders are young or new, they need to be able to assert themselves; in other words, to make that transition from the unknown to the known, from outsider to insider, and to get out of that negative position of being the junior trader who is allocated little and who generates little profit. As one salesperson recounted, "He tests you [when you are new], that's for sure! He says to himself, he's just started, he won't make a fuss, I'll quote him a 5-point spread! He won't make a fuss, even though it's worth 2 points on the market!" This strategy is even more obvious to this salesperson because he used to be a trader and knows both the prices and the trader's strategy of increasing the bid–ask spread to the seller's detriment.[14] One of the resources available to prevent opportunistic exploitation of junior traders is to ask the head of desk to intervene. Heads of desk, thanks to the high level of redeployability of their total assets, are less vulnerable to being exploited by traders and can threaten the opportunistic trader with reprisals. Even so, turning to the head of desk for help can only be a last resort. It could demonstrate an inability to negotiate or a failure to increase one's assets.

Lewis's account *Liar's Poker* provides a striking illustration of the way in which a senior trader may exploit the redeployability differential of a junior salesperson (Lewis 1989, Chap. 8). In early 1986, Lewis was working as a junior bond salesperson at Salomon Brothers in London, in charge of French and English clients, "small" money managers with less than 100 million dollars (the senior salespeople keep the big clients for themselves). As he almost never finds any new clients, his boss eventually passes on the name of a small fund manager, Herman, at the English branch of an Austrian bank, to whom nobody on his desk wants to sell. Once a relationship with Herman has been established, a trader in the room accosts Lewis and suggests he sell Herman an idea he claims will be profitable: buy cheap 30-year AT&T bonds and sell short 30-year US treasury bonds. Excited by the idea, Lewis persuades his Austrian customer to come on board and do the trade with Salomon Brothers. Once the transaction has gone through, however, he realises that his trader has not sold AT&T bonds bought on the market but AT&Ts dumped in his own portfolio, which he has been trying to get rid of for months[15]. According to his boss, everyone in the trading room knew this. Lewis then understands that he has "blown up" his customer. The client waits before getting rid of the troublesome bonds. After a month, if Lewis is to be believed, Herman's loss reaches 140,000 dollars, his boss is bothered by his positions and fires him.

In the case recounted by Lewis, the outcome of the exploitation of the redeployability differential is not so much the sharing of the margin and pricing as the respective opportunity presented by the transaction for the trader's portfolio or the portfolio of the salesperson's client. The head of the sales desk explains that he's just a "geek" who has been "fucked". On the other hand, when the young trader complains, the senior trader responds with a commonly-used question: "Who do you work for? This guy or Salomon Brothers?" (Lewis 1989, p. 195). Even if the head of bond trading at Salomon, as well as the trader, thinks it is acceptable to "screw" customers to the bank's benefit because clients have a short memory, it is not in the salesperson's interest to do so. The condition for salespeople's increased power over traders, and over the bank, is that they make their assets – the clients – completely redeployable in relation to the firm that has allocated them. This means forming a secure attachment with clients by working in accordance with their interests, even if that may sometimes mean working independently of their employer's interests.

Two years on, Lewis is an experienced trader. At the firm's express request, he agrees to sacrifice one of his customers by persuading him to buy bonds that Salomon wants to get rid of by any means, which earns Lewis the honorary, virile title of "Big Swinging Dick". This deliberately opportunistic strategy, which goes against his long-term interests as a salesperson, is considered an exception, which the author resolves to make and for which he feels ashamed on account of having gone against his own long-term interests and code of honour. Of course, salespeople can and must exaggerate the prices of the bonds they sell to clients, but they must not sell products they believe will severely compromise a client's financial health.

The advantage that comes with redeployability is used in a wide range of strategies. The most famous example is the big trader who widens the spread beyond the market price to capture the profit that comes with the work of soliciting clients. A senior salesperson, meanwhile, could obtain tighter prices from a small trader than those available elsewhere. Lewis's example illustrates the question of the suitability of the transaction for different portfolios (clients or securities). Finally, there is a third issue that arises from the kind of information that passes between the trader and the salesperson. The trader often requests information from the salesperson and then draws conclusions about price movements and how he should manage the price spread. As one salesperson told me, "The trader says 'Who's it for?' . . . They think to themselves, 'Ah, it's EDF calling me, he's an exporter, he's going to sell dollars, and if he sells dollars that means he buys euros.' . . . He'll say to himself, 'Look at that, he's just bought an option, maybe he'll get his gamma position. He becomes gamma positive. If it goes up he'll buy.'" However, there is a fine line between using information to get a better position in the market and front-running (Abolafia 1996, p. 19),[16] which involves conducting transactions just before the customer and to the customer's detriment. My informer also highlighted the relatively common phenomenon of "traders who quote prices according to the client's direction": "If we know a customer always buys eurodollars, if the price is between .00 and .02 on the market then he'll quote .01 to .03." Also, the desire to protect the client's interests (and therefore her own) may make the salesperson unwilling to share information with the trader, such as the customer's identity or the direction of the discounted transaction (buy or sell); in other words, information that generally gives the trader a good idea of any changes in the markets, but which serve as invitations to trade against the customer's interests. In the reverse direction, although traders are obliged to provide prices, if price requests are too insistent and transactions do not follow, they may become irate, suspecting a speculative, "predatory" customer who is monitoring their strategies so as to better counter them.

Although, from an analytical point of view, we can identify the specific effect of asset redeployability in the relations between traders and salespeople, we shall analyse this relationship carefully, for it rarely occurs in isolation. The trading room is a space in which strategic advantages, bounded rationality, rules of social opportunism and social affinities and antagonism overlap and combine. Salespeople commonly underline the fact that the quality of their relations with traders depends largely on the quality of the traders' results, as if their P&L influenced the speed at which they make prices, their congeniality and the quality of their current prices.[17] The salesperson at Neptune Bank told me that when he was a trader, "I'd sometimes quote a shit price", for example when he'd had "a bad day". When he was having a good day, however, "I'd drop 'return prices', that is, 'choice prices'. In other words, my bid and ask prices were the same. The salesperson really loves this because he widened the spread on both sides." He conceded that "normally . . . there should be consistent pricing that shouldn't depend on variations in the trader's P&L". He justifies this by adding, "But we're only human." In other words, traders are *homo sapiens* rather than *homo economicus*, adopting mental accounting techniques symptomatic of a rationality that is bounded rather than perfect. Equivalences are established between P&L flows without always providing up-to-date totals; in addition, the results are evaluated *one day at a time* with no real intertemporal substitution (Camerer *et al.* 1997). The result of this phenomenon is that the propensity for opportunistic behaviour also depends on different days and cycles in the economic situation. Positive economic conditions bring goodwill, while negative conditions promote greed.

This exploitation of the profitability differential not only varies day by day but also according to the individual. Friendly relations between certain traders and salespeople, often based on the logic of social affinity, create pockets of reciprocal collaboration in which it is forbidden to exploit this redeployability differential too directly (Uzzi 1996). It is not uncommon to hear traders (or salespeople) explain that they do not get along with salespeople (or traders) apart from two or three who are the exception – salespeople who are not like the rest: close friends who are more likely to be similar to them in one of many possible ways such as classmates or old friends from preparatory classes, former colleagues who used to work on the same desk or at the same firm and recently left, friends who play sport or socialise together, and people with similar social backgrounds and outlooks. The salesperson at Neptune Bank explained that the choice prices he quoted as a trader were saved for good days and for people he chose, salespeople who could widen the spread – some did not have the instinct – and with whom he got on well. Although these relationships with like-minded people are based more on the logic of elective matching than on instrumental reason, they nonetheless have a considerable impact on the organisation of power in the room. Their presence helps to outline a continuum of relations between traders and salespeople, ranging from the most harmonious and cooperative partnerships to the most uncooperative ones. The former make the latter stand out all the more, and enable their control, sanction and etiology (individualistic rather than structuralist). Particularly in the long-term, cooperative behaviour allows small groups to form which, when the competition within them is regulated, gain independence from the structure that employs them. I will return to this point in the following chapters.

Different pricing methods

The relations between traders and salespeople also appear in a different light depending on the different accounting methods used in the distribution of profit. Although the organisation of trading rooms and work is relatively uniform, and is the result of a process of rationalisation, competition through imitation and a very active labour market, which allows any employees hired by a competitor to find their feet very quickly in their new firm, the method for calculating a salesperson's performance remains heterogeneous. This heterogeneity undermines the quality of any comparison of traders' and salespeople's performances, although such comparisons are still made.

I identified the following methods:

- To each her margin: The trader quotes a price to the salesperson and receives the usual P&L statement for the transaction. The salesperson adds a "sales margin" and will be paid on that basis. This accounting method corresponds to the paradigmatic case described above. It may cause conflict because, as seen previously, there is a chance that one of the two parties will encroach on the other's results. This is certainly not the most widely used system because overall it requires the establishment of a complex registration system for internal transactions, two profit centres (sales and trading) and the clear allocation of profit flows to one centre or the other. Saturn Bank adopted this system in its equity derivatives trading room for most of its internal transactions between traders and salespeople.
- Fixed sharing of the margin: For transactions involving more sophisticated products (such as those developed for a single client), at both Saturn Bank and Mars Bank the share of the margin was established beforehand between traders and salespeople. For some very specific types of products sold by the equity derivatives trading at Saturn Bank, the salesperson's account was credited with 85% of the transaction while 15% appeared on the trader's P&L. The profit-sharing ratio for traders may, however, range from 10% to 50% depending on the trading room and product, and seems to be based more on the state of the balance of power between the two groups in a given situation (generally speaking when the product in question is launched) than on its analytical relevance in the breakdown of profit. Furthermore,

this same system of division can be coupled with two pricing systems: two-stage pricing, first with the product development price quoted from trader to salesperson, and then the sales price quoted from salesperson to client, or else an all-in-one price offered by the trader alone and simply passed on by the salesperson.

- Crediting the salesperson: In fact, most banks adopt the sales credit system. In this system, the salesperson is given some of the responsibility for profit and credited with part of the transaction volume or overall margin. However, this form of accounting is only valid as a technique for measuring the salesperson's performance and not as a way of measuring profit. Profit is accounted for at trading level. The forms taken by this transfer of sales credit vary greatly from one trading room to the next, both in the way it is calculated and in the degree to which its establishment is managed. As a basis for calculation, sometimes half of the trader's bid-offer price is taken, and sometimes the margin added by the salesperson is taken into account. Given that the same margin on products with different risk levels does not have the same economic significance, the rate applied is not the same for all products. Some trading rooms develop managed pricing frameworks for the transfer of sales credit by main product category,[18] and even manage both the transfer of sales credit and the spread width that the trader quotes the salesperson. More often than not, the trader is left to determine the sales credit amount either exclusively or by negotiating with the salesperson. In the latter case, a different accounting method is used, closer to the case of "to each her margin" described above.

Traders and salespeople, how can they share profit?

The head of the fixed income trading room at Neptune Bank, a former trader (who started out on foreign exchange in the mid-1970s and referred to himself as a "survivor"), did not seem to like salespeople much. For him, trading was the noble side of the profession. He was asked about the method used to share profit between traders and salespeople. The method used in his trading room was sales credit. He put forward a notion of profit responsibility that tied in with his conception of the nobility of his activity. For him, profit was the trader's domain.

> . . . Obviously, the trader has to pay his fees. And sales are included in the trader's fees. The overall costs charged to a trader are around 3 to 5 million.

> *Why are sales included in a trader's costs?*

> A salesperson doesn't actually make any money. They're not a profit centre! For us, sales profits fall into the traders' hands. So, if they

(continued)

(continued)

get the profit, of course they also have the costs. Which also annoys
them because they say the salespeople are no good and the clients
corner them.

Could the trader be considered as included in the salesperson's costs?

No, because then you'd have to allocate a P&L to the salespeople.
Profit for the salesperson? How would you go about it? Profit for the
trader is simple. You have the client's price and the rollover price, and
you know how much is left over. So the trader makes money, mostly
thanks to the salesperson when there's a margin or through pure trading. How do you allocate a net banking income to salespeople? We
tried a hundred times. All the banks in the world have tried it. It's
impossible. The trader says, there's a customer margin, but I made
a good price in relation to the market and I turned things around and
made money too. And that's true enough. The final profit is a combination of the two. How can they be separated? It's impossible. They'd
have to separate every single transaction, and there's a transaction
every ten seconds. They'd have to build a huge labyrinthine system
and spend millions on software all for nothing. There's no point. It
wouldn't bring in a single penny. And it would be incorrect and would
cause endless fights between traders and salespeople. The only real
P&L is the customer's price minus the rollover price, which gives you
the trader's result. You can't go any further than that.

Note: This head of trading room was greatly exaggerating the impossibility
of separate accounting for sales and trade profit. The system implemented
by Saturn Bank, albeit only for equity derivative products (which are
slower-paced), shows that banks always try (against their competitors) to
push the breakdown of profit between trading and sales as far as possible.

What can be said of the organisation of such transactions? Do the different methods of organising internal transactions act as contractual solutions to the risk of
internal hold ups? From a distance, Williamson's explanation seems relevant.
He considers that transactions will be all the more controlled by hierarchical
arrangements because the transactions are based on specific assets, take place in
an uncertain environment and are repeated (Williamson 1985). The few examples
found, which by no means constitute a robust statistical test, may give the impression that the organisation of trader–sales relations varies according to some of the
dimensions characterised by Williamson.

When analysing the different ways of processing transactions in the equity
derivatives trading room at Saturn Bank, it appears that the more illiquid the product (for example structured products) the more likely it is that internal transactions

will be managed by a bureaucratic pricing framework. When there is no external market price to guide the sharing of the margin between traders and salespeople (in cases when the product is highly particular), then the sharing of the margin is pre-established before the transaction is concluded, which makes it less sensitive to the definition of the "production price" that the trader is supposed to quote the salesperson. Pre-establishing the framework for the exchange could prevent one of the parties from playing the redeployability differential and capturing the overall profit generated by the exchange. At Saturn Bank, on the contrary, when the product is commonplace in the market, and therefore less specific, the market provides a benchmark for identifying any potential encroachment by the trader on the profit usually credited to the salesperson.

Likewise, if we read accounts[19] of the way in which English banks active in fixed income and foreign exchange products – on which transactions are made at a very fast pace – have a tendency to manage trader and sales transactions by pre-establishing internal trading spreads and sales credit transfer rates, we might conclude that there is greater management of transactions as exchanges become more repetitive.

These two observed trends, however, are fragile and need to be backed up by more general statistical tests. Moreover, they should be put into perspective along with two other considerably more robust trends seen during interviews and observations: first, managing transaction relations does not eliminate power struggles and conflict between traders and salespeople; second, the choice of one method of managing transactions over another depends just as much, if not more so, on the trading room's past activity and orientation as on "transaction costs".

For a trader or salesperson, a change of firm, when it involves a shift from a system of free negotiation to a managed system that organises internal transactions, is a way of testing the extent to which relations alter when pricing changes.[20] Some, like the novice salesperson at Neptune Bank, appear to view the shift to a more managed system as an ideal solution to pacify relations between traders and sales: "Like that [with that kind of system], it's obvious! With up to 20 million eurodollars the spread is predefined! I think it's a good thing, because there's no dispute. Afterwards you have to identify the good spreads . . . " he exclaimed. One trader saw a major difference in trader–sales relations when he switched from a small French brokerage firm (Titan) to a large American bank in London (Orion). "At Titan, everyone worked for themselves. The problem with the system was that no one cared, in fact they liked it that way. Here, everyone wants to improve things and shares the feeling of all being in the same boat," he stated. The different atmosphere depends on several factors: the difference in size and past activity, more managed transfers of sales credit, and a weaker correlation between the bonus and the individual performance index. At the Titan brokerage firm, as in many small organisations, the traders benefit from a P&L formula and the salespeople get commission on sales, which may increase their incentive to capture the profit from the bilateral relationship at the other party's expense. At Orion Bank, on the other hand, as is the case in many large English banks, the bonus distribution process is highly discretionary, secretive and mysterious. The managers delight in repeating the fact that the bonus depends on overall efficiency (and takes account of a number of "qualitative" factors) and the junior traders at these large banks are generally ready to believe them.

Nevertheless, price management does not eliminate the power differential in favour of the party with the most redeployable assets. For the transfer price is only one element that determines the return on a bilateral transaction: the information passed on, the speed of execution and the suitability of the transaction to the managed portfolio (securities or client) are just some of the other elements, which barely change with managed pricing. The hold-up situation may be based on these terms of internal exchange rather than on the transaction price. As one trader explained, the sales credit system "changes nothing!" and does not prevent "the typical trader–sales arguments":

> The usual dispute is between salespeople who always try to explain to the traders what should be bought in the trading book and the traders who think the salespeople don't manage their customers properly and are utterly incapable of making them buy products at the correct price, and that they are content to trade at the traders' prices without ever trying to improve on a product and get more value added.

For traders, gaining the loyalty of clients or sales staff by quoting promotional prices or carrying out transactions that are matched to the client's portfolio structure is only a minor element in the overall profit they must look after. For the salespeople, however, this is a vital strategy through which they connect with customers and are able to detach them from the firm that has allocated them. Moreover, not only does managed pricing fail to eliminate all power relations and conflicts between traders and salespeople, but also it is often the case that sales managers or heads of trading desks, keen to argue in favour of changing a pre-established balance between units (pricing, sharing of bonus budgets, etc.), redevelop a "real" accounting system that breaks down the internal transaction flows that the management had chosen not to decompose. In the same trading room, where the head claimed it was "stupid" to try to analyse and decompose the share of profit between trading and sales, one salesperson explained that in his team they decomposed the transaction into the sales credit – in which "the flow, the volume are compensated" – and the markup (sales margin) – in which the margin added by the salesperson is accounted for. "The real money is made when you widen the spread. When you are going to ask for a pay increase, you say 'I brought in 10 million dollars in markups alone!'" This is the reason why, even if an internal pricing system is established at a specific moment in time in order to prevent power relations between the two parties, the bonus distribution system and the organisation of activities in profit centres tend to covertly restore an analytical accounting system considered more "real" but also more contentious on a day-to-day level.

Although it seems clear that the management of internal transactions only partly eliminates the possibility that one of the parties may benefit from a greater redeployability of assets granted by the firm, a comparison of financial establishments with a very similar product positioning, such as Saturn Bank and Mars Bank, would suggest that the different methods of managing internal transactions are more a result of the trading room's past activities than the transaction costs they face. In the equity derivatives room at Mars Bank, the head of trading claimed that, "the money stays in the same cash register". "There's no sales P&L here like at Saturn. At the end of the day, everything goes to trading. So, we use sales credit. At Saturn, it's not like that. Some goes to sales and some to trading." The head of management control of market activities at Saturn Bank confirmed there was a well-established organisational strategy of separate accounting for sales profit and trading profit, based on a free discussion on internal pricing between traders and salespeople:

> The sales desks are profit centres. So, justifiably, we're very attached to them. It allows us to monitor the balance . . . In our results we always look at the balance between sales desks and trading desks. Why? Because we base things on the principle that the sales result is recurring and less risky because a margin is set at the beginning.

The particular system of organisation used at Saturn Bank needs to be reinterpreted in the light of its history. During the late 1980s and early 1990s, the bank's policy was to establish an industrial style of organisation to manage risk and develop a very broad range of derivative products, focusing on the process and production, building the different stages of risk management from scratch and opting for a distinctive industrial policy that focused on leadership. From the mid-1990s, once the different stages of risk management were in place, Saturn Bank invested in selling its derivative products by subsidising its sales activities right from the start. As the head of equity derivatives at the bank explained, "At one point, we looked carefully at the balance between trading and sales [from the perspective of bonus distribution] and established a system in favour of sales in order to promote development." At Saturn Bank, the voluntaristic policy of developing sales activities resulted in the adoption of this highly analytical method of profit accounting. This policy was promoted by the trading room's managers – a handful of engineers from the very best *grandes écoles* who had "left" the market and saw themselves more as market organisers than as traders or salespeople, and who supported the production base but competed with each other to establish authority in the room, replace the head of trading room and eventually lead the markets. This was certainly a contributing factor in the bank's establishment of an accounting system that counted each employee's points. The trading room at Mars Bank joined the equity derivatives market at a later stage. It was developed in the early 1990s, not from scratch but by incorporating a number of teams from the established world of brokerage firms and the bank's own stockbroking activities. It first competed with its rivals by copying the banks that had already entered the market rather than by innovating. It was geared more towards trading, and invested less in the sales side than Saturn Bank. Moreover, the trading room at Mars was led by a core group of "buddies" who supported each other and, in their individual domains, remained relatively close to the production side. The bank had a tacit policy to develop – or, for teams already established, to maintain – a kind of home from home, with a family atmosphere that was less competitive. These were all factors in the bank's history that led it to opt for a managed method of internal transactions: sales credit.

Research and trading: transfer and monopoly of knowledge

Using trading–sales relations as an example, I have shown that greater redeployability of allocated assets (all things being equal) results in increased power for the user over the other parties. Similarly, within the organisation an internal monopoly also leads to a type of power over others. This more classic phenomenon has been proven many times in the past in the field of organisational sociology (Crozier 1964; Crozier and Friedberg 1980).

By focusing on the relations between research and trading, I will analyse cases in which a monopoly over technical know-how has been maintained or lost, and examine the consequences for a definition of internal power relations. In the previous chapter, I explained how the production process gives asset users (traders, salespeople) a greater sense of ownership of profit than inventors. This unfavourable structuring of the sense of ownership is perpetuated by a balance of power in favour of trading that is equally unfavourable. Indeed, research workers generally find themselves in a situation in which they systematically concede the technical and intellectual assets they develop. As one head of a R&D team commented, the transferral of information and, in particular, of expertise only ever takes place in one direction: from engineers to traders.

> In any case, the teams of IT engineers are never told what is done with the software we produce. It's like a diode. We can pass info on to the traders, but they never pass any back! Everything happens in a context in which our activity is increasingly usurped by traders.

As engineers have no access to the market or to customers, they are unable to hold on to their research products or even threaten to do so. With no assets such as clients or market access, the value of their inventions is itself restricted to the internal firm. It stems more from the quantity of skilled work that resulted in the invention (the input) than from the profit flows generated by the implementation of their invention. Engineers can certainly try to capture the profit linked to the use of their inventions, but they have little support for such action. In the worst-case scenario, they relinquish their discovery to the trader in one fell swoop. In some cases, they can redeploy their invention on the market but, once again, they may find themselves in the same situation with their new employer: having to concede their invention all at once. Quants who develop a software product that "trades" on the market by itself have, in a way, already relinquished it to the trader who ordered it, thus losing all control over the profits that the product may generate. Within the organisation, product developers do not usually benefit from any legal provision, such as copyright, that protects their rights over the use of their invention.

Therefore, the best way to defend one's intellectual property rights in a context in which they are not properly guaranteed by the collective is to organise exclusive control on an individual basis. There are two possible strategies, which usually go hand in hand: *limiting their transfer* and *acquiring the assets* through which the invention gains value.

Limiting transfer

With no access to the market assets (clients, products), the strategy of limiting the transfer of technology is risky and has little scope. Inventors generally have client–provider relationships with the front office and their relations are usually conceived as such within the management structure: in most appraisal systems, and even when the bonus budgets are being drawn up, the front office assesses the quality of its providers' activity, whereas the reverse rarely happens. In this management system, all sorts of sanctions may be applied (relating to bonuses, employment positions, etc.) if employees show an intention not to provide what is required in their job description. However, it is possible to avoid conceding all of one's know-how or technology at once and, by routinely repeating minor transfers, to transform a relationship based on transfer into one of dependence, which puts the inventor in a far more favourable position to capture the profits generated by the market transaction.

This was the basis on which one head of a R&D team distinguished between profitable IT projects and other projects. In the first group, he included the Monte Carlo algorithm, "particularly Monte Carlo for exotic options". The Monte Carlo simulation is a method of pricing options by generating a large number of scenarios. It is used in finance to assess certain parameters such as volatility, risk, sensitivity to price fluctuations, etc., when traditional probability tools (normal and log-normal processes) cannot be used. On sophisticated products in particular (exotic options, structured products), it is widely used and requires large amounts of machine resources. Lépinay recounts that the exotic traders he observed might spend several hours every morning waiting for the results of a simulation of the exposure parameters of the securities portfolios they were managing (Lépinay 2011). When it "crashes", as happens quite often, they explain, "we go and find [the head of R&D] and hang him". In these situations, the traders are dependent on the IT engineers: the engineers do not concede everything by creating a Monte Carlo simulation model. They concede a software program without giving up the technology required to create it, and this is extremely beneficial in strategic terms when the software, algorithm or data are incorrect. They still have to deal with traders' anger when the machine's errors prevent them from accessing the market – a return to the harsh reality of material exchange – but even so, being in a position in which the transfer is repeated and renewed, particularly in market situations where the market operator is working under increased pressure, makes IT engineers a vital link in the trading process and sets them apart from their colleagues. Nevertheless, this scenario is quite rare. Engineers generally work on projects, which are a one-off collaboration between a few engineers and a few front office operators. These projects usually precede transactions and once they are completed they give way to other projects and collaborations with other financial operators. This organisational method, which is more in line with engineers' method of working and, more broadly, with the world of research to which they remain closely linked, is less favourable to their strategic positioning.

The transfer of and monopoly over intangible assets is not only an issue for engineer–trader relations. It also arises within the front office itself. The financial and technical career path of the trader from Orion Bank provides a useful illustration of this. This particular trader had graduated from an elite business school in the provinces and was drawn to academia, particularly the social sciences. He found that finance was his only area of interest while he was a student. He made up for his academic inferiority complex with regard to finance by investing much of his free time in mathematics and computing, which eventually led him to develop his own pricing software for convertible bonds.[21] He explained that, to start out with, he hired an intern who worked on the software full-time. The intern, who subsequently left, was in a situation in which he had to hand over his invention in one go. The trader appropriated the software completely, both by overseeing its initial preparation and then by continuing to develop it alone, to the point where he considered it "his". He was in a position to control the timing of the transfer to his work colleagues and then to his new employer. Thus, the software was a factor he used when negotiating the terms of his move from the small French brokerage firm Titan to Orion Bank, a major American bank with offices in London, and he was eventually hired partly thanks to the software program. He installed it on his new colleagues' computers, but they never acquired the knowledge required to do anything other than use it. They remained reliant on its developer to update, modify or repair the software. Similarly, he let Titan use the program and continued to help his former work colleagues. It was a way for him to maintain a good relationship with them and also a strategic means of knowing what they were doing in the market.

Acquiring assets

In the last example, the trader from Orion Bank was very successful in gradually transforming a one-off acquisition into a step-by-step redistributed product, because he controlled the key assets that gave the product its value. Product developers, generally quants and sometimes analysts (strategists, economists, chartists) say that they would like to be given a securities portfolio to manage, both to test out the empirical correctness of their arbitrage and speculation forecasts and to put an end to a situation in which they are stripped of the fruit of their own inventions. In most financial organisations, however, particularly in the oldest and largest, the somewhat strict organisation of labour prevents the role of engineer–researcher from merging with that of market operator. The only way of acquiring strategic assets is to change jobs, even if this means renouncing the values and culture of R&D, which partly defines itself as being opposed to the front office model (Godechot, Hassoun and Muniesa 2000; Godechot 2001). The members of research teams (and, by extension, all technical roles such as risk control) often wish to join front office teams after two or three years, so as to "work for themselves" at last and put a stop to the capturing of profit at their own expense. In small organisations (which may be internal divisions of large firms), it is easier both to retain a monopoly over inventions and be allocated market assets (clients, securities) to develop. The trader from Proxima Bank, who worked on statistical arbitrage in a hedge fund managed by an Anglo-American bank, was in a situation in which he had a double monopoly over the statistical correlations he discovered (and whose secret he jealously guarded to the point where he refused to explain them even in general terms) and over a securities portfolio.

I will now look at another example of a strategy designed to maintain exclusivity. A team of semi-professional financiers made up of a statistician, an IT engineer and a former individual floor trader, built a technical device, successfully set up a small financial firm and were given capital by the Titan brokerage firm. They sold part of their "discoveries" without losing their monopoly over them. According to the trader responsible for evaluating their techniques on behalf of Titan, the team had developed a toolbox of statistical models. Each morning the program made an estimation for each type of model thus allowing the best price prediction to be made on the basis of past data and, out of hundreds of models, it identified the one that made the best predictions. This team faced a dilemma with regard to the trader: tell him enough to convince him, and therefore Titan, while not revealing the entire secret. In the end they obtained funds and retained their technical monopoly. The software program remained with them.

However, as soon as this type of organisation grows and the hedge fund becomes more sizeable, only the firm's leaders retain the double monopoly of technical assets and market assets, and they tend to carry out a division of labour for new employees below them that often re-establishes relations of automatic transfer between those who look for links between prices and those who do transactions.

By analysing imperfect and provisional monopolies, we can make an implicit assessment of the role of exclusivity as a source of power. Researchers have a monopoly over their invention that is both temporary (there is an obligation to transfer them) and limited within the organisation (they lack the assets required for their implementation). They are therefore in an unfavourable situation of dependence with regard to the front office, which, in contrast, can build upon the allocation of well-protected assets in order to benefit from the research carried out. Research can only get around this asymmetry by transforming the complete, combined and automatic transfer into a partial, repeated transfer or by acquiring the assets required for its own development.

***

Analysing the allocation of company assets to employees is not only vital for understanding their sense of ownership of profit but also the relations they establish and the outcome of the distribution process. In the race to appropriate profit, the volume of assets is important as well as their structure. Monopolising assets and being able to redeploy them easily puts their holders in a privileged position in relation to the peers with whom they co-produce. The latter depend on the asset holders, but not vice versa. This asymmetry creates power and thus enables asset holders to be in a position to capture collective profit simply by threatening to end the collaboration (a hold-up situation). This chapter has focused on the internal redeployment of assets: on the one hand, I have shown that, in the real world, there is no reason to believe that hierarchy is the solution to situations of relational dependence and, on the other hand, to highlight the link between this origin of power and the internal distribution of bonuses.

However, redeployability in finance does not only take place internally – far from it. It is found above all in the labour market. We now have the tools to understand that market, which its actors invoke so often but which classical theories do not explain satisfactorily.

Notes

1 I borrow from Boltanski and Thévenot (2006) the term "grammar" to refer to the set rules that an action, like an utterance, must respect in order to seem correct.
2 The "model must assume for all its members an identical *power* of access to all the states that we shall designate by their common *dignity*".
3 *The New Spirit of Capitalism* aims to change this irenic dimension of *Economies of Worth* (Boltanski and Chiapello 2006, p. 27).
4 An example would be the seemingly opportunistic behaviour of the team leader who deliberately forgot the bonus of one of his employees who had been on unpaid leave when the bonuses were distributed, so as to better compensate himself or others.
5 The hold-up concept has been explored by Goldberg (1976), who analyses its chronological development. It is often associated with Williamson, but Williamson prefers the term "opportunism".
6 "For example, one would not build a house on land rented for a short term. After the rental agreement expires the landowner could raise the rental price to reflect the costs of moving the house to another lot" explains Klein (1980, p. 357).
7 The "differences in levels of opportunism that are observed among financial markets are explained by social conditions rather than by the psychological or moral inclinations of individual traders" (Abolafia 1996, p. 10).
8 I can thus reinterpret the theory of structural holes developed in the analysis of networks (Burt 1992). The "bridge" – who controls numerous structural holes – holds a resource that is both rare and redeployable (an investment made in a contact may be

redeployed in another contact) whereas those who are in contact with the bridge hold a relational resource that is potentially common and hard to redeploy.

9 The use of the labour market as a hold-up weapon will be analysed in greater detail in Chapters 6 and 7.

10 In the rest of this chapter, when I speak of what competing parties "make", I am referring not to their fixed wages or end-of-year bonus but rather to the accounting measures used for financial operators – P&L, sales credit, net banking income and gross operating income – which, for the firm, represent the flows of profit that originate with them. The link between the accounting measures and the bonus can be fairly weak.

11 For this reason, each "market community" is a small, closed world in which everyone knows each other. For example, all the traders of French convertible bonds know one another. There are probably only around 20 of them globally.

12 The relationship between medium Salesperson *b* and medium Trader *c* is more complex to analyse. It illustrates the way in which the power of redeployability and monopolistic power exist simultaneously. Although the asymmetry of redeployability is in Trader *c*'s favour, it may be partly compensated for by the monopolistic power of Salesperson *c* over one of the biggest clients (Client *2*). A hold-up by Trader *c* would not be credible, because it could jeopardise the trader's access to a particularly important client.

13 It is often the case that salespeople, clients and traders of the same (new) product get older together and are active in the same field. The young trader is allocated clients of minor importance, who are often young themselves. As they get older together, the importance of one is reflected by the importance of the other.

14 He adds: "I'm in an awkward position because I used to be a trader. I get asked what I think but I don't want to get involved. I sort out my problems with traders. But when I'm asked, 'Isn't it a bit wide?' I answer, 'Yeah, it's a bit wide . . . ' But I don't go and complain on his behalf. [My boss] will go and plead his cause."

15 To understand this manoeuvre, we must note that the 30-year bonds of private firms are highly illiquid products. There is no centralised market as such but rather a somewhat opaque over-the-counter market in which traders offer one-off product trades. The one-off trade proposed by the trader to Michael's customer was manifestly in his favour. He sold him 3 million dollars' worth of AT&T bonds at 97. The following day, when the concerned customer had realised and asked him to buy back the AT&T bonds, he offered him a price two basis points lower (95), incurring a loss of 65,000 dollars.

16 Although front running is hard to properly detect, Abolafia claims that it was very common on the bond market in the late 1980s.

17 As one salesperson commented: "Especially because some of the traders get screwed from time to time, so they're not in the best mood!"

18 One trader told me that at Orion Bank, traders allocated one-eighth of the sales credit margin to the salesperson for low-risk transactions and one-sixteenth for high-risk transactions. However, he then thought better of it, stating that it was one-sixteenth, thus showing that even in a managed situation such as this, he still had the freedom to characterise and classify the transaction in question.

19 For example, the trader at Neptune Bank, speaking of Anglo-American banks, had the following to say: "Now it's done through pricing grids. For a particular client and a particular desk, according to the amounts and the maturity there's a spread the trader has to respect."

20 Except that the individual experience of change is never "all things being equal", because the differences in organisation between one firm and another is never based on one element alone.

21 This software carried out pricing and a large number of accounting tasks, as well as monitoring the overall position. This gave the software program a certain industrial interest, because it carried out pricing and monitoring in one go, unlike rival software programs on the market.

References

Abolafia, M 1996, *Making Markets. Opportunism and Restraint on Wall Street*, Harvard University Press, Cambridge MA.

Baker, W 1984a, 'Floor Trading and Crowd Dynamics' in *The Social Dynamics of Financial Markets*, eds P Adler and P Adler, JAI Press, Greenwich, CT. pp. 107–128.

Baker, W 1984b, 'The Social Structure of a National Securities Market', *American Journal of Sociology*, vol. 89, n° 4, pp. 775–811.

Boltanski, L and Chiapello, E 2006, *The New Spirit of Capitalism*, Verso, London.

Boltanski, L and Thévenot, L 2006, *On Justification: Economies of Worth*, Princeton University Press, Princeton NJ.

Burt, R 1992, *Structural Holes: The Social Structure of Competition*, Harvard University Press, Cambridge MA.

Camerer, C, Babcock, L, Loewenstein, G and Thaler, R 1997, 'Labor Supply of New York City Cabdrivers: One Day at a Time', *Quarterly Journal of Economics*, vol. 112, n°2, pp. 407–441.

Crozier, M 1964, *The Bureaucratic Phenomenon*, University of Chicago Press, Chicago IL.

Crozier, M and Friedberg, E 1980, *Actors and Systems: The Politics of Collective Action*, University of Chicago Press, Chicago IL.

Eccles, R and White, H 1988, 'Price and Authority in Inter-Profit Center Transactions', *American Journal of Sociology*, vol. 94 (July), pp. S17–S51.

Gabrié, H and Jacquier, JL 1994, *La Théorie moderne de l'entreprise. L'approche institutionnelle*, Economica, Paris.

Godechot, O 2001, *Les Traders. Essai de sociologie des marchés financiers*, La Découverte, Paris.

Godechot, O, Hassoun, JP and Muniesa, F 2000, 'La volatilité des postes. Professionnels des marchés financiers et informatisation', *Actes de la recherche en sciences sociales*, n°134, pp. 45–55.

Goldberg, V 1976, 'Regulation and Administered Contracts', *Bell Journal of Economics*, vol. 7, n°2, pp. 426–448.

Granovetter, M 1985, 'Economic Action and Social Structure: the Problem of Embeddedness', vol. 91, n°3, pp. 481–510.

Granovetter, M 1995, 'The Economic Sociology of Firms and Entrepreneurs' in *The Economic Sociology of Immigration*, ed A Portes, Russell Sage Foundation, New York, pp.128–165.

Klein, B 1980, 'Transaction Cost Determinants of "Unfair" Contractual Arrangements', *American Economic Review*, vol. 70, n°2, pp. 356–362.

Lépinay, VA 2011, *Codes of Finance: Engineering Derivatives in a Global Bank*, Princeton University Press, Princeton NJ.

Lewis, M 1989, *Liar's Poker*, Hodder and Stoughton, London.

Malcomson, J 1997, 'Contracts, Hold-Up, and Labor Markets', *Journal of Economic Literature*, vol. 35, n° 4, pp. 1916–1957.

Uzzi, B 1996, 'The Sources and Consequences of Embeddedness for the Economic Performance of Organizations: The Network Effect', *American Sociological Review*, vol. 61, n°4, pp. 674–698.

Williamson, O 1975, *Markets and Hierarchy. Analysis and Antitrust Implications*, The Free Press, New York.

Williamson, O 1985, *The Economic Institutions of Capitalism*, The Free Press, New York.

Williamson, O 1993, 'Calculativeness, Trust, and Economic Organization', *Journal of Law & Economics*, vol. 34, n°1, pp. 453–502.

Williamson, O 1994, 'Transaction Cost Economics and Organization Theory' in *The Handbook of Economic Sociology*, eds N Smelser and R Swedberd, Princeton University Press, Princeton NJ, pp. 77–108.

Part III

Hold-up and labour market

6   A hold-up case

In June 2001, the financial press reported a scandal that was causing a stir at Neptune Bank. The head of the equity derivatives trading room and his deputy had just been paid bonuses of 10 million euros and 7 million euros each for the year 2000. The sums were disclosed by a Confédération Générale du Travail trade unionist and threw the bank into turmoil right up to the highest echelons. How had it been possible for such vast sums to be paid? The two beneficiaries declined to comment, but accounts given by several employees – in particular the head of equity derivatives' previous line manager, his rival in fixed income and foreign exchange and his former head of back office – allowed me to make a fairly accurate reconstruction of the case.[1]

Piecing together the various accounts, it would seem that these sums of money were paid out after a particularly intense showdown. Some interviewees were quick to use expressions such as "blackmail" and "hold-up", with their framework of interpretation appearing to match the conceptualisations of Williamsonian economists mentioned in the previous chapter (Williamson 1985; Malcomson 1997). Once the different elements of the case had been reconstructed, it stood as a symbol of the hold-up power acquired by some financial operators – a critical and spectacular form of the power that assets confer on an individual.

In order to understand this case, I will both analyse the specific mechanics of power relations and re-establish the context in which they function. The chapter will first describe the feeling of indignation in the firm following the disclosure of those two bonuses. It will clarify how those bonuses originated and then explain why they could be analytically considered as the result of a hold-up. Here, the two heads exploited the power to redeploy the trading activity elsewhere. Finally, the aftermath of this case shows the further use of the hold-up power and some of its limits.

The bonus outrage

When trying to make contact with the main actors of this "affair", I was quickly put in touch with the trade unionist who had disclosed and denounced these payouts. In the April edition of the 4-page monthly bulletin, a CGT trade unionist published an "Open Letter to the CEO of Neptune Bank. Dear Sir, we want to earn millions too". In the letter, he revealed the sum of the two bonuses, stating that it was "information that we believe will not be refuted", but did not give the recipients' names or exact positions in the firm (it was only known that they worked in the trading rooms). However, as the trade unionist recounted, "in the bank it was hardly a secret!"

The positions of the two beneficiaries were quickly exposed in the French press, and their names were revealed in the Anglo-American press. The trade union article, which was deliberately sarcastic and demanded a "non-dogmatic approach to bonuses", put forward arguments that it hoped would resonate with both employees and management: the relation between work done and compensation was disproportionate; compensation was the result of individuals exploiting others' work; it was in no way the fruit of any risk-taking by those involved (since it was the bank that assumed all risks); the "labour cost" of these two individuals was astonishing; the lack of fairness was damaging to the bank's overall performance. The open letter was followed by a series of comparisons with wage bills and the evolution of wages at Neptune Bank: the highest wage was almost "750 times the lowest"; these two amounts were compared with "the modest salary increase of 0.5% and the gross wage premium of 150 euros at the start of the year", and it was pointed out that "these bonuses would have allowed staff to receive 596 euros each if they had been distributed among the 28,642 employees at Neptune". Finally, he also compared the bonus of the two heads with Neptune's 18-million-euro[2] bonus pool, operators' sales commission pool [22 million euros] and the performance pay pool [6 million euros].

Everything suggests that this disclosure caused a major stir at Neptune Bank, particularly given that in the mid-1990s the bank's financial difficulties had forced its directors to ask employees to make an "effort", which involved redundancy plans and wage freezes. When the bank's results improved in the late 1990s, however, pay levels still failed to match those of its main competitors. A young professional at Neptune, who was working in the HR service of the capital markets department, made an assessment of the wage levels of different support function jobs. He reported that the wages for some positions such as back office management were (according to remuneration surveys) 10–30% lower than those of the bank's major competitors.

Although the link established between the sacrifices demanded on the one hand and the generous bonuses on the other hand did contribute to the scandal, the main catalyst was the incommensurability of the sums received by the two employees in relation to the ordinary amounts given to ordinary employees, whether in trading rooms, support functions or retail banking. "In HR, people talked about it for at least a week . . . They always described it as a 'scandal'. Very few people really understood. 'It's scandalous' they said. That was the term used the most," one HR professional told me. This comparative process did not oppose two social groups, as is sometimes the case with disclosures of the compensation of executives or high-level professionals in industrial firms. Nor was it an abstract revelation of a CEO's salary, which, in this specific case at Neptune Bank, happened to be 11 times lower than the better paid of these two beneficiaries (Chocron and Pinson 2001).

At every level of the hierarchy, this comparison, far from being refuted, was made possible and even encouraged by a working environment that was becoming increasingly individualised. At all levels, from ordinary employees to directors, the result of the comparison gave rise to a disproportionate scale and a failure to grasp its foundation. Faced with an internal and external scandal (shareholders' discontent),[3] the bank's executives neither denied nor confirmed the amounts, but they tried to justify market-wide pay levels, invoking market and value creation logics.[4] However, I know from the account given by the head of the capital markets department that market remuneration, particularly for heads of equity derivatives, was only accepted grudgingly.

> So the bonus amounts I had to present to the executive committee for approval started to cause dreadful jealousy within the bank, and also to concern and even shock the two people in charge of approvals at the time, the CEO of Neptune Bank and his deputy. For the latter, who was a socialist, a technocrat and a high-ranking civil servant, these market pay levels were unbelievable – and he was right, in my opinion. The CEO was a different story. He'd always been addicted to money – it was his personal obsession. So he was more understanding . . .

He was a socialist?

> He was, but isn't now. Whereas his deputy is radically and profoundly socialist. The CEO was a socialist because that's what his career was based on . . . His career kick-started with nationalisation. So he'd been a socialist and had maintained some links, but apparently he wrote a book that says "Long live Chirac!" I guess he changed tack, but I don't know any more about it . . . So it wasn't as if the CEO had a problem with giving people money, because that was his whole way of thinking. But as CEO, he started to think that it was a lot of money, and rightly so. In comparison with what he got it certainly was, and he made a huge fuss, but even so, he was more dignified than that. They got a lot more than the members of the executive committee, that's for sure. And it created a lot of ill-feeling in the bank. As CEO, he thought to himself, "Now the shit's going to hit the fan!"

The management's awkward justifications could not conceal their belief that the bonuses were excessive. At the lower end of the hierarchy, the survey on employees' perception of bonuses conducted jointly with Neptune's trade unionist gave an idea of the scale of people's disbelief and the opinion of those working alongside the two beneficiaries. The disclosure itself, which could be seen as a violation and an accusation, was supported by those who read the article. They almost unanimously (96%) agreed that the unionist had been right to reveal the two bonuses. Likewise, the majority of those surveyed (88%) said they were shocked by the amounts. While those working in support functions were unanimously shocked (97%), front office professionals were more divided. The majority said they were shocked, whereas a significant minority (8 out of 19) did not answer positively. The fact that they were not shocked does not necessarily mean they approved of the payouts, but rather that they were not surprised and did not want to unilaterally denounce them.

When asked to express themselves freely on the reasons for their shock or lack thereof, those who were not shocked, particularly front office professionals, generally cited results logic ("Because the results followed"; "We live in a free-market economy and we have to accept its advantages and disadvantages. Bonuses like these are common in any profession where performance is indexed to results"). Some tempered their view by stating they did not know enough about the real results or bonus distribution method to form an opinion ("I don't find them shocking if they are the real result of a value added and of profit generated for the bank; but they are shocking if these amounts are taken away from teams").

The mixed feelings expressed by the front office are understandable. The existence of such high bonuses can mean several things at once. First, there is a feeling of excess, even if this is more moderate than in other professions in the capital markets division. Unlike in the support functions and, a fortiori, the rest of the bank, where there is no need to try to measure excess, those who are familiar with bonuses measure excess according to several key points: the bonuses that are usually awarded in a particular bank, market prices and contribution to results. In addition to their relative frustration at not being treated in the same way, they may also have had a persistent feeling that the remuneration of the two heads of trading room was only possible thanks to the direct exploitation of their work ("amounts taken away from teams"). Second, these two bonus sums paved the way for levels of remuneration that most had never even imagined. Therefore, if they believed that either there was a possible continuum between heads of trading room and basic financial operators or that the position of head of trading room was not an impossibility for them, these two bonuses provided an insight and gave them hope as regards their own future remuneration chances (Hirschman and Rotschild 1973).

> "It takes us closer to the top. It probably isn't considered so bad in the trading room. People see it as a chance to say, 'I can ask for more'. People in the room will just think it's shocking but that's it," recounted one fixed income trader.

Among those who claimed to be shocked (the majority), several common themes emerged. First of all, their answers expressed their astonishment, which was still apparent three months later, including among front office professionals.

> When the same trader was asked again about the matter in an interview several months after the revelation, he still seemed unable to believe the enormity of the sums: "You wonder why you're still bothering to work. What progress are you making? It's unbelievable ... It's a huge sum ... huge! It's hard to justify. It's really huge. How can it be justified? Especially the

result . . . If they bring in money, fine, but this is confusing the bonus with their wages. Afterwards they can come and work for free. Even if they'd got half these amounts I still would have been shocked."

The excessiveness of the sums was a recurring theme in employees' answers. Almost 50% of respondents mentioned the notion of incommensurability in some form or another. More so than front office professionals, support and IT staff highlighted the loss of all proportionality: "Too excessive"; "Appalling"; "It's exorbitant and obscene"; "For most of us these bonuses are excessive. They're higher than the salary of several lifetimes"; "17 million euros is how many years of work for you? Personally I don't even want to think about it!"

Injustice was the second most common theme. For example, some respondents added the following precisions: "Because the rich get richer and the poor get poorer"; "Considering the bank's recent problems, it would be beneficial to share some of it with all the employees who have suffered and are still suffering every day in the bank's branches"; "The lowest-paid employees got nothing!" This theme was mentioned more often by IT specialists than by back or front office professionals. First, their origins, career path and position in the firm made them more open to a discourse that questioned the distribution method and, second, they generally held positions in which they would benefit from such a questioning. IT specialists were also most likely to question the link between pay levels and work carried out: "I don't get the feeling they've contributed 6,500 or 4,700 times more than me (compared with a bonus of 1,500 euros)"; "These bonuses are hard to believe considering the work they did in comparison with the crumbs left over for us".

Front office and support professionals were no doubt more aware of market prices than technicians, and thus tended to use market prices as a benchmark against which excessive payouts were measured and found to be shocking. "Neptune is not known for being a bank that pays high wages, and these two bonuses are the highest in the French market"; "Exceptionally high, even in relation to the market". The bank's rocky history was often mentioned directly: "Too high for a bank that's supposed to be having difficulties", but often remained implicit.

The origin of the case

Establishing the scandalous nature of this particular case is not enough to identify a hold-up situation. Now I have taken stock of the emotions it stirred up, I will explain how such payouts were possible considering that they clearly came as a surprise to almost every level of the bank's hierarchy.

The head of the equity derivatives had started out at Saturn Bank, like many of those working in the capital markets. At the end of the 1980s, he was in charge of the Tokyo office. According to the former head of options trading, who at the time oversaw derivatives trading at Saturn Bank, he learned "his trade by watching how things were done, because he really had no idea at the beginning". Right at the end of the 1980s, Saturn Bank seemed to have a considerable advantage

over its competitors in the field of derivatives: "We dominated the equity derivatives market in Japan!" recounted the former head of options trading at Saturn
Bank, who was keen to glorify his heroic past as head of a leading department.
At that time, the options department saw itself as an integrated whole, working
entirely under the guidance of its charismatic leader and independent in relation
to traditional bank offices. The head of options at Saturn Bank was thus in dispute
with the head of the Tokyo office over whether the branch was merely a shelter
for derivatives activities or whether it had a say in the capital markets activities
taking place within it. Therefore, in 1990, when the head of capital markets at
Neptune Bank hired the man who would later become head of equity derivatives
(which caused [the DG of Saturn Bank] to make "a major fuss . . . a real scene on
the telephone"), the latter explained that he wanted to leave Saturn Bank because
he "directly clashed" with the head of options. He also made out that he was self-
taught, when in fact he had studied at a major business school in Paris:

> He said to me, "I didn't do any *Grande École*!" I had to look at his CV to see
> that he'd gone to [a major business school in Paris] . . . which is a very good
> school. Why did he pretend he was self-taught? Because he hadn't gone to
> the *École Polytechnique* or the *École Nationale d'Administration* (ENA) and
> he thought that in French banks, at Saturn, it was hell for those who hadn't
> gone to the *École Polytechnique* in particular. He always said to me that he
> believed his career path was blocked because of that. There are some CEOs
> who went to ENA, but he admitted there were very few in the markets so it
> didn't bother him. It was more within the banks' headquarters that there were
> so many ENA graduates among the managers. But in his niche market, there
> were only Polytechnique graduates, and he hated them for that reason. But he
> couldn't avoid having a few in equity derivatives.

At Neptune Bank, he was hired on two specific missions: to become the "boss
of Tokyo" and to "specialise in equity derivatives and create the start of the
equity derivatives product line". "And he completed those two tasks perfectly,"
he concluded. The team only had a handful of people in it to start with, but it
expanded quickly and had some major successes. Although it did not match
the considerable size of the derivatives product lines of the major banks in the
sector such as Saturn, Mars or Sirius, with just 100 employees it had become a
noteworthy actor in the market. After establishing business in Japan, the future
head of equity derivatives oversaw a global product line that moved its base to
London in the mid-1990s rather than in Paris, for tax reasons. The employees
working on this product line were grouped in a subsidiary devoted to equities
and equity derivatives, a subsidiary that provided market access (thanks to its
simplified management as a brokerage firm) and strengthened its independence
from the parent firm.

The business line led by the head of equity derivatives was, by all accounts, a
great deal more independent and protective of its autonomy than the trading room
devoted to fixed income, foreign exchange and commodities. This difference in

status could be seen, for example, in the bonus distribution process. Whereas the head of capital markets discussed the bonus distribution proposed for staff with the head of fixed income, she recalled that such discussion was generally impossible with the head of equity derivatives: "For him, it was all or nothing, make or break. The year it broke, the pool was too small and he was scared everyone would resign, so that time he said, 'I can't do it, let's do it together!'" Similarly, at the end of the 1990s, the head of the fixed income and equities back offices reported that the fixed income front office was much more cooperative that the equities front office, both in terms of agreeing to risk control solutions proposed by the back office and submitting to its budgetary requests for IT investment.

The head of capital markets admitted that the equity derivatives department was a fortress, but:

> No more than anyone else! In all banks around the world, equity derivatives were a fortress. They brought down UBS. UBS was in crisis and was taken over by SBC. Of course, it was also because of retail banking structuring problems, but it was mostly due to equity derivatives. The equity derivatives barony had started to make huge losses, but it had become a state within a state and was effectively running the bank. My head of equity derivatives never did that. At Saturn, the head of options [in the late 1980s] had become a state within a state, which the bank found intolerable. That's the tendency with equity derivatives, given the specialised nature of the profession and the major risks and results generated by the sector. All banks have had problems managing this product line. And my head of equity trading was no more of a nutcase or a baron than the rest. He was just like the others, no more no less.

The head's personality type, whether it was the result of his career path in the world of finance[5] or the fruit of previous determinations, no doubt contributed to the rebellious, separatist tendencies of the equity derivatives trading room. According to his line manager, he combined "[Anglo-American] value creation and French hierarchical structure",[6] which, she maintained, consisted not only in desiring high wages when profit existed but also in protecting them against losses and making them dependent on a hierarchical position.

One year, the equity derivatives market performed extremely well in New York whereas Tokyo saw major losses, which caused a considerable reduction in the global bonus pool. The head of capital markets recalled:

> That was when I could test his limits. He still wanted a maximum bonus pool. I told him, "When times are tough, we have to tighten our belts." I also wanted to hold on to the guy from New York who had over-performed. He said to me, "No way. I want to get the most, and I want my deputy to get less than me but more than the rest." I said, "OK! But don't come to me later saying that the guy in New York wants to resign!" In the end, the guy in New York didn't resign, even though he got the same amount in francs that he'd

expected in dollars. We promised him solidarity went both ways. I had some unlikely conversations with him when I told him that things hadn't gone his way this year, he'd lost out, but that next year things would definitely go in his favour. Which is what happened. So he didn't resign, but one more year like that . . . And that was when I realised the limitations of the [equity derivates head's] system." When she tried to make the head of equity derivatives see reason by giving him a glimpse of her own low bonus, he mocked her for her lack of skill in bargaining to defend her own interests:[7] "He told me the same thing 50 times. He really took me for a total fool. 'That's not the way to play things with the executive committee [of Neptune Bank]. You have to put it to them like this [*makes a cut-throat gesture*] and say, It's make or break! With people like them that's all they care about!' So he found my approach absolutely ridiculous."

The hold-up

At Neptune Bank in the 1990s, the bonuses paid to the head of equity derivatives and his deputy were high in comparison with those of ordinary operators but moderate in relation to those of other equity derivatives heads. They were distributed following the usual discretionary procedure. The head of the capital markets department suggested an amount to be agreed on by the CEO. The highest bonus paid to other less senior employees for that period was 1.5 million euros. Both the amount and the procedure irritated the head of equity derivatives. As the head of fixed income trading noted, "[The equity derivatives head] and his deputy believed [in 1999] that for several years they'd been ripped off and that they should have been receiving higher bonuses."

On the eve of a corporate action that was vital to the future of Neptune, the head of equity derivatives resigned with his deputy, giving Neptune Bank 48 hours to rehire them and match the conditions a competitor was offering them. The two heads announced they were leaving "for a German bank operating in London. That's it, we're going. We've got a contract". The name of the bank had been erased, but the entire contract was forwarded to Neptune. The implicit threat was that they would take the whole team with them. According to the head of fixed income, who did not take part in the negotiations, they said, "We're leaving together, and naturally we're taking the team with us. But we like [Neptune], so we're giving you 48 hours to align" – in other words, to match the German bank's contract offer. The new contract included a predetermined bonus formula: the head of the trading room was to receive 8.5% of the bonus pool reserved for equity derivatives products (the bonus pool represented 30% of profit before taxes and bonuses) and his colleague 6% of the bonus pool – that is, 14.5% of the bonus pool for the two alone, or 4.5% of the trading room's profit (before taxes and bonuses). The contract did not require the bank to pay out any exceptional bonuses for the year 1999. That year the head of equities had received 1.7 million euros and his deputy 1.2 million. In 2000 the financial bubble swelled and burst, increasing equity derivatives activities and generating extremely high profits. In all banks, profits on equity derivatives were especially high. Neptune had also benefited from these favourable economic conditions: according to the head of fixed income,[8] profits before taxes and after bonuses came to 230 million euros. The application of the predetermined formula – which had not been revised between 1999 and 2000 – enabled the two heads to receive the two major bonuses mentioned, which contrasted sharply with the bank's past pay practices.

Every aspect of the negotiation, whether deliberate or not, proved judicious and favourable to them. The head of fixed income acknowledged that given the way things proceeded, the two had "played their cards right".

First and foremost, *resigning together*. Hence, resigning showed their willpower. The fact that this was a resignation and not a threat to resign made their determination much more plausible. By taking a much greater risk, the two sent a clear signal that they were not willing to return to their former employer unless their conditions were met. As Schelling remarked, it is sometimes by willingly surrendering a degree of freedom (in this case, "we've left" and not "we might be leaving") – "to burn the bridges behind me as I face an enemy" (Schelling 1980, p. 195) – that one can send the most effective sign of one's determination and thereby obtain the best bargaining conditions.

What is more, this resignation was collective. It was collective in a first sense, because the two resigned together. Were the equities head and his collaborator particularly close friends? It was sometimes said that they were "pals". The fact is that whether they were friends – which seems most likely – or not (which is also possible), their joint departure was a crucial element in the success of their coup. As their former line manager explained:

> If he'd resigned alone we could have managed. But as soon as it became the whole team, it wasn't so doable. If it had just been him, we could have managed just fine – we would have appointed [his deputy]. But losing the two managers at the same time would have been very damaging for the team. And they would've taken everyone along with them.

> *Couldn't you have promoted the people under [the deputy]?*

> No. There was a really gifted guy below [the deputy], he was working in Hong Kong at the time and I knew him well. But he wasn't up to managing a global product line. He was 29. Both of them – it was impossible. One of them, OK, we could've handled it. But not the two of them. And since they were leaving for a European bank, the team would have gone with them six months later.

Replacing the two with an external head of equity derivatives would also have been fairly risky. First, Neptune would have had to attract one, which would have been extremely costly in terms of guaranteed bonuses; second, the trading teams would have been wary of the newcomer and therefore just as tempted to leave for their former bosses' new bank.

The resignation was collective in a second sense, even more critical, because the two managers threatened to take their whole teams with them. Their joint resignation thus made the threat to bring about the collective departure of the equity derivatives trading room much more credible. Most of their key colleagues, from heads of desk all the way down to junior employees, would have joined them soon enough. By taking all their teams to a competitor, the two heads were actually organising a full-scale transfer of activity. At the rival bank, the head of equities and his deputy would soon have had virtually intact production capacity at their disposal.

At Neptune, on the other hand, the better part of several years' worth of investments – development of technical and practical know-how, market share acquisition, client loyalty, etc. – was likely to be seriously damaged if not wiped out by the transfer. Thanks to their social capital (in this case, their ability to poach their own teams), the two heads had company assets at their disposal; those assets were eminently transferable for them, whereas for the firm (particularly the back office) they were eminently specific.

Second, the *timing*. The fact that they resigned in the middle of a major corporate action put the company in an extremely difficult situation and would have made their departure extremely costly. Precisely because of the corporate action, the bank's directors were very preoccupied with contacting and meeting investors, and had little time to think of alternative solutions (such as calling in headhunters), particularly since they were given so little time to respond.

Moreover, allowing the two heads to leave and risking the loss of the whole trading room would have sent out a negative signal to the financial community. The danger of losing the bank's most profitable department – even if, in global terms, the department was of fairly limited importance – could have indicated low asset sustainability and severely compromised the success of the corporate action. Lastly, the two were taking advantage of a vacuum in the bank's senior management: the bank's second highest executive was due to leave for a high political office in the European Union. The executives, who were busy preparing the upcoming road shows, eventually granted the capital markets department complete freedom to negotiate, with the result that Neptune simply accepted all the two heads' conditions for staying on.

Next, the *choice of bank*. The head of equity's game was to give enough information about the bank that was ready to hire them without revealing its name. It was a European bank operating in London that had chosen to set up a derivatives centre. This information indicated that the resignation of the two heads and their threat to take the entire team with them were very real. The two heads would not be required to reorganise and manage an activity that was already in operation but rather to create one from scratch. Clearly the fastest way to achieve this was to ask their usual colleagues to join them. At the same time, keeping the competitor's name a secret prevented Neptune from trying to negotiate in secret with that bank to convince it to withdraw its offer.[9] By leaning on shared business and financial interests and possibly personal relationships, Neptune might (this is only a supposition) have worked to develop a credible retaliatory move against its rival that would have put an end to the threat from its two rebel heads.

Next, *the percentage*. By establishing their bonus levels in a contract, the two were protecting themselves against discretionary intervention by the head of capital markets and the deputy chief executive and thus profiting fully from the soaring rise in these activities in the late 1990s. The sharp increase in stock prices in 1999 and the profitability of equity derivatives was leading banks to invest in this lucrative sector, raise risk limits, and increase equity capital and team size. Establishing bonus amounts contractually enabled them to profit from these increases (risk limits, equity capital, etc.) and protect their bonuses from the high number of new staff laying claim to one. Moreover, they demanded that their bonuses be determined by a *rate*, even though the bases for applying that rate were very likely to be different. Considering the head of equity derivatives and his deputy would have had to reconstruct their activity at the rival bank, bring along all their former staff, and above all be allocated capital and operational support (back office and IT support), they would probably have been unable to generate the same level of activity or obtain the same bonus levels in 1999 and 2000, even under the exact same formula. For Neptune Bank, accepting the rival bank's formula with no discount probably meant paying much more to keep the two heads than the rival bank was offering them.

However, although the two made sure they would receive a very sizeable share of the profits by setting the percentages in advance, they were clever enough to present things in such a way as to keep the agreement acceptable for their former bank. The share of the bonus pool they would receive was to be deducted from a single base – the bonuses for equity derivative products – that had not been adjusted in the bonus negotiation of spring 1999. As the head of fixed income trading remarked, the only problem this caused for the bank at time t was distribution: "It didn't cost the bank anything, because in any case it was within the 30%. The trick is distributing within the 30%. But the bank always pays out the 30. In fact, rather cynically, the bank couldn't care less whether it pays out x or y amounts. So, faced with this problem, [the CEO] balked, but he signed." The executives of a bank, as they embody the firm, tend to reason in terms of overall cost, seeing distribution as a problem to be resolved between heads of teams and their staff.[10] However, when they shift from reasoning in terms of a budget to reasoning in terms of individuals, they find the difference with their own pay unbearable.

Lastly, *the economic situation*. 1999 was a good year for the equities market and the derivatives industry. The near-continuous rise in equity, in the order of 50%, and the even greater rise in volumes, both in underlying assets and derivative products, was attracting a large number of financial institutions wanting to capture some of the rent being generated by this type of business. These last movers, handicapped by their very late start, had little hope of catching up with the leaders by building a business line from scratch. As a result, their primary means of entering the equity derivatives market and profiting from the fallout of the financial markets bubble was to buy whole teams by poaching heads of trading room, for example. Not willing to let an excellent opportunity pass them by, these institutions were ready to offer extremely high prices (guaranteed bonuses, fixed wages or, in this case, handover of profit) in order to acquire teams.

This situation gave the heads a solid basis on which to renegotiate conditions for remaining at Neptune Bank. Furthermore, in that kind of economic situation, the extent to which their threats were real was more likely to be overestimated than underestimated (particularly considering that the bank's top management was unfamiliar with the markets). Even if it is impossible to predict exactly when a financial bubble will burst and the market will shift, in 1999 it seemed clear that it would do so by the time the productive teams had moved to the rival bank. Instead, by renegotiating the conditions of their continued employment at the highest price, the two heads were ensuring that they would gain maximum profit from the peaks of euphoria in the equities market while remaining within the same productive organisation.

Although I do not know the explicit reasoning and strategies of the two equity derivatives heads, by reconstructing the conditions of their negotiation, which constituted a full-scale hold-up for Neptune Bank, it is clear that they had a keen sense of how to position themselves and of the Greek concept of *kairos*, the tactical moment that decisively determines the success or failure of an action; in short, as traders themselves would say, they had the feeling of the timing of the operation.

A perspective on the case

The head of fixed income trading gave his opinion on the remuneration level of his counterpart in equity derivatives:

"Two things shocked me the most at Neptune. First, the sudden jump from 1.5 million to 10 million. That came as a surprise. Second, the fact that he didn't deserve 10 million. That's where things get subjective. It wasn't deserved for two reasons. An objective reason, which was the market conditions. The market was working so well and things were so easy that we shouldn't have given so much money to the traders, to all the traders in general but especially those who already had the most. The second reason is a lot more honest in my opinion. The first one is subjective; a trader can answer, 'When the market's bad, you don't give me a bonus even though I worked like a dog . . . ' So, that argument can be refuted. The second argument is better. It goes like this: it's not right that he got 10 million euros, which is about the same as the 11 million that his counterpart at Saturn got. The difference is that he brought in 230 million euros after bonuses but before tax, whereas at Saturn they made 2.1 billion less expenses, which worked out at between 1 and 1.2 billion euros. Let's say 1.1 billion for the sake of simplicity. Neptune's result was five times lower than Saturn's, and that's down to market shares or whatever, but it's a fact. So if their result was five times lower, the boss should earn five times less.

Saturn paid out 11 million on profits of 1.1 billion euros, which meant it paid its head of derivatives 1% of the profit. Neptune paid out 10 million on profits of 230 million euros, which was 5% of the profit. That's what's so shocking. There are no rules as such, as it depends on how popular you are, but 1% for the head of capital markets is a fairly common amount. Basically, the amount they would usually get is between 0.5% and 1% of the profit. And for the head of a product line, it's a bit more, as high as 2%. I've rarely seen it go higher. I don't know everything though. There are always exceptions to the rule, especially considering that there aren't actually any rules in this case.".

The aftermath of the hold-up

To complete the picture of the two heads of trading room, particularly the first of the two (as little is known of his deputy, other than his position as second-in-command and the fact that, according to his line manager, he was a "a really sweet guy at the beginning . . . but he became completely addicted to money . . . under his boss's influence"), it is helpful to take a look back at the situation with the capital markets senior management at the end of the year 2000 and the conditions under which these supposedly secret bonuses were revealed.

At the end of 2000, the head of capital markets resigned after a dispute with the CEO of Neptune Bank over the latter's refusal to grant greater autonomy to the capital markets department. In the wake of her departure, the bank carried out a major reorganisation of the department: activities involving M&A and securities issuance were no longer managed by the capital markets department, and the head of equity derivatives was appointed as the department head, despite the lack of loyalty he had shown just 18 months before. "The head of fixed income could easily have replaced me, but he wasn't in a strong enough position to do so," explained the former head of capital markets, on account of the major losses incurred that year in the treasury management, which was one of the product lines he oversaw. However, she continued:

> The two heads of trading room had hated each other for years, and the head of equity derivatives had particularly loathed the head of fixed income for a long time . . . He also hated the head of back office . . . He'd stipulated three key conditions for replacing me. First, he wanted to keep the same bonus formula despite changing jobs. Second, fire the head of fixed income. And third, fire the head of back office.

According to the CGT trade unionist, not only did he keep his bonus formula on equity derivatives but also had it supplemented by a separate formula on fixed income and foreign exchange products (albeit less profitable). Because of the often negative correlation between the equity market and fixed income market performances, this formula enabled him to earn a high bonus year after year.

The fact that a head of capital markets kept a limitless bonus formula (or, in this case, two) was severely criticised by the three individuals who made way for him (for a variety of reasons) at the end of 2000. "Continuing to pay someone for one of the product lines he oversees, when he's responsible for the entire department, well that's unheard of. It's the supreme offence," exclaimed the head of capital markets.

The head of back office was equally critical, and went into further detail:

> What shocks me the most now is that my boss was replaced by someone from front office who kept his front office bonus formula! I believe it's extremely dangerous to give a head of capital markets a limitless bonus formula. To give an example, my previous boss wanted to maintain our recurring profit, so she made sure we invested in IT. She didn't spend vast amounts, but she was sure to spend a minimum on investment. The front office was only interested in instant profit. What's the point of investing if we're being taken over by Venus Bank in a year? In other words, there is no counter-power these days to short-term profit. And that's very risky, because it means that the people who make investment decisions are also those responsible for – and incapable of – mediating between the front office, who want to spend as little as possible, and operations, who may tend to be too perfectionist. And my previous boss played that role, because her own bonuses had an upper limit. From a certain threshold, she was prepared to spend in order to guarantee future activity, whereas today, anyone whose head of capital markets has a limitless bonus formula will say, "everything's short term" and "the day things slow down, well it's tough luck, we've already had our bonuses". The only action taken by the executives which I find completely reckless was its choice of capital markets head. That's where Neptune got caught. They'd appointed [the head of equity derivatives] as head of capital markets, and it's obvious that he then said 'I'm not switching from a limitless bonus formula to one that's capped at 800,000 euros!' . . . And if they wanted to keep him, they were forced to pay him like that. At that point, he shouldn't have been given the job. To my mind, the mistake they made was saying, "You're head of capital markets!" The head of equity derivatives reasoned like this: "I don't want any support functions. I didn't ask for them!" And he meant it, because he couldn't have cared less. He told me, "You know why I took them on? Because I was worried that after you left they'd put some technocrat in charge who'd do anything." And his concerns were justified. His reasoning was correct, but the consequence of his reasoning was that he has support functions with no counter-power, because he wanted to stop people from spending hundreds of millions, and I can understand his concern.

The conditions under which the head of equity derivatives kept and extended his contract after he was promoted were the subject of considerable speculation. As the protagonists were forced to speculate *in absentia* and from a distance, their conjecture was clearly less reliable than accounts of the first negotiation.

Whether or not it was borne out, however, the simple fact that it was expressed highlights both the head of trading room's tactical thinking and a number of vital mechanisms of the hold-up situation: it showed that the negotiation took place in a context of uncertainty and that the actors formed their own beliefs as regards the credibility of the threat and the determination of those involved in the negotiation.

> But he played the same card again and said, "You either pay me or I'm leaving!" Quite simply, the big difference is that you have to be in the markets. The CEO of Neptune has never been in them, and his deputy chief executive even less so. When my head of equity derivatives said to me in May or June 1999, "I'm leaving for another bank" (it hardly mattered if he didn't tell me the name), I knew it was plausible and true, especially a bank that was establishing an activity. But when he had to say, a year and a half after I left, "Blablabla . . . " No! It wasn't true! Because no one would buy him at that price! But you have to be in the markets to know that. His advantage came from dealing with people like the CEO and the deputy chief executive of Neptune Bank, because they had no idea what was going on in the markets. When you're talking to the new head of the executive committee and he's a commercial banker who's never had a clue about the markets, if you say to him, "I'm leaving. Such and such a bank is offering me the same deal," then he'll believe you, because he doesn't know. He's never experienced the markets. You need experience to know if it's plausible or not.
>
> (Former head of capital markets)

The hold-up situation is particularly difficult to manage because most of the negotiation issues at stake are uncertain and need to be assessed, which cannot usually be done within a stable, robust framework. The head of equity derivatives would certainly have based his plan to be promoted on the idea that the deputy chief executive believed the success of the equity derivatives department was down to its leader's talent and methods, and that he would be able to apply his lucrative methods to reorganising the fixed income and foreign exchange trading room. His promotion was all the more necessary considering that an external head of capital markets would have resulted in a revival of the secessionist tendencies of the equity derivatives department.

Once the negotiation was underway, the directors of Neptune Bank, if indeed they really were being blackmailed for a second time by their head of trading room, had to assess the following points. Was any bank willing to give him an equivalent formula? Was that formula likely to generate the same sum in the very short term? If need be, would that bank be able to guarantee a bonus of around 10 million euros? Was the head of equity derivatives really as disposed to leaving the bank as he would have them believe? Did he really have so much power over his own troops that he would be able to persuade them to join him on an uncertain adventure? These considerations demanded practical knowledge of the financial markets in order to be properly weighed up.

Outsiders often waver between an excessive lack of trust and excessive confidence in the necessity of the order of things, failing to see frameworks of reference, the constructed nature of equilibriums, risks of errors or of hoaxes and influence strategies in the same way that insiders do. Executives may therefore swing from considerations of the arbitrary and surrealistic nature of remuneration to assertions that remuneration conforms perfectly with value creation. In this game, there is a chance they will indeed overestimate the risk that their head of trading room precisely wants them to overestimate (Groysberg, Lee and Nanda 2008). In such a chain of assessment, they may either wrongly conclude that there is a rival willing to recruit their employee with such a formula or, otherwise, if a buyer does exist, as in 1999, that existence may lead them to conclude positively on subsequent questions: a buyer who guarantees a sufficient activity or bonus level, a head of trading room who is absolutely determined to leave and staff who really are willing to follow him. Perhaps we should also consider the short-termism of the directors who, while waiting for an imminent alliance with another bank, may have decided that accepting the head of trading room's conditions would allow them to negotiate the alliance from a stronger position than if he resigned, even if it meant getting rid of the intruder when the alliance came about and the capital markets departments merged.[11]

To conclude the account of this case, I should briefly describe the conditions under which the two bonuses were finally revealed. In the spring of 2001, the CGT trade unionist first heard talk of "50 million francs" (8 million euros), which he initially dismissed as impossible and absurd, thinking "they must be talking about old francs". Once the information had been verified by a number of sources, he began to write the open letter, taking the utmost care not to give rise to a legal complaint from those involved. He also warned the bank's executives of the imminent publication of his letter so as not to present them with a fait accompli.

I told the executives that we would make a statement on the bonuses . . . I got a call from the head of the equity derivatives trading room in London. He buttonholed me for half an hour then he went nuts. The threats he made! They weren't direct threats, but threats nonetheless. He pulled out all the stops. What we were denouncing was a principle. It wasn't a question of exposing people. It was about denouncing something that wasn't right. In any case, we didn't include their names because I didn't want to find myself in court. The fact alone was reprehensible no matter who was involved. It was the principle of the thing that we were denouncing. "It's got nothing to do with you. Good for you, I say. But I believe that it has to be exposed for the sake of Neptune." He didn't like it at all. . . . He said, "It's hypocritical to talk about my bonus and then say you're not talking about me!" He wanted me to give him some names to make a counter-attack. Then he said, "If you talk about my bonus I'll shut down our activities, jobs will be lost and it'll be your fault." It was the kind of situation where the trade unionist can walk away if . . . anyway. I let him talk. Afterwards he threatened to take the union to court. He was really nuts, because then he said, "If you publish my bonus

I'll take the president to court for divulging my pay!" It was crazy. He was threatening to take [Neptune's CEO] to court. At the time I wasn't laughing. I thought to myself, "What's wrong with this guy?" I stayed calm. I could sense that he was worked up. Half an hour getting shouted at by someone who earns that much dough, it's enough. He was pretty worked up. He was talking at me and I had to go along with it. After a while he started repeating himself. I said to him, "Look, I'm going to think about it! I'll let you know what I decide." And at the end of the month I played my card. I warned him first. It was decided that we'd let the news out. That really pissed him off.

Even if it is biased, this account of the confrontation between the head of equity derivatives and the trade unionist shows two things. First, it illustrates the head's hot-headed character, which may be the result of a position in finance, a career path and perhaps also of pre-existing dispositions (of which I know nothing), such as a readiness to make threats, hold a knife to people's throats and try to take action against others by subjecting them to the most imperative moral, legal and financial constraints.

Second, however, this confrontation placed the head of equity derivatives in an unprecedented position: although he seemed to enjoy a significant tactical advantage, he lost ground for making the credible threats that would serve his interest. Although the assets he managed gave him considerable control over the bank's top management, he found himself incapable of influencing a minor staff representative. He could hardly threaten to have the man fired because he was protected as a trade unionist. Nor could he threaten to take him to court for invasion of privacy because no names had been published. He made a few implausible threats, all the more so because he swung from one to the next without taking the time to assess their overall coherence: threats of collective dismissals carried out in reprisal and a threat to take the CEO to court (which would have implicitly had repercussions for the trade unionist). This situation was particularly infuriating for the head of equity derivatives: on the one hand his remuneration was being made public and was accompanied by a moral denunciation of its level and, by extension, of his entire person, which jeopardised the social stability on which the secret pact of profit distribution was based. On the other hand, he found himself in the unprecedented situation of being unable to control others with threats. Ultimately, the failure of this particular hold-up proves the fact that there are specific structural conditions (a certain transfer of assets) on which its success depends.

Notes

1 My reconstruction is particularly reliable given that at the time of the interviews these three individuals no longer worked at Neptune Bank. The first had left for reasons unrelated to the case, while the other two resigned after the head of equity derivatives was promoted. These former employees were thus no longer bound by any withholding and reporting obligation, which is commonly enforced in the banking environment.

Interviews were also conducted with the trade union leader who had revealed the case and two of his colleagues, as well as a HR professional, an equities risk controller and two fixed income traders.

2 This figure no doubt reflects the bonuses of employees in head office and not those of subsidiaries. Equity derivatives employees, starting with the two recipients, belonged to a subsidiary of Neptune Bank established in London "for taxation reasons", according to the head of the capital markets department.

3 One HR professional told me that, at the general meeting of shareholders, no questions were asked on the matter. However, the general meeting took place after the disclosure had been made internally but before the press had found out. At the board of directors' meeting the following month, the directors requested information on the bonus payment criteria. The president did not respond to their request but agreed that the board of directors' remuneration committee should be given information on the matter and draw up a report.

4 "'If we don't match market prices, the best employees will leave for an institution that does' someone pointed out [at Neptune Bank]" (Chocron and Pinson 2001).

5 The growing feeling of frustration at Saturn Bank may have strengthened his belief that in the world of derivatives, if one is not a graduate of the *École Polytechnique* or even an engineer, nor an ENA graduate in a managerial position, the advantages can only be obtained by taking them for oneself.

6 It is necessary to examine the cultural nature of this attitude in context. Close-up, Anglo-American banks prove to be extremely hierarchical. Anglo-American managers drag their feet just as much as French managers in an effort to apply the logic of value creation when value is not there. The degree to which particular models are invoked may vary more from one continent to another than the degree to which they are applied.

7 The head of the capital markets department also applied a bonus formula to her own bonus, which involved indexing her bonus to the capital markets department's results and applying a maximum in absolute value. She said this formula had never really worked, apart from in "the last two years". The reason she gave for not applying it was that she was too preoccupied with her colleagues' problems to worry about her own formula: "The head of equity derivatives trading first argued his own case and then that of others, which seemed like a sensible way to resolve things. He would say, 'First we negotiate the bonus, then once that's done, we'll talk business.' Whereas I, rather stupidly, I might add, would start by solving all my teams' problems and then say 'Now me!' But once everything's settled, you're not in such a strong position."

8 On the basis of the bonus formulas, the bonus pool for equity derivatives can be estimated at 119 million euros (17/14.5%) and profits before taxes and bonuses at 400 million euros (119/30%). To arrive at the figure of 230 million euros, we have to subtract the bonuses and employer contributions on them. The head of fixed income noted that, considering the equity derivatives room was "consuming" 115 million euros in share capital and that it was posting profits of 230 million euros, its return on equity was 200%!

9 Ten years earlier, when the department head hired the man who would later became head of the equity derivatives trading room, she came under intense pressure from the director general of Saturn Bank, the head's former employer.

10 Although information on this is lacking, it is possible that this new bonus distribution would have been insufficient for the rest of the team, leading to resignations, hurting group productivity, and in the medium term leading the two managers to demand an increase in the bonus pool for the whole team.

11 Indeed, after Neptune's capital markets activities merged with those of Uranus Bank, the former head of equity derivatives was both isolated from his troops and in competition with the head of capital markets at Uranus Bank. This conflictive situation led to his departure and that of his former deputy. While at the time they had no alternative plan to take their teams elsewhere, their departures in 2004 caused a pause in activity, leading to scattered defections that were devastating for the equity derivatives department.

References

Chocron, V and Pinson, G 2001, 'Grogne autour des bonus record versés par les banques', *La Tribune*, 29 May.

Groysberg, B, Lee, LE and Nanda, A 2008, 'Can They Take It with Them? The Portability of Star Knowledge Workers' Performance: Myth or Reality', *Management Science*, vol. 54, n°7, pp. 1213–1230.

Hirschman, A and Rotschild, M 1973, 'The Changing Tolerance for Income Inequality in the Course of Economic Development', *Quarterly Journal of Economics*, vol. 87, n°4, pp. 544–566.

Malcomson, J 1997, 'Contracts, Hold-Up, and Labor Markets', *Journal of Economic Literature*, vol. 35, n°4, pp. 1916–1957.

Schelling, T 1980, *The Strategy of Conflict*, Harvard University Press, Cambridge MA.

Williamson, O 1985, *The Economic Institutions of Capitalism*, The Free Press, New York.

7 Towards a model of hold-up

The spectacular case described in the previous chapter is exemplary of transactions occurring in this labour market. How can I speak of a hold-up situation when these are in fact freely agreed and non-violent? In addition to cleverly exploiting the economic context, the two heads used the rival bank's offer as leverage for credibly threatening the other party (the bank) with disaster (the loss of its equity derivatives activity) if it refused to do what they were demanding (renegotiate their contract).[1] By bringing along a close-knit team, the two employees were in a position to take a significant segment of the bank's activity to a rival bank.

The hold-up mechanism employed here in an exemplary fashion operates on a smaller scale in other professions and at other hierarchical levels within the financial industry. A fixed income trader in the same bank secured himself a raise twice by threatening – competitor's contract in hand – to leave and practise his art in a rival bank. Through this leverage effect, renegotiation allows an employee to obtain far more than a mere individual contribution to the whole (assuming that such a contribution can actually be measured). In the case described in Chapter 6, the heads were also able to capture part of the trading room's value by threatening to redeploy its full activity. Similarly, by threatening to leave, the fixed income trader was able to capture part of the trading expertise that his bank had allowed him to accumulate by granting him access to assets that required learning, sharing collective knowledge with him and financing that accumulation of expertise by paying his wages.

I shall first present the hold-up mechanism and then discuss possible protection methods that can reduce hold-up risk, and the limitations of these protections.

The hold-up mechanism in finance

Over the past 20 years, many economists have vested interest in establishing a model for the hold-up phenomena (Klein, Crawford and Alchian 1978; Williamson 1985; Malcomson 1997). If an economic actor who is engaged in a collaborative relationship invests in an asset that cannot easily be redeployed, her partner can blackmail her: revise the terms of the exchange or break off the relationship and lose the value of her investment. The first consequence of this situation, if it had been anticipated, is that it leads the economic actor – in this case the firm – to invest less in this type of asset (Grout 1984). The second consequence is of more relevance here: the other party, in this case the financial operators, makes a sizeable profit. The operators then receive higher wages than the market wage that would apply if the hold-up had not taken place.

The general idea of a hold-up in the case of redeployable assets is as follows: if the firm's investment in financial activity can be entirely or partially redeployed by an employee moving to a rival firm, then that employee will be able to renegotiate her salary, demand and obtain an alternative redistribution of value, and appropriate collective investment profits. The "firm" should be seen here as a collective entity representing all parties: shareholders, of course, but primarily employees. In the case that I have just analysed, the employees working under the two heads of trading room were, without knowing it, also direct short-term victims of the less egalitarian distribution imposed by their bosses.[2]

I will clarify the way in which a hold-up unfolds by analysing the career path of a salesperson in a bank or brokerage firm. The work contracts that firms sign with new employees are fairly standard, which means they are fundamentally *incomplete* in the sense that there are few clauses in them specifying how the exchange terms (i.e. wages, conditions for breaking the contract) will evolve in response to changes in either external environment or internal organisation. In many cases, even the job itself is not defined in the contract but rather assigned gradually as the new employee becomes integrated into the work group. That integration determines whether the new employee will become a trader, a salesperson or a back office administrator. The contract is incomplete first of all because of the uncertainty of the external environment and internal organisation. Not only is the financial world constantly shifting but there is no pre-existing stabilised nomenclature for all of the employee's future states at the time the contract is signed. Even for the dimensions of the future that can be most easily measured and therefore probabilised, establishing the indicators on which to index contract clauses can be a complex matter, and it can be even more difficult to get these indicators verified by a third party. Hence, it is not possible to prevent hold-ups with a more detailed, if not complete, labour contract (Hart and Moore 1988; Stole and Zwiebel 1996).

Let us assume that this junior professional has become an efficient financial products salesperson. To get her to perform well, the firm has to invest in training her as well as putting her in a position to attract customers. Junior employees selling sophisticated products can often only carry out their first financial transactions after several months of soliciting clients. The firm's investment not only consists in the employee's first months' wages (which it pays out without a return), it is much greater than that, and is both continuous and multiform: it involves "wining and dining" clients, marketing new financial products and explaining them to customers, and investing in the trading and back office teams so as to facilitate financial product arbitrage, transaction settlement and delivery. Investment in an employee, based as it is on general investment in the firm's financial platform, is thus difficult to isolate as such and it is hard to imagine contract clauses that would be a priori conditional on that overall investment.

In contrast with general (or ongoing) training, investment of this sort cannot be handled by the employee alone outside of any financial structure. It is consubstantial with integration into a financial activity, and the firm cannot offload its responsibilities onto an external training structure funded by the employee.

While the simplest formalised models emphasise investment by one of the parties (in this case the firm), it is more accurate to assume here, as with more sophisticated models, that both the firm and the employee are investing in production (Hart and Moore 1988; Rajan and Zingales 1998; Rajan and Zingales 2001). Not only is the employee granted the firm's assets, she also needs to specialise in the management of those assets. In other words, she acquires skills and attracts customers, and she will do this even more intensely if she plans to appropriate part of the return on overall investment for herself. Even on the most standard financial products, salespeople succeed in making this collective and individual investment and thereby attracting clients (usually portfolio managers from financial institutions) by producing highly personalised information. Thanks to their monopoly over the external environment (that is, clients), these "marginal secants" of the organisation (Crozier and Friedberg 1980) acquire clients (thereby detaching them from the firm) by learning to provide them with the type of daily information most likely to hold their attention on the telephone. This ranges from technical information on market prices to jokes, and includes topics of conversation on extra-occupational areas of interest such as sport and film. When portfolio managers engaged in daily transactions involving large sums of money have to choose between 15 telephone salespeople offering identical products at virtually identical prices, they tend to favour those to whom they most enjoy talking and with whom they have the greatest number of affinities, both professional (the same ideas about the market and the same way of selecting relevant financial information) or extra-occupational, such as conversations on sport and cultural activities (Ortiz, 2005 and 2014).

After some time (usually 2–3 years), the salesperson is no longer a junior; she is now aware of the economic situation in her financial niche and she observes, if not the collective investment, at least the financial activity and the transaction and trading flows that pass through her hands. She starts to believe that such financial activity could not take place if she were not there to mediate it, and in many cases she becomes convinced that she is the only truly legitimate owner of the profit generated, especially if she underestimates or forgets the collective dimension of the investment. She may therefore demand that the firm give her a share of the profits and threaten to redeploy her activity elsewhere if her new wage conditions are not met. Hold-up here operates on the basis of two mechanisms: the *specificity* of assets for the firm (Klein, Crawford and Alchian 1978; Williamson 1985) and the *transferability* of assets for the employee (Rajan and Zingales 2001). If the employee left, she would cause the firm's assets to lose value. Even if she left for another sector or stopped working altogether, the firm would have to bear a high cost for its disorganisation, the loss of its point of contact for clients and a loss of expertise. The classic problem of specificity is compounded by a *transferability* issue: by leaving to work for a competitor, the salesperson removes herself as an employee but also a share of the firm's assets, in this case some of its clients (Malcomson 1997). If the firm's anticipated loss is higher than the profit share the employee is claiming in the form of a bonus, it will be in the firm's interest to accept the renegotiation conditions. Beliefs play a major role in power struggles where the threat to resign is used as the main argument. Financial operators who are planning to leave often strengthen their position by dramatising the impact of their departure on the firm.

Pure power struggles of similar intensity to the one imposed by the two heads at Neptune Bank do not occur very often if we consider total annual employee wage transactions in the financial industry. Even so, the resignation threat functions as a kind of regulating horizon. By gradually increasing bonuses (trying to "keep people happy") at the different hierarchy levels in an investment bank, line managers try to avoid reaching this dually critical point. Although it is often more a matter of abrupt mood changes than complex renegotiation plans, when the annual bonus negotiation and distribution process takes place a significant number of financial operators (traders and sales) express dissatisfaction with their bonus, stating to their line managers, "If that's how it is, I'm resigning!"

To summarise, the primary effect[3] of the particular hold-up mechanism described here is that it explains how financial operators constitute a micro labour market whose level is disconnected from that of other job markets (cf. the mathematical model included in the Annex). This is a market not only of people but also of asset transfers, captured by financial operators but generated by group investment. Here, the group that I have modelled as "the firm" encompasses all employees in addition to the CEO and the shareholders.

Protection limitations

Can a firm protect itself against the transfer and bargaining power an employee may acquire from gaining control over certain key assets? What occurs when the firm anticipates an employee's potential hold-up power? Some economists have argued that even if employment contracts remain fundamentally incomplete, hold-ups can be avoided through appropriate contractual terms: at the start of the period, the firm may try to exchange under its own favourable terms the power that the employee could acquire for an entrance fee (Carmichael 1990); and at the end of the period, it may limit the chances of defection by establishing non-compete clauses, deferred bonuses or garden leaves (Edlin and Reichelstein 1996). However, those protections appear difficult to implement in the finance labour market and offer at best a poor protection against hold-up power.

Exchanging bargaining power

One of the points that has not yet been addressed concerns the establishing of a junior employee's starting wage. If the firm knows that the new employee will acquire a high level of internal bargaining power, it may, in an unregulated labour market, take the initiative and try to introduce this future bargaining power into the current terms of exchange, either by selling the position as a franchise or by requesting that the employee pay a bond or deposit to be recovered at the end of the period if she still works for the firm, but which she would lose if she left the firm prematurely (Cahuc *et al.* 2014, pp. 353–355). In that event, the employee would lose her bargaining power and only receive the market wage with no additional wage premium.

The first challenge in this radically uncertain environment is to define the initial amount the employee should pay. If it is below the amount she could capture by leaving, it will of course be in the employee's interest to force a renegotiation by brandishing the threat of resignation. Conversely, if it is above that amount, the firm may take advantage of the situation by renegotiating the work contract in its own favour or not making adjustments in line with wider professional market wages. As a result, it is no simple matter to get the employee to commit to paying such a potentially high sum, as it would put her in an extremely vulnerable position in relation to the firm. She would be paying in advance for an uncertain investment to which it is impossible to commit by contract. Indeed, it would be too difficult to describe the investment and the set of states-of-the-world in which it would assume value. If the investment in kind and in monetary terms is not the one anticipated, her bargaining power would be severely weakened. How could an employee accept to pay to become a French convertible bond salesperson when the firm cannot commit on the kind of investment it will make? First, will it or will it not invest? Second, will it invest a significant amount in the *processes*, in the quality of execution, settlement and delivery – which would diminish the salesperson's overall bargaining power – or in winning over clients (cases of wine, football matches, restaurants), which, on the contrary, would increase the employee's overall bargaining power? The firm's opportunism also plays a role: a head of desk or trading room sometimes promises prospective employees "developments" that do not materialise, leaving the employee feeling resentful (even without having to buy her position).[4]

To commit to such a contract and keep it from being broken opportunistically by the firm, the employee has to be certain of recovering the deposit if the company fires her before term. However, the line between being fired and resigning, and therefore between a salary renegotiation initiated by the employee and one initiated by the firm, is hard to distinguish. A cautious employee will try to protect herself from all the techniques the company may utilise to force her to resign (sidelining, moral harassment, transfer, deteriorated working conditions) by trying to recover the deposit exploiting any breach of contract whatever its cause. However, the deposit would then no longer be an effective incentive to prevent the employee from carrying out a hold-up.

Even in a highly deregulated environment, then, there are major obstacles to making an employee sign a work contract that would force her to pay for or guarantee the investment she might capture from her future position in the organisation.[5] Moreover, a generally inefficient economic world could make it impossible to fund such deposits. Employees have to deal with credit rationing: banks seldom lend large sums of money without requiring a collateral. Existing labour legislation on work contracts means that employers cannot make employees pay for their job and requires them to pay their employees higher first-period wages than the minimum wage for the industry sector. Other types of contracts, such as franchise or sales agreements, can be recategorised as work contracts by employment tribunals if it is proven that the financial operator is subordinate to the firm.

Lastly, the bounded rationality of ordinary economic actors and the intellectual and economic costs of finding solutions at the contractual level in a changing economic world also explain why little energy is ultimately devoted to improving the initial contracts of junior employees in the world of finance. At Saturn Bank, when a junior professional graduating from a *Grande École* was hired, the HR professional scanned the salary range for new employees and applied the indicated rates,[6] regardless of whether the employee had applied for a position in the back office, middle office, front office, as a financial engineer, risk control officer, etc., despite the fact that redeployment risk was very different for the various jobs. To secure one's first job on the financial markets, one usually has to have completed an internship, and in a few cases to have worked as a temp in a trading room. The internships vary from one to two months full-time to a year part-time and are completed while pursuing the last year of university study.[7] In the trading room at Universal Company, I calculated that 10% of the staff were interns whose work capacity was being used to the full, generally in exchange for half the wage they could claim for their first job (Godechot 2001). Even so, according to ENSAE students, the firms that paid their interns the highest wage were banks and financial institutions. Also, despite the fact that internships as a first stage in employment are more widespread in finance than in other sectors, and even though they last longer and may generate a greater workload, employees themselves pay for very little of the investment being made in them, an investment they will be able to capture later on.

Limiting defections

If, at the start of the period, the employee cannot be made to pay the price of the bargaining power she will acquire through the working relationship, it may be possible to have her pay for it at the end of the period. For example, a non-compete clause can be used to make her pay for breach of contract (Bessy 2009). As protection, this applies more directly to the firm's asset transfer risk than its specificity problem (loss of value if the relationship is broken off). Non-compete clauses are only effective for the firm when their violation is sufficiently costly in moral, judicial or financial terms for the employee. If the clause specifies a fixed fine only in case of early departure for another firm, that fine has to be higher than or equal to the maximum gain the employee could expect from threatening to leave the company. If this is not the case, the firm also should retain the right to sue the employee for anticipated commercial damages.[8] In certain non-compete clause models, a fixed sum is combined with reparation for damages inflicted by breach of contract.

Having the employee sign this type of contract at the start of the period would effectively protect the firm against hold-up, and it would not have to pay employees any more than the market wage. However, work contracts that include non-compete clauses are rare in the financial industry. This has to do with the history of the sector (inertia of contract practices that do not use non-compete clauses) and above all the difficulty of making these clauses legally enforceable.

In societies with free-market economies, the legitimacy and legality of non-compete clauses are likely to be problematic. They highlight the conflict between one of the foundations of labour law, that is, the freedom to work, and one of the principles of common law, the freedom to enter into a contract. In some American states such as California, such clauses are legally nul and void (Gilson 1999). Other states tolerate them but strictly regulate the scope of their application and make contract freedom subordinate to principles of public order such as freedom to work, often deemed a fundamental human right in itself. If these clauses are given too much scope, they can put the ill-informed, unsuspecting employee who signs them in a situation close to slavery.

In France, non-compete clauses have to be shown to be indispensable to the protection of the company's legitimate interests; they have to be limited in time and space, take into account the specificity of the employee's job (in other words, the clause has to allow her to exercise her profession) and, since the Court of Cassation's ruling of 10 July 2002, they must contain an obligation for the employer to financially compensate the employee (Vatinet 2002a). The legislation itself offers no more than very general guiding principles. In practice, space is counted as *départements* and time is measured in months (6, 12 or, most commonly, 24 months, but rarely more). It is up to the judge to examine the proportionality of the clause and decide whether the actual specifications and general principles are consistent. Firms that require their employees to sign a non-compete clause must therefore anticipate legal costs. Although the time criterion may be appropriate for protecting company assets against hold-up (2 years is long enough for the unused assets to depreciate almost entirely), there are two limitations to this type of clause that can make it impossible to enforce them in the financial industry: job specificity protection and spatial limitation.

First, an employee cannot be prevented from practising her profession.[9] Everything therefore depends on the way that profession or job is defined. In the financial industry, a job is defined not only by the activity but also by the products traded therein. A convertible bond trader is neither a bond trader nor an equity trader. A convertible bond trader might even be able to argue that she was being prevented from doing her job even if the clause were restricted to French convertible bonds. Moreover, when the restriction bears on certain products and clients only, it is not easy to check whether it has been complied with.

The space limitation is becoming increasingly difficult to apply in a world where financial activities are on the cutting edge of globalisation. In general, this limitation means that the competition clause cannot apply beyond the national territory. In Europe, most financial activities can be carried out in one of the following locations: Paris, London, Frankfurt and Amsterdam. A limited number of activities are carried out in American (or Japanese) offices, but here the problem of different time zones arises. In order to be truly effective, therefore, a non-compete clause should not include any spatial restrictions. However, in the framework of current French legislation, this type of clause would then be difficult to enforce legally. For example, a large team from a major French commercial bank special-ising in structured operations was subject to a non-compete clause in London, and collectively resigned in 2001 to set up a rival financial company in Dublin, where such clauses of course no longer applied.

In the English-speaking world, non-compete clauses are very seldom used. In the United Kingdom their use is very restricting, which led firms to adopt long notice of departure and garden leaves instead (Lazar 2008). Employees' freedom to work is seen as the counterpart to employers' freedom to fire staff. In con-tinental Europe, non-compete clauses are more likely to be used. They are not frequently encountered in the financial industry, though they do exist. One head-hunter interviewed said she hardly ever encountered them. A HR professional at Saturn Bank said that up until 2001 the bank never included such clauses for two reasons: first, the heads of trading room expressed no need for them, and second, the bank's legal services advised against them because the risk of their being invalidated by French industrial tribunals was too great. One possible rea-son for the lack of interest shown by heads of trading room in this kind of contract clause (in addition to the lack of historical precedent) may have to do with their ambivalent relation to them. First, the company could impose such clauses on the managers as well as their junior staff. Second, imposing them only on more junior staff would not necessarily benefit managers. They would of course be protect-ing themselves against staff resignations, but they would also considerably limit their own bargaining power, which consists in implicitly threatening to leave with those same employees.

According to the same HR manager, contacted in late 2003, the head of the equity derivatives department began imposing non-compete clauses when the financial crisis began. After several tries, the clauses were imposed at the end of November for all new professionals hired by the investment bank: traders, sales people, financial engineers, IT specialists and support function professionals. The bank's legal experts – pusillanimous, in the words of the HR professional – deliberately restricted the scope of the limitations: the time limit was six months and the space restriction was the Île-de-France region. The clauses were not applied to employees hired before November 2002. Despite the fact that there have been some resignations, the bank has hardly activated these clauses. In 2008, a quant of this bank told me that his bank was now trying to subject financial workers to international non-compete agreements, forbidding them to work dur-ing six months for a defined set of competitors in a defined list of financial centres in the world. However, cross-border non-compete clauses still remain very fragile because, first, they raise the question of the competent jurisdiction and, second, they may not be enforced due to their wide geographical scope (Lazar 2008). Hence, the quant considered that the clauses were imposed more for their psycho-logical impact than for their legal force. While Saturn is famous in Paris for its "annoying" non-compete agreements, a trader from another bank told me that he was still not subject to such contractual terms in 2016.

Given financial operators' ability to turn to the courts or even the unions to defend their interests, and given the interests at stake for headhunting firms, it is unlikely that non-compete clauses will put an end to the hold-up phenomenon and the disconnection between the financial industry labour market and other markets. At most it might slow development of the phenomenon, lengthen circulation paths and substitute Paris–Paris transfers for Paris–London–Paris ones.

Besides non-compete clauses, two other common retention devices may prevent hold-ups: long notices of departure and deferred bonuses.

In the British financial labour market, it is quite common to ask for a long notice of departure that usually lasts one to three months, and more rarely up to six months. When a competitor poaches a financial operator, her firm can ask her either to continue working for it or to stay at home on "garden leave". Garden leave prevents the financial operator serving her notice from working in advance for the interests of her future employer or to transfer to this firm too quickly assets, such as trade secrets or clients. A small survey among the United States top 100 financial firms (DA Kreuter 2013) showed that 43% of those firms were using garden leaves in 2012, often for less than three months. Their typical duration was two months.

However, this policy faces several limitations and cannot fully prevent hold-ups. First, this policy is expensive since the firm must pay its financial operator during the garden leave period. Second, its typical duration may not be sufficient to prevent a transfer of assets. Even after three months, it is still possible to implement previous trading techniques or to successfully call back a client. Third, the policy is rather fragile since courts do not enforce such measures in every case.[10]

Deferred bonuses, already in use in the early 2000s, became fairly common in the financial industry in the aftermath of 2008 crisis, and were highly recommended in 2009 by the G20 FSB as a means for limiting risks (FSB 2009). In the European Union, the CRD III Directive (2010/76/EU), which implemented those principles in 2010, requires 40% to 60% of the variable to be deferred over a period of at least three to five years. Hence, in the European Union financial industry, 45% of the bonuses of "high earners" (earning more than 1 million euros) were deferred in 2011, 51% in 2012 and 53% in 2013 (EBA 2015).

Could deferred bonuses prevent hold-ups and transfers of assets from one firm to another? An investment banker who moves to another firm just after receiving her yearly bonus may lose an amount of deferred bonus equivalent to 80% of a yearly bonus if 40% of her bonuses are deferred over a period of three years. This loss increases to 1.8 times the yearly bonus when 60% of the bonuses are deferred over a period of five years. This policy could deter people who transfer little assets to exercise their outside option. Nonetheless, even if high deferred bonuses prevent financial workers from moving, these people still benefit from a wage premium in the long run thanks to this retention policy. Moreover, when the estimated value of the transferred assets is larger than the amount of the loss, it is still worthwhile to jump ship. New employers often offer "sign-in" or "welcome" bonuses that cover the loss of deferred bonuses. Some financial operatives try to recover those bonuses either by suing their firm, sometimes successfully, to make it pay its due or by trying to get fired instead of having to resign. One equity derivatives trader from Sirius Bank interviewed in 2002, thanks to a credible threat issued by his father, head of one of the biggest law firms in Paris, obtained the right to be fired and thereby recover the 2 million dollars in accumulated shares and stock options released by this "non-voluntary" departure. He went on to set up a hedge fund in direct competition with his former bank.

The composition of pay has also changed in recent years and therefore weakened the efficacy of deferred bonus for preventing hold-ups. Banks, in order to circumvent the European Union regulations on deferred bonus and moreover the new 2014 bonus cap (cf. Chapter 1), increased fixed wages substantially. Therefore, the proportion of total remuneration eligible to deferral largely decreased. To summarise, although deferred bonuses may decrease turnover, it only slightly weakens hold-up power and appropriation of profit.[11]

In order to measure mobility in finance and the impact of these retention devices, I launched an online survey with efinancialcareers.fr in September 2008 (Godechot 2013 and 2014), which collected 768 useable answers, broadly representative of the diversity of the financial industry (although with a junior bias). I can rely on 454 complete and 78 incomplete questionnaires for those who did change job in finance, and 209 complete and 28 incomplete questionnaires for those who never changed job. In the questionnaire I asked if, before their move, people were subject to conditions that could hamper it: 8% said they were subject to deferred bonuses, 13% to non-compete clauses, 10% to long notice of departure and 4% to "other" devices. Altogether 28% were subject to at least one retention device, i.e. 21 % to one device and 7% to two or more devices.

As transaction costs theory predicts, people who are likely to move key assets or productive teams are generally more subject to retention devices than other workers (Table 7.1). This result applies in particular in the case of deferred bonuses and long notices of departure, but does not apply in the case of non-compete clauses. Among those devices, deferred bonuses seem the most efficient. With the help of a regression model, I showed that this device appears to prevent people who can take their team with them from moving. Moreover, when comparing people who moved with people who did not, I found that, for the latter, deferred bonuses were twice as common as for the former (16% against 8%). This differential turned into a factor of three in a logistic regression when I controlled for sector, function, experience in finance, age, sex and diploma. This result suggests that deferred bonus did prevent part of the turnover.

However, my survey also shows that in practice the efficacy of those retention devices is undermined by workers' ability to renegotiate their removal. Non-compete clauses, long notices of departures and not paying deferred bonuses to those who resign are not only legally fragile and highly susceptible to being overturned in the courts but also because, even without any trial or threat of trials, firms can simply exempt the departing worker from respecting the contractual clauses or agree nevertheless to pay her the accumulated deferred bonuses.

Table 7.1 Retention devices and their removal

Independent variable → Dependent variables ↓	Net impact of combined moveable assets index (Odds ratio)
Deferred bonuses	×1.7 ***
Non-compete clauses	×0.99
Long notice of departure	×1.6 ***
At least one type of retention device	×1.3**
Retention device successfully removed	×1.4**
Retention device successfully removed for those subjected to it	×1.2

Note: I model the impact of a moveable assets index (cf. Table 8.1) on the probability of being subjected to various retention devices and of being able to successfully renegotiate their removal. One standard deviation of the combined moveable assets index multiplies the probability of being subjected to deferred bonuses by 1.7. Each cell corresponds to a different logistic regression. All models contain the following control variables: sector (two categories: investment bank versus others banking activities), function (four categories: front office, financial experts, IT, back office), experience and experience squared in finance, age and age squared, sex and diploma (nine categories). $N = 441$, except for the last row where $N = 115$. *$p < 0.1$, **$p < 0.01$, ***$p < 0.001$.

Employees are aware of this fragility and of the possible removal of those devices through renegotiations. Among those transferring to new jobs and subject to such retentions, 42% successfully negotiated their removal, 21% renegotiated unsuccessfully and 37% did not renegotiate. Among the workers who did not move, 40% think that it is possible to obtain the removal of the retention devices, 54% find those devices somewhat annoying but not enough to prevent departure, and only 4% think that they really inhibit mobility. Long notices of departure are quite easy to remove (I estimate that the rate of successful removal is 60%) and it is quite common in the financial industry to exempt the worker from respecting her notice of departure once she finds a job elsewhere. However, non-compete clauses and deferred bonuses do not represent a significant hurdle either, with 35% of successful renegotiation.

Although the employees who can more easily move their workforce and the assets they have acquired are also those that the firm will try the hardest to retain, those people are, by various means, the most successful in circumventing retention devices. Renegotiation with the firm is not a highly abstract process. It generally takes place with the supervisor and sometimes with the latter's line manager. Someone departing to a new firm with assets and collaboration ties could be, for many of her contacts, a person worth following immediately, worth doing business with in the future or worth collaborating with again a few years later. Far from being a scapegoat that everyone will try to punish, the employee leaving with assets is like a magnet to whom everybody wants to remain connected. In a regression (Table 7.1, two last rows), I estimate the impact of moveable workforce and of moveable assets on the probability of successfully renegotiating the removal of retention devices. Moving workforce or moving financial assets such as knowledge or clients significantly increases the likelihood of success.[12]

Clearly, though some types of protection in question – such as non-compete clauses or deferred bonuses – can have real effects (effects that the banks have only recently begun to realise and test), they also have limitations, and they do not seem capable of ensuring the total protection of a company's assets and preventing the financial operators in charge of those assets from appropriating rent from them. The individuation process underway in financial work and accounting is surely a significant obstacle to determining effective protection measures. There is an increasing tendency to forget the fact that key assets are continually being ceded to employees. Hold-ups may elicit indignation. However employees are still individually credited with the profits generated by the assets they hold. "He earned it, he deserves it!" exclaimed the head of back office at Neptune Bank, referring to the head of equity derivatives in the above-cited case, even though the speaker himself was one of the first victims of the derivative head's further promotion. The symbolic hierarchy of what is understood as individual merit simultaneously confirms and veils the economic foundations of this domination. And even if the truth of this unequal economic exchange were to become fully evident, it would be difficult for the actors concerned to protect themselves from its effects.

Annex

Outline of a simple hold-up model

By making limited changes to the Grout model (Grout 1984; Malcomson 1997), I adapted it to employee relations in the financial industry and characterised the profit-capturing power acquired by financial operators. My model considers a risk-neutral financial firm during a particular economic period at the end of which it sells financial products. It employs L financial operators, all identical, such as financial products salespeople, who have a linear utility function in income (and are therefore risk-neutral). On date 0, the firm signs a work contract – incomplete on account of its uncertainty – with an employee it hires for ω_0 wages in order to train her as a financial operator. The firm invests K amount in marketing financial products. When the two parties observe both K the capital invested and s the state of the world, they may on date r decide to renegotiate the contract.

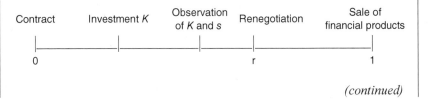

(continued)

(continued)

Profit π at the end of the period is expressed as the difference between the sale of financial products $F(L, K, s)$ and the input cost, wage costs ωL and investment cost K.

$$\pi = F(L, K, s) - \omega.L - K \qquad (1)$$

To simplify, the renegotiation applies to wage ω_R only and does not impact the capital K and the level of employment L.

It is supposed that the employee can resell to another employer a fraction γ of the profits, that is $\gamma. F(L, K, s)/L$.

When the employee leaves, the firm only retains a fraction β of the profit, that is $\beta. F(L, K, s)/L$, first because that profit is partly redeployed externally and second on account of the costs of disorganisation and retraining a new employee in financial techniques and routines.

To gauge the outcome of the renegotiation, I use a generalised Nash equilibrium[13]. In the event that the negotiation breaks down on date r, the employee may obtain $[w.t_{r-1} + \gamma.F(L, K, s)/L]$ elsewhere, in other words the market wage for the remaining time period t_{r-1} plus the part γ of the profits which she "sells" to her new employer. She must, however, bear a syncretic mobility cost C (risk cost, psychological cost, cost of professional retraining, etc.). Similarly, if the negotiation breaks down, the firm will gain the fraction β of the sale of the financial products. The Nash solution can be written as follows:

$$\underset{\omega_R}{Max}(\omega_R - (w.t_{r-1} + \gamma.F(K, L, s)/L - C))^\alpha. \ (F(L, K, s)/L - \omega_R - \beta.F(K, L, s)/L)^{1-\alpha} \qquad (2)$$

This programme finds a solution when the first derivative of (2) in ω_R is null:

$$\omega_R{}^* = (w.t_{r-1} + \gamma.F(K, L, s)/L - C) + \alpha. \ ((1 - \beta - \gamma). F(L, K, s)/L - w.t_{r-1} + C) \qquad (3)$$

The employee therefore receives both compensation from her external option (market salary plus sale of redeployable profit) minus the mobility cost $[w.t_{r-1} + \gamma.F(L, K, s)/L - C]$, and in keeping with her bargaining power, part of the residual profit from the continuation of the relation $[\alpha. (1 - \beta - \gamma). F(L, K, s)/L - w.t_{r-1} + C]$.

In my model, the employee's hold-up power does not lie so much in her intrinsic bargaining power α as in her capacity to capture part of the investment and redeploy it elsewhere. Thus, even when α is zero, the employee captures at least the fraction γ of the yield.

The employee's compensation over the whole period is therefore equal to $(\omega_0 + \omega_R)$. The profit the employee receives depends on how ω_0 is established. If the firm has not anticipated the hold-up configuration on date 0, the rent captured unexpectedly by the employee will be at the maximum level because on date 0 it pays the employee market wage w and because the level of investment is at its maximum:

$$\omega = (w.t_{0-t} + \gamma.F(K, L, s)/L - C + \alpha. ((1 - \beta - \gamma). (F(L, K, s)/L - w.t_{r-1} + C \qquad (4)$$

Notes

1 In an actual hold-up, the leverage is the firearm, the disaster is death and the demand is for the contents of the cash register.
2 Shareholders are indirectly harmed by the destabilising nature of the new distribution method and the risk of having to increase the bonus pool that funds this activity.
3 The second effect of the hold-up model, the one that generally attracts the most attention, is that it results in suboptimal levels of investment (Hart and Moore 1988) and, in some cases, suboptimal employment rates (Cahuc *et al.* 2014, pp. 445–448).
4 An exchange broker recounts how he followed a "pal" to another brokerage firm and was ultimately "fooled" by promises of career prospects. "I left for less than what I was getting (fixed wage plus a percentage), thinking that since they were going to develop the department, my percentage was going to soar . . . It's true that I left because I let them talk me into believing there were real development possibilities. That was what I wanted to hear. I'm so naive!" Nevertheless, his contribution was modest: a slight fall in wages (partially compensated for by his "best year" two years later).
5 On this point see also Hart and Moore's demonstration that dual specific investment can lead to suboptimal contract relations (Hart and Moore 1988).
6 In June and July 2000, HR professionals each had a small file containing the papers sent in by the centres and dated 1 June 2000, giving the following starting salary ranges for graduates of the main universities and business schools: *École Polytechnique*: 35–40,000 euros; ESCP, HEC, ESSEC: 30–35,000 euros, etc. HR professionals complained that the document was not up to date and that they had to set starting wages that were higher than the indicated ranges.
7 At the ENSAE (*École Nationale de la Statistique et de l'Administration Économique*) in the late 1990s it was very common for students to work part-time in their third year. The study program was explicitly designed to allow for this kind of combined work/study.
8 See, for example, the studies made by Edlin and Reichelstein (1996) on the efficiency of contracts that enable charges to be incurred in line with anticipated damages.
9 The Court of Cassation ruling of 18 September 2002 states that a judge can limit the scope of a non-compete clause if it prevents "an employee from practising an activity consistent with his training and professional experience by limiting its application and its effect in time and space or its other terms and conditions" (Vatinet 2002b).
10 Cf. Bear, Stearns & Co., Inc. v. Sharon, 550 F.Supp. 2d 174 (D. Mass. 2008).
11 Partnerships have similar effects and limitations as deferred bonuses. In a partnership, partners, as long as they stay in the firm, earn the profit of the firm corresponding to the share of capital they own. This profit flow helps to substantially diminish turnover and assets transfer. However, most financial partnerships went public in the 1980s and the 1990s, because old partners wanted to resell their preferred stock at its market price rather than at its bought value (Auletta 1986).

12 In the last column, when I restrict the estimation to the population subjected to retention devices, the parameter is positive, but due to the small size of the sample (n = 115) and the important number of control variables (k = 17), the parameter is not significant. It is worth noting that without those control variables, correlation between successful renegotiation and my combined index of moveable assets is positive and significant (Godechot 2013).

13 This problem was solved as follows. A solution to the negotiation was sought that would maximise the outcome (offset by bargaining power α) of the differences for the two players between the value of a solution and the value of a failed negotiation: $\text{Max}_{\text{solution}} (U_{\text{solution}} - U_{\text{failure}})^{\alpha} (V_{\text{solution}} - V_{\text{failure}})^{1-\alpha}$ (Cahuc *et al.* 2014, pp. 445–448).

References

Auletta, K 1986, *Greed and Glory on Wall Street. The Fall of the House of Lehman*, Random House, New York.

Bessy, C 2009, 'L'usage des clauses de non-concurrence dans les contrats de travail', *Revue d'économie industrielle*, n°125, pp. 9–40.

Cahuc, P, Carcillo, S, Zylberberg, A and McCuaig, W 2014, *Labor Economics*, MIT Press, Cambridge MA.

Carmichael, H 1990, 'Efficiency Wage Models of Unemployment – One View', *Economic Inquiry*, vol. 28, n°2, pp. 269–295.

Crozier, M and Friedberg, E 1980 *Actors and Systems: The Politics of Collective Action*, University of Chicago Press, Chicago IL.

DA Kreuter 2013, *Garden Leave Study*, December, http://www.dakassociates.com/garden-leave-study-june-2012/, accessed 1 April 2016.

EBA 2015, *Report on Benchmarking of Remuneration and on High Earners 2013*, 7 September, http://www.eba.europa.eu/documents/10180/950548/Report+on+Benchmarking+of+Remuneration+and+on+High+Earners+2013.pdf, accessed 1 April 2016.

Edlin, A and S Reichelstein 1996. "Holdups, Standard Breach Remedies and Investment," *American Economic Review*, vol. 86, n°3, pp. 478–501.FSB 2009, *FSB Principles for Sound Compensation Practices. Implementation Standards*, 25 September, http://www.fsb.org/wp-content/uploads/r_090925c.pdf?page_moved=1, accessed 1 April 2010.

Gilson, R 1999, 'Legal Infrastructure of High Technology Industrial Districts: Silicon Valley, Route 128, and Covenants Not to Compete', *New-York University Law Review, vol.* 74, n°3, pp. 575–629.

Godechot, O 2001, *Les Traders. Essai de sociologie des marchés financiers*, La Découverte, Paris.

Godechot, O 2013, 'Can the Immobile Stop the Mobile?', *Economic Sociology, the European Electronic Newsletter*, vol. 14, n°3, pp. 27–33.

Godechot, O 2014, 'Getting a Job in Finance. The Role of Collaboration Ties', *European Journal of Sociology*, vol. 55, n°1, pp. 25–56.

Grout, P 1984, 'Investment and Wages in the Absence of Binding Contracts', *Econometrica*, vol. 52, n°2, pp. 755–785.

Hart, O and Moore, J 1988, 'Incomplete Contracts and Renegotiation', *Econometrica*, vol. 56, n°4, pp. 755–785.

Klein, B, Crawford, R and Alchian, A 1978, 'Vertical Integration, Appropriable Rents and the Competitive Contracting Process', *Journal of Law and Economics*, vol. 21, n°2, pp. 297–326.

Lazar, W 2008, 'Employment Agreements and Cross Border Employment Confidentiality, Trade Secret, and Other Restrictive Covenants in a Global Economy', *The Labor Lawyer*, vol. 24, n°2, pp. 195–211.

Malcomson, J 1997, 'Contracts, Hold-Up, and Labor Markets', *Journal of Economic Literature*, vol. 35, n°4, pp. 1916–1957.

Ortiz, H 2005, 'Évaluer, apprécier: les relations entre les brokers et gérants de fonds d'investissement', *Économie rurale*, n°286–287, pp. 57–71.

Ortiz, H 2014, *Valeur financière et vérité: Enquête d'anthropologie politique sur l'évaluation des entreprises cotées en Bourse*, Presses de Sciences Po, Paris.

Rajan, R and Zingales, L 1998, 'Power in a Theory of the Firm', *Quarterly Journal of Economics*, vol. 133, n°2, pp. 387–432.

Rajan, R and Zingales, L 2001, 'The Firm as a Dedicated Hierarchy: A Theory of the Origins and Growth of the Firm', *Quarterly Journal of Economics*, vol. 136, n°3, pp. 805–851.

Stole, L and Zwiebel, J 1996, 'Intra-firm Bargaining under Non-binding Contracts', *The Review of Economic Studies*, vol. 63, n°3, pp. 375–410.

Vatinet, R 2002a, 'Clause de non-concurrence. Champ d'application. Réduction', *Droit social*, n°11, November, pp. 1007–1008.

Vatinet, R 2002b, 'Les conditions de validité des clauses de non-concurrence: l'imbroglio', *Droit social*, n°11, November, pp. 949–954.

Williamson, O 1985, *The Economic Institutions of Capitalism*, The Free Press, New York.

8   The labour market as asset transfer

In the mechanism described in the previous chapter, I simplified matters by taking for granted the renegotiation outcome. Indeed, renegotiations occur and are not seen as signs of disloyalty. Headhunters know that such practices are common in the financial industry and that the hiring process can be brought to a halt in its final stages by last-minute renegotiation with a former employer.[1] One director of a headhunting firm specialised in finance mentioned that roughly one employee in ten renegotiates with his former employer rather than going to work for the new one.

The option to renegotiate plays a structuring role in the financial services job market. However, the process is not systematic. Two firms might have different estimations of the value implied in a transfer and, in such a case, the firm that the employee is leaving or threatening to leave will make no effort to retain its operator. This is particularly true when the recruiting firm overestimates the volume of business the employee will bring with her, as Groysberg has shown often happens with star financial analysts (Groysberg 2010). Generally, the employee who is resigning refuses to be put up for auction, preferring to leave straightforwardly rather than engage in a bargaining process that may feel degrading. Even in the world of finance, many people prefer to avoid transforming personal relations into market relations. Thus, renegotiation, when it does take place, is usually on the firm's initiative; that is, the initiative of the employee's former line managers.

For all these reasons, the labour market in this sector is very active and transfers are frequent. On the basis of data provided by Jupiter Bank, it can be estimated that 16% to 17% of traders and salespeople left that bank at some point in 1999, a year of expansion characterised by a high level of recruitment. Thanks to the online survey with efinancialcareers.fr, I estimated just before Lehman Brothers' bankruptcy that 25% of employees working in finance changed jobs each year. This industry-wide proportion is much larger than that found for either French employees (7%), or for French managers and professionals (Amossé 2003). After five years, 65% of French financial operators had changed employers. The flourishing activity in this market hardly makes it the model of a perfect job market, however.

Operators do not leave by themselves. When they resign, they remove their physical person, which had been a repository of assets that give those operators great value on the job market. They also leave with information, knowledge and know-how. They leave with clients and teams. The financial labour market is, therefore, composed of a fundamentally dual structure: it consists of a market of individuals *and* a market for what those individuals take away with them. What accounts for the value of a transfer lies more in the assets transferred than in the intrinsic skills of the individuals who hold those assets.

> Former CEO of the Bankers' Trust Charles Sanford, revisiting his experience of the transformation of the bank into an investment bank, makes a very similar observation:
> "The problem with having innovation and ideas at the centre of your business as opposed to, say automobiles, is that your capital is made up of people rather than physical inventory. *Your assets walk out the door at the end of every day.* And there is no copyright or patent protection available to ensure that employees cannot take their ideas and talents to another firm and start competing with you. This is especially easy on Wall Street because changing jobs often doesn't mean uprooting your family and leaving your friends. It simply means walking across the street."
>
> (Sanford 1996, p. 17)

To understand how the financial industry job market is first and foremost a market for assets produced by group investments – and to thereby explain why it is not correlated with surrounding job markets – I will first detail the different ways an individual may move these assets. Second, I will show how these transfers come about in the framework of a Malthusian market that also contributes to wage increases.

Moving assets

Extensions of the physical person

Financial knowledge is probably the most fully incorporated element in the financial production process. The focus on skills and human capital in scientific literature over the last four decades has led researchers to seek out the individual foundations of social orders. We should, of course, analyse all the implications of the individual dimension of knowledge. It generates individuation, belief in the individual origin of profit and a legitimation of the demand for profit and profit capture. Still, it is important not to forget the collective origin of this individuated knowledge, which is acquired through on-the-job training in a collective environment. To judge the effectiveness of pay policies based on individuated knowledge, it is necessary to ask whether the constituting of that knowledge was actually paid for by the individuals who become productive thanks to that process.

In *Les Traders*, I described the space of winning strategies in which financial operators move (Godechot 2001). Those strategies amount for the most part to practical knowledge. Even when this knowledge is highly formalised, as is the case with mathematical arbitrage, these operators still develop the practical knowledge required for using those mathematical models. In the noisy environment of the non-partitioned trading room with its lack of privacy, knowledge circulates in complex ways. For example, during the morning meeting, knowledge flows, circulates and sedimentates.

However, the trading room is hardly an ideal communication society where knowledge is fully shared. Two antithetical types of behaviour play a role in establishing that knowledge: withholding knowledge and divulging it distinctively. As in many highly competitive environments, it is advantageous to know what others do not yet know. Revealing knowledge to someone can also be a means of establishing one's authority over a person. Being the source of a valued piece of information provides a form of "distinction" that can strengthen a person's position within the trading room's symbolic hierarchy. While financial operators may balk at sharing knowledge or information with colleagues from other desks, they often will share it within the same desk. This is because a collective constitution of that knowledge is facilitated through rivalry among senior operators in an attempt to establish authority (during the morning meeting "jousts", for example), as well as through friendships among operators. One common channel of information distribution occurs between a mentor and a mentee, often a desk senior showing someone more junior the ropes of the job in exchange for affection and loyalty (Lewis 1989, pp. 204–217).

Employees who own a durable monopoly on fruitful financial assets benefit the most from accessing a collectively constituted knowledge. To provide a sense of the relationship between capturing collective knowledge and individual profit, I shall take the borderline example of the divulgation of a valuable secret. In simplified terms, financial strategies like arbitrage techniques, conception and mastery of a new financial product, or developing a statistical arbitrage formula can each be seen as a small secret (of differing quality) used to generate profit.

However, these productive secrets – the ideal type being the statistical arbitrage model – cannot be protected by a system of patents and intellectual property rights as in the pharmaceutical industry. Using a secret to one's advantage is a delicate matter and can hardly go on for long. Any employee who is party to the secret – regardless of her contribution to its discovery or whether she used it productively – can sell it to a competitor at its marginal value and thereby weaken its productivity (Zábojník 2002). When a trader working on statistical arbitrage discovers a recurrent anomaly in market prices (such as a correlation between the stock prices of two firms in the same sector), this of course enables her to make a prediction. However, she can only earn money with her "thing" as long as it remains a secret. Divulging the information would lead, through a simple arbitrage mechanism, to the elimination of the arbitrage opportunity.[2] By leaving to work for the competition, any member of her team could sell this lucrative knowledge externally, increasing exploitation of it and thereby hastening its disappearance. Moreover, competition on the labour market is highly effective in diffusing knowledge of arbitrage opportunities and thereby causing them to disappear. "If I had no competitors, the model I developed two years ago would still be working and making huge profits today," exclaimed one trader specialised in statistical arbitrage.

Mastering an innovative financial product is a kind of knowledge similar to the "open sesame" that will open the thieves' cave. When a sophisticated new financial product such as an exotic option or a structured product is launched on the market and the team in charge makes the effort required to master the mathematical price-setting formulas and the relevant dedicated software while learning how the product behaves in practical terms and what its commercial value is, that team acquires a monopoly power that one of its members could in turn sell externally. Mastering strategic assets becomes more important to the exchange than the asset holder's intrinsic skill. One headhunter I interviewed recalled how a client of hers who wanted to hire a trader working within a particular product area would only settle for "a person from Saturn Bank"; "beyond that, he didn't care whether it was x or y". Since Saturn Bank dominated the market for that type of product, the best way its competitor could think of getting a foothold in the market was to hire an operator from Saturn.

The transfer between firms of incorporated assets, such as knowledge, techniques and know-how, is often accompanied by the transfer of more clearly external assets. In 2002 a trader specialised in convertible bonds brought with him a laptop computer containing pricing software and programs for handling derivatives – a whole set of computer routines which he then made available to his new desk. Two traders in high frequency trading (an activity relying exclusively on automatic algorithms), Sergey Aleynikov at Goldman Sachs in 2009 and Samarth Agrawal at Société Générale in 2010, were found copying or printing algorithms in order to transfer them from their previous employer to their new one (Demos 2010; Lewis 2014). As algorithms are protected by intellectual property law in contrast to most financial techniques, the two were sentenced to jail for code theft. Yet for every legal condemnation, we may suspect many more successful transfers of assets, remaining invisible and/or non-prosecutable.

Financial operators bring with them a whole range of assets. This includes both practical and technical knowledge, a range of organisational and computer routines, pricing software and client databases, as well as colleagues and clients. While traders move around with a whole set of disparate types of market knowledge and organisational and computer routines, salespeople are also known for transferring their address books. Analysts, and particularly star analysts, whose fame is the complex dual product of the press and the financial community, bring with them clients and fame. They often possess both clients and good rankings from clients, two factors that are having an increasing impact on the orientation of brokerage flows.[3] When we move from financial operators (traders, sales) to financial engineers, quants, and above all risk controllers and back office administrators, we encounter people who, though certainly knowledgeable, control a smaller share of the collective assets. While front office operators control detachable assets that could almost be sold externally by themselves, middle and back office actors usually have a much smaller repository of moveable assets.

They may have control over assets such as computer programs, mathematical models and settlement-and-delivery systems, but these assets are merely the cogs of a greater organisational whole that exceeds them and, as such, are not readily transferable.

Seeing the labour market as an assets market thus makes it possible to understand the hierarchy of financial jobs and the reason why, within financial operator professions, the value of a job fluctuates if not with the market prices at least with the activity prevailing in the micro-market in which these operators are specialised.

Collective departure as a profitable takeover bid

Job market transfers do not always take the simple, paradigmatic form of selling knowledge of where the treasure trove is hidden. Since the secret of rents is complex and based on highly disparate elements that includes clients, organisation, knowledge and know-how, a transfer through mere displacement of an employee is highly unlikely to be complete and will tend to involve some loss of the total initial asset. The collective departure of an existing team is a means of endowing the transfer with greater value and thereby containing that loss. Taken together, the components of the team as a whole are worth more than they would be as a sum of separate parts. For instance, Groysberg and his co-authors have shown that while financial analysts generally suffer a loss of reputation when they move alone from one firm to another, this is not the case when they move in teams with other colleagues (Groysberg, Lee and Nanda 2008). In the financial industry, moving in teams and hiring teams are quite common phenomena. For instance, Frank Quattrone in Private Equity is reported to have moved from Morgan Stanley to Deutsche Bank Securities with eight colleagues in 1996 and to have then moved again with two other bankers and their 100-strong team in 1998 to Crédit Suisse (Hamm and Burrows 2003). Team moves are also at the origin of most hedge funds (MacKenzie 2003). From an Internet survey launched with efinancialcareers.fr in September 2008, I found that 14% of those who changed job in the financial industry had later helped to hire former colleagues and that 15% of them had already moved in teams (Table 8.1). Although the collective aspect of financial recruitment is generally limited to small numbers (a team of two or three members) and does not include the most spectacular ones, its prevalence makes it worth investigating further. Moreover, Groysberg and his co-authors remark that investment bankers commonly refer to this as "block trading in people". Of the 366 analyst moves collected in their database, 100 are team moves involving colleagues categorised as "other ranked analysts, junior analysts, institutional salespeople, and traders". This figure is all the more impressive since the job of financial analyst would not at first sight appear to be team-based, at least compared to other jobs such as traders or salespeople.

This characteristic gives social relations, and particularly work relations, a strategic importance. The financial industry is sometimes presented as a jungle where everyone is permanently at war with everyone else – the noisy juxtaposition of individual solitudes, a recurring theme in Rozan's novel (Rozan 1999). The alternative vision of a world of personal relations, insider tips and pals is one more regularly used to denounce the "mafias" of the finance world. Although this vision can certainly become a caricature, in many ways it more accurately depicts the reality of the financial world.

Although the cult of friendship is not an explicit theme, the presence and importance of professional friendships is a point that comes through loud and clear in the interviews. In particular and perhaps more than elsewhere the effect of friendship plays an important role in the functioning of the job market.[4] Even among financial operators who say they make a point of distancing themselves from their professional world, refusing to be assimilated with their colleagues and the mercantile, opportunistic, mundane world of money, we find market-related friendships that play a combined social, affective and economic role:

> We were making a lot of money, and the ECU really took off – it was astounding . . . Then we were approached by another firm. Somebody I'd known before, somebody came out to me and said . . . "Come and work with us and do ECU!" So there were the four of us, there was the guy called Burny, there was Dave, my best friend in the market, and Angus . . . We had lunch together and talked things over. It would double our wages! It would get us really nice cars, and a chance to travel in Europe. So yeah, we took it in the end, and the four of us went. And at that time, I was on about 17 or 18 thousand pounds a year . . . And they offered me about 40 thousand pounds to join them.
>
> (Steve, ECU salesperson in the 1980s in London,
> Godechot 2001, p. 147–148)

The way social relations operate in the financial labour market is particularly complex. Weak ties, whose importance was stressed by Mark Granovetter (1973), do of course play an important role. They serve to circulate singular, original information which strong ties, often involving redundant contact, are less likely to circulate. Relations with superiors in finance are not always warm (though often they are). In these professions where the hierarchy is relatively flat (the links in the chain are operators, team managers and heads of trading room), managers and more junior staff are potentially in competition with each other. Lower-level staff wait for their managers to resign or move up, while senior staff may dread juniors' master strokes or attempts to resign. Financial operators' straight talk and crude language are well known; they blame each other in rough terms that people would find shocking in any other sector.

Nevertheless, while this behaviour is visible and striking to any observer accustomed to the more univocal circulation of discontent found in large organisational hierarchies, it is counterbalanced by the importance of maintaining ties. An operator who has decided to resign knows that her former manager and especially her colleagues, with whom she has never had particularly warm relations, will remain her market partners in financial transactions – they will continue to furnish products, clients, exchanges – and that they will also remain her partners on the job market. Indeed, former colleagues are sometimes used by headhunting firms as "sources" on that market, to certify former colleagues' results and performance or give an opinion on their personality. And former colleagues are highly likely to not only run into each other again on this ultimately tight-knit job market, but are likely to follow each other and end up working together again one, two or three years later in the same organisation. In this way, the importance of weak ties is preserved on this job market as a vehicle for the circulation of information.

However, because of their productive efficiency,[5] strong ties too remain extremely important, particularly those formed on the job. Friendly relations that boost financial co-production within a team constitute economic modes of productive "matching". Familiarity, common knowledge, the shared experience of organisational modes, knowledge of the implicit limits of each person's domain of activity, trust, cooperative goodwill and the limiting of competition are all qualities that allow the team to be more productive as a group and thus give it much greater power to move and sell itself as a team on the job market.[6]

There are many accounts of group moves: collective team departures, group resignations, scaled regroupings and buying back teams. Well before moving to Orion Bank in London, the aforementioned convertible bonds trader made an attempt to leave Titan brokerage firm with a colleague–friend and negotiate a collective hire using a headhunter in a bank that had no convertible bond business at the time and was keen to acquire one. "Setting up a desk, that's everyone's dream," he explained. It was seen as an opportunity to break free from the head of desk, a person no one really trusted, and create the activity from scratch on virgin territory. Not only was this an exciting intellectual experience in that it broke with the repetition of financial transactions and kindled the hope of major gains if the activity took off and multiplied, but it allowed members of the group to imagine themselves as becoming team managers, heads of room, heads of department: in other words, internal entrepreneurs with a financial mushroom pushing up beneath them. Yet for the trader in question, the negotiation ultimately failed. Surprised that his headhunter was not calling, he found out that the bank in question had acquired a team from Mars Bank instead. In the end, he and his friend from the brokerage firm only managed to find positions in London separately in existing convertible bond teams, one in a major American bank, the other in a hedge fund.

Close co-productive relations in finance are a strong asset not only when it comes to leaving as an existing team but also for setting up full-scale financial enterprises, particularly hedge funds. The extremely high bonuses distributed in the early 2000s, together with favourable financial organisation, encouraged the formation of hedge funds, organisations in which financial operators can become even more autonomous and allow them to independently increase the value of the assets they have captured within the financial organisation. For example, the trader from Sirius Bank mentioned in the previous chapter, was in spring 2002 manoeuvring to get himself fired so as to collect a large share package. He was aiming to set up a hedge fund with a friend from his bank and hire ten or so colleagues and friends from that same bank.[7] "What interested me is that we got along really well," he explained.

Strong, cohesive relations make it possible to develop a stable, mobile core which ultimately attracts – like a flame passing from candle to candle, from managers to subordinates, from subordinates to their closest colleagues – all the activity in a given market department. This is why the unity of the trading room management and the quality of relations between the head and her direct lieutenants are so important in determining the head's bargaining power. The hold-up by the two heads of trading room analysed in Chapter 6 was successful because they were threatening to recruit all their former teams once they had got things running at the rival bank. They were not necessarily friends with all the traders and salespeople in their rooms, but they had enough confidence in the quality of their relations with their heads of desk, and the quality of relations between those heads of desk and their staff, to believe they could recruit perhaps not the entire trading room but at least the most useful, productive part.

In some cases, moving teams by buying them up or establishing a new business actually amounts to displacing business activities and even transferring an entire firm. The job market can therefore stand as an alternative to the stock market in the acquisition of financial firms or their departments. With respect to immaterial assets, in the extreme hypothetical case of the whole set of employees leaving one company for another, the company itself would change hands without any exchange of shares on the stock market.

The head of Neptune Bank's capital markets department recounted that one of her English "market-making" teams collectively resigned and left for Mars Bank when she tried to impose a "RAROC threshold" on the collective bonus formula – in other words a risk-adjusted remuneration of capital threshold below which the trading team would not receive any bonus: "They were told, 'We're going to put a RAROC threshold on the bonus formula.' 'Fine!' they said, and they all left . . . They left together for Mars Bank which didn't have enough market makers at the time . . . They all left – 50 of them. Even the ones on holiday sent in their letters of resignation."

In *Homme du marché*, Lepetit, former Deputy Chief Executive of Indosuez, offers a highly detailed description of a team-purchasing operation (Lepetit 2002, pp. 115–117). In March 1990, Lepetit met Richard Sandor at a cocktail party. As Drexel Burnham Lambert had just gone bankrupt, Sandor was in the process of negotiating with another French bank for the sale of three complete teams, which he had previously headed, totalling 60 staff. The first was in swaps activities, the second in structured operations, and the third in futures in Chicago. Sandor thought Indosuez was already very active in derivative products and therefore would not be interested in taking on the teams. He nonetheless suggested to Lepetit that they strike a deal over the weekend before giving the other bank an answer. With the CEO's support, Lepetit left with a few collaborators and lawyers to negotiate a contract "in the finest Wall Street tradition of merger–acquisition operations":

The coach negotiated with us. When we had agreed on one point, he left to consult with his three heads of team, who then got in touch with their troops. . . . On Sunday at about 5pm I called AJG to tell him I was ready to close on wages and two-year guaranteed bonuses amounting to 40 million dollars, a sum totally out of line with what we were used to. The contract also stipulated the bonus distribution; the team heads, and especially the coach, had planned hefty bonuses for themselves.

(Lepetit 2002, p. 117)

Lepetit recounted this incident when he was interviewed in 2001, adding: "I thought I had done a very good deal because I was buying a business, not goodwill,[8] and the only thing I had to pay for was the people." Buying up teams as described here does indeed resemble buying up activities, and it cannot be equated to mere hiring. When the team is sold as a pre-existing, productive team, it acquires much greater value than the sum of individual transactions. To take advantage of this leverage effect, Sandor used three features of the situation: his camaraderie with Lepetit (they had already worked together to launch Indosuez's options department in New York in the mid-1980s), the competition between two rival banks, and the fact that the allotted bargaining time was so short. What appears just as determinant in the transaction, however, is the centralised nature of the negotiation. Sandor brought in and represented the group, and gained an advantage for both the entire group and himself. A year later, however, when Sandor's role as team provider and unifier was less salient, his lieutenants revolted and brought him down like pirates throwing overboard their captain who had become too greedy when the booty was being shared out. "The funniest thing about it all is that Richard Sandor was thrown out. By whom? Not by me! By those guys!" commented Lepetit bluntly in our interview. Having the power to bring entire teams along during employee movements on the job market did not prevent the representative of one of those subordinate teams, when an opportunity presents itself, from trying to turn that power to his own advantage and to the detriment of the first go-between. Although in terms of content and process there is nothing military or feudal about relations in the financial industry, they do have points in common with political–military relations in the early Middle Ages (Lebecq 1990). Being at the head of a hierarchically ordered set of relations does of course mean having a certain amount of power, but that power is never fully safe from felonious attack or from being undermined by scissiparity.

While collective hiring can indeed be seen as a kind of transfer of activities, or another way of implementing an acquisitions policy or a kind of cheap takeover, the gain involved in this kind of transfer is perhaps lower for the firm that buys an existing group than for the group that has a monopoly over the rents of its own activity. By buying an existing group, the firm integrates a close-knit team into a new, larger whole with which that team shares fewer solder points than it did with the whole from which it extricated itself. It is therefore more mobile and detachable than it was in the previous configuration, and teams often use this leverage effect to obtain either internal or external advantages. This is why replacing the team that had left for Mars Bank by one from Uranus Bank, as the head of capital markets did, or even buying an activity as a whole, as in the case of Lepetit, is not necessarily a good deal for the firm. Investments in this new entity might not be as lasting as they would have been if they had been made in a collective composed of employees gradually hired one by one and coming into their first job. The three teams hired by Lepetit left Indosuez after two to three years, which Lepetit put down to bad luck (Lepetit 2002, p. 117).

Firms do not always gain from buying teams that already exist, and may even suffer further defections. The teams, on the other hand, capture a larger relative share of the financial profit when they sell themselves as a ready-made unit. The survey carried out in 2008 on the website efinancialcareers.fr showed that the capacity to bring along a team is, all things being equal, closely linked to higher wages (Table 8.1): total compensation increases by 10% per former colleague recruited. Based on this estimation, a head of desk who hires his whole team of ten employees increases her wages by 100%. Hence, because the two heads of a trading room, as seen in my previous hold-up case study, had the potential to move 100 traders and salespersons, they could multiply their wages five-fold.

Moving individuated assets and moving collaborations

To go one step further, I will therefore draw a distinction between two types of transferable assets analysed in the two previous subsections. The first type is constituted of those assets that may be individually appropriated and transferred. They can be human assets such as knowledge, know-how or routines; electronic assets such as algorithms, software, databases or even computers; and social assets such as reputation, contacts and clients. I call these *moveable individuated assets*. The second type is more fuzzy, but no less essential. It is rooted in work collaborations and involves past and present co-workers inside and outside the firm. When two employees produce more together than separately, they have a clear interest in continuing, moving or resuming their collaboration. I will therefore talk of *moveable collaboration ties* for those moveable assets that consist in collaborations and need some coordination between co-workers in order to acquire value.

Moveable collaboration ties are more likely to be significant when two persons linked together share a common individuated asset (for example a client), when they organise a division of labour in order to exploit and value this shared asset and when it is possible to move this asset from one firm to another. In such cases, when moving together, they move a much larger fraction (per capita) of the shared asset than when moving separately. What is more, moveable collaboration ties also demultiply beyond shared assets the quantity of individuated assets moved. Therefore, I expect *moveable individuated assets and moveable collaboration ties to be highly correlated.*

As shown in previous chapters, moveable assets are not evenly distributed throughout the financial firm. They are to be found at the core of the financial markets in front office positions. The first reason for this is that front office jobs are highly specialised and their incumbents enjoy great autonomy. An employee is more likely to appropriate an individuated asset if she has been working long term with such assets. Strong autonomy and high specialisation also favour the creation of strong, long-term collaboration ties and a close-knit team ready to defect. The final reason is that the organisation of work is fairly standardised in front offices whereas it is more firm-specific in support departments. The more similar the organisations, the easier it is to move assets and to value them inside a new environment. Therefore, my second hypothesis states that *working in front office favours the accumulation of both moveable individuated assets and moveable collaboration ties.*

Previously, I have explained how the ability to move assets in finance increases wages. In addition to personal, original skills, the market also values what an employee takes away from previous jobs and brings with her. The pay premium for this input can be achieved either when the employee moves to another firm, when she successfully renegotiates a pay increase in order not to move – as in the hold-up case – or when the firm matches on its own initiative the pay level that will keep her from moving. Moreover, according to the findings of Groysberg, Lee and Nanda (2008), firms that are trying to poach a financial analyst frequently overestimate the assets the financial analyst is moving, and overbid in order to get the full package. These two arguments, i.e. that of assets-moving and over-bidding, converge in the case of mobile financial operatives. Therefore, I lastly assume that *the moving of individuated assets, collaboration ties and notably the combination of these two dimensions all increase wages.*

To provide statistical evidence of my claims regarding asset transferability in the financial industry, I will rely here on the online survey launched with *efinancialcareers.fr*. This survey, compiled in September 2008, particularly targeted French financial employees who had recently moved from one firm to another.

Asking questions on moveable individuated assets held by employees is not an easy task since the concepts are highly abstract and may sound unfamiliar to the respondents; moreover, employees may not always be conscious that in a sense they can appropriate assets from the firm. For this reason, I have tried to find a proxy by asking some questions on the elements that were at stake during their last move (Table 8.1, question A). I interpret the last four answers of this question as a proxy of the individuated assets held by the employees. If the reason for the recruitment was to bring something "new" to their employer, whether that be "new techniques", "new clients", "new strategies" or "new business", it is most likely that those assets were based on assets acquired during their career in finance. In order to measure collaboration ties, I rely mainly on three questions concerning the role of contacts during their last recruitment (Table 8.1, questions C, D, E). Being hired in a service where one already knows a former colleague or business partner, moving in teams and hiring former colleagues are clear examples of collaboration ties. Those cases reveal situations where people are somehow more productive when they work with contacts with whom they are used to collaborating than they are with other colleagues, whether they share

Table 8.1 Assets moved in finance and their link with front office positions and total pay

Questions		Items	Freq.	Net impact of front office positions on variables A to G (n = 441)	Net impact of variables A to G on current total pay (n = 429)
A	What was at stake during your last recruitment? (n = 489)	1 Replacing someone	27%	×1.1	−10%
		2 Strengthening a team	55%	×0.8	+4%
		3 Bringing new techniques	21%	×1.8*	+3%
		4 Bringing new clients	7%	×3.7***	+17%(*)
		5 Providing new strategies	11%	×1.3	+9%
		6 Developing new business	25%	×2.4***	+10%(*)
B	Moveable individuated assets index std[std(A3) + std(A4) + std(A5) + std(A6)]			+0.5*** (on s.d.)	+6%** (per s.d.)
C	Did you know employees in the service where you were hired? (n = 531)	1 Former colleagues	22%	×1.4	+12%*
		2 Business partners	13%	×1.8(*)	+24%***
		3 Former classmates	13%	×1.4	−3%
		4 Friends	8%		
		5 Others	15%		
D	When you changed jobs, did you ever move with other colleagues to another firm? (n = 469)	1 No	85%	+0.1* (on number of colleagues)	+6% (per colleague)
		2 Yes, with one or two colleagues	12%		
		3 Yes, with three or more	3%		

(continued)

Table 8.1 (continued)

Questions	Items	Freq.	Net impact of front office positions on variables A to G (n = 441)	Net impact of variables A to G on current total pay (n = 429)
E Once in your new job, did you help to hire some former colleagues? (n = 469)	1 No, I did not try 2 I tried with no success 3 Yes, one or two colleagues 4 Yes, three or more	76% 10% 12% 2%	−0.01 (on number hired)	+10%** (per colleague)
F Moveable collaboration ties index std[std(C1 + C2) + std(D2 + 3 × D3) + std(0.5 × E2 + E3 + 3 × E4)]			+0.2* (on s.d.)	+10%*** (per s.d.)
G Combined moveable assets std(B + F)			+0.4*** (on s.d.)	+10%*** (per s.d.)

Note: This table provides statistics on proxy indicators of employees' capacity to move assets in finance from one firm to another – more details to be found in Godechot (2014). In the two first columns, I detail the questions and the response items I used and the indexes I constructed for the analysis. The "std" abbreviation stands for standardisation (i.e. dividing a variable by its own standard deviation). In the third column, I display frequency percentages of respondents' answers. In the fourth column, I model the probability to do those transfers or the quantity of assets transferred with regressions. The key independent variable here is working in a front office position rather than a back office position. Besides function (four categories: front office, financial experts, IT, back office), I also control for sector (two categories: investment bank versus others banking activities), experience and experience squared in finance, age and age squared, sex and diploma (nine categories). Each cell corresponds to a different regression. For qualitative dependent variables, I use logistic regressions and I display the odds-ratios. For quantitative variables such as indexes, or number of persons moving or hired, I use ordinary least squares. Hence, working in a front office position multiplies by 3.7 the probability of bringing new clients and increases by half a standard deviation my moveable individuated assets index. In the last column I model the impact of different types of assets on total compensation. Each box corresponds to a different regression. All column five models also use the same independent variables listed above for column four models. I model the logarithm of current total compensation with interval regressions. Hence, having a business partner in the team where one was hired increases by 24% total compensation relatively to employees who did not have such ties. Regarding the small size of the sample, I take the liberty of signalling with (*) nearly significant parameters such as the ones on the rows C2 in column four (p = 12.1%), A4 and A6 in column five (p = 10.1%).

idiosyncratic routines or more fundamental assets such as knowledge, technology, market share or customers.

I first find that moveable assets and collaboration ties are indeed strongly correlated. The gross correlation coefficient amounts to 0.3*** and is highly significant. The strong and significant partial correlation of 0.22*** indicates that the correlation does not hold only because of the high similarity of their prediction based on the same set of variables.

Second, the analysis of Table 8.1 (column four) clearly confirms the link, stated in my second hypothesis, between working at the core of financial markets and accumulating individuated assets on the one hand and collaboration ties on the other. Controlling for human capital and experience, working in front office jobs such as trader, salesperson or asset manager rather than in the back office significantly increases by half a standard deviation my indicator of moveable individuated assets and by 0.2 standard deviation my indicator of moveable collaboration ties. More specifically, a front office position is tied to the moving of clients and of activity, the pursuit of collaboration with former business partners and the ability to embark on team moves.

Third, as posited, both moveable individuated assets and moveable collaboration ties have a positive and significant impact on wages. One standard deviation increase in collaboration ties index results in total wages being 10% higher. At a slightly lower 6%, the moveable assets index also has a significant impact. More specifically, bringing new clients and developing new business, the presence of former colleagues, and particularly former business partners in the new service, and hiring former colleagues all contribute positively and significantly to the wage premium.

In the end, the statistical confirmation of my hypotheses and the amount of qualitative evidence clearly show that on this market a great deal more is exchanged than just personal skills. It is a market that also transfers assets from one firm to another. Those assets are carried by employees – alone or particularly in team – who earn hefty profits for this carriage.

A Malthusian labour market

As well as enabling finance employees to capture higher wages, one of the outcomes of the hold-up model developed in the previous chapter is underinvestment by financial firms (Grout 1984, Malcomson 1997). The high profitability of some financial sectors (for example, option products in the 1980s, structured products in the latter half of the 1990s) motivated some financial firms to make massive investments. But the investment, while significant, was still less than it would have been if hold-ups had not been a threat. This is difficult to measure in quantitative terms. Some evidence of it can be seen in the rates of financial profitability required in order for a financial activity to be considered profitable. In equity derivatives, for instance, it is sometimes said that a return of 40% on equity capital is needed before any money can be made. Such a high rate is of course linked to the financial risks involved in these activities. However, it also stems from turnover rates, the high risk of collective departure and, ultimately, from the impermanence of financial activities. If an activity only functions for an average of two or three years before it is seized by a rival firm, the profitability horizon is reduced and far higher rates of return are required than for other sectors if a firm is to consider investing.

The impermanence of financial activities can be seen in Lepetit's account, whether that be teams bought, such as those of Richard Sandor, those built up gradually such as Rozan's options desk in New York (Rozan 1999; Lepetit 2002, p. 132), or the Indosuez team on the Matif (Lepetit 2002, p. 137). In all three cases, teams were profitable for a number of years before abandoning Indosuez and leaving behind a seriously handicapped bank. Admittedly, Indosuez was an extreme case. The former head of options at Saturn Bank gave a harsh view of its former competitor, explaining that it had never been able to build anything permanent and that it had given itself over to star traders who then left it in ruins. Even for banks that choose to pursue large-scale industrialisation and a rationalised division of labour that makes the activity more durable, as was the case with Saturn Bank, the risk of departures and renegotiations looms permanently on the horizon, influencing investment decisions and ultimately limiting their scope. In the financial industry, investment is largely immaterial. Investment and labour are not substitutes. They are complementary. Investing in a trading room primarily means recruiting: defining roles, recruiting people, establishing teams, developing knowledge and know-how, soliciting clients and – beyond recruitment but still complementary to it – acquiring material assets such as software, machines and buildings. Underinvestment therefore usually implies underemployment.

In the financial labour market, the likelihood of capturing financial assets is increased by a self-sustaining relative rarity in that labour market. First, the possibility of entering the market is limited by firms' relative underinvestment; second, the rapid exclusion of unemployed operators from that same market sustains that rarity and also plays a role in the high wages distributed within it. In the end, it is the institutions driving the labour market, especially headhunters and remuneration consultancy firms, that support and strengthen a Malthusian job market that functions more as a market of assets than one of people.

The tendency towards underemployment

Underemployment in this sector is evidenced less by data than by gathering observations and anecdotes on the financial world. Those who witnessed the demise in the 1980s of the traditional stockbrokers company (*Compagnie des Agents de Change*) on the Paris stock exchange stressed the fact that, due to the highly favourable clauses in the sector's collective agreement, which made it extremely difficult to fire employees,[9] as well as the size of bonuses, the corporative order went hand in hand with a kind of Malthusianism.

According to a manager from the Société des Bourses Françaises, this system of large-scale, contract-based profit-sharing resulted in a slow-down in the recruitment process during the 1980s, driven by a fear among HR managers that such a system would lead to further sharing of the profits ceded:

> In other words, it caused a Malthusian reaction in people's minds. "Since we were being asked to receive a share of the profit generated by a position, the fewer people there were to share the profit the more we would each receive." So at the time there was a kind of objective alliance between executives and employees to avoid any further recruitment.

This Malthusian reaction is not specific to the traditional French stockbrokers company (*Compagnie des Agents de Change*). In modern financial markets, it is fuelled more by a fear of distribution than by any protective measures set out in the agreements. At every level, the prospect of not collecting full marginal return on a new job (due to the fact that the future employee is expected to capture some profit) leads to cutbacks in recruitment. There is also an added risk of competition from within the team to control the most profitable assets and, if the new recruit proves to be talented and lucky, there is a risk that the line manager's authority comes under threat. For example, the head of the Belgian desk of Universal Company was highly suspicious of potential interns because, if the intern proved to be competent, the head of trading room might take the person on and force the head of desk to share the bonus with them.

This Malthusianism is intensified by the decentralised nature of the recruitment process. The role of the HR department at Saturn Bank (and most banks) is merely to provide advice and services. They distribute the CVs they receive, draw up employment contracts and serve as intermediaries between frontline staff and headhunters. In many ways, these frontline managers define the firm's recruitment needs. They receive support primarily from the head of desk and the head of trading room. The choice of candidate is down to the frontline staff: during the recruitment process, the person is hired after interviews with the head of desk, the head of trading room and team members. In large Anglo-American banks, some of my informers claimed to have been through as many as 20 interviews before being hired, generally with operators or members of the trading room management.

The role of HR is more that of orchestrator than decision-maker. At Saturn Bank, candidates are required to have a meeting with the psychologist who either gives a favourable assessment (the usual outcome) or else expresses reservations. Sometimes, however, frontline managers who are particularly keen on hiring an individual, especially for market activities, have managed to impose their will despite HR managers' reservations. In short, the recruitment process is in fact a collegial process of cooptation.

Favouritism at entry-level

Even though the recruitment process might appear to be based on a candidate's degree and depends largely on the human capital it reveals, in this elitist environment, degrees and even skill sets are at best a necessary but not a sufficient condition for recruitment. In a context of relative underemployment at entry level to this labour market and a huge rise in all kinds of finance degrees from the mid-1990s onwards (including Master's degrees, and specialisation modules studied in a business or engineering school), recruitment took on the form of a *favour* done for those with a connection of some sort: friends, family members, former *Grande École* and preparatory school classmates.

At Jupiter Bank, this kind of bias in favour of those with the same degree was apparent when I examined the composition of a group of professionals according to their degree type. I found that a line manager and her subordinate hold the same degree more often than when I randomly picked two professionals in the overall investment bank's population. This favouritism was also evident in the accounts given by financial actors. All too often, those who had been excluded tended to blame their exclusion on various forms of favouritism. One female trader from Saturn Bank recalled how difficult it was for a woman to become a trader and establish her own legitimacy. One salesperson criticised the fact that, in Saturn Bank, trader positions were completely off-limits to business school graduates and open only to those with engineering degrees:

> Coming from a business school, you didn't feel like going to work in a firm where you knew from day one you had no chance of promotion . . . Even the heads of sales desks were engineering graduates . . . And I got the feeling that as the head of sales was a graduate of the *École Centrale*, he was valued less than someone from the *École Polytechnique* and so they'd given him the sales desk.

Biased favouritism is mentioned more often in critical evaluations than in evaluations made by decision-makers, who usually either deny any form of favouritism or else give practical reasons for anything that might be perceived externally as such. When observing Saturn equity derivatives trading room in the late 1990s, I was struck by the uniformity of style of its members. The staff was largely made up of men who resembled the members of a boys' choir, with their faces so clean-shaven as to appear almost pre-pubescent; their hair cut to just the right length, not too long but not too short, carefully parted and coiffed; their classic, plain, well-fitting suits; their serious, determined, affable demeanour. A thousand minor, evanescent details that, together, were the clear sign of a "good, Catholic education".

The recruitment method adopted by the founder of equity derivatives at Saturn Bank enables one to understand the origin of this impression of uniformity. The head of options, a man who recruited most of the trading rooms' managerial staff in the late 1980s was the son of a small businessman. He attended a Jesuit boarding school and then went on to the Sainte-Geneviève Jesuit preparatory school in Versailles (known as "Ginette"), which had a profound effect on him: "I had a strong Jesuit education. I don't know whether it's of much use but it was important for me." He graduated from ENSAE, rather than the *École Polytechnique* that produced so many of the professionals he went on to recruit. However, he favoured those who had attended the same preparatory school over those from the same *Grande École*: the confined environment of the preparatory schools tends to create solidarity and a shared identity, whereas the *Grandes Écoles* are institutions that confer degrees making the results of a preparatory school competition official rather than places where new identities are forged (Bourdieu 1998).

Yes, because there are lots of people from Ginette.

For me Ginette was a very important recruitment hub. I had two sets of people I used to call the pirates and the faithful. Those from Ginette were the faithful and the rest were the pirates . . .

So the faithful were from Ginette . . . ?

It's a bit of a stereotype. But what I liked about Ginette . . . was the idea of the shared project and the Catholic idea of making a sacrifice for a shared goal. It's like saying, "What we do together is worth more than what I get out of something personally. I'm making a contribution to the group's project." I really like that idea.

A kind of "boy scout" approach?

Yes, that's it, a kind of Catholic, boy scout thing. I really like that idea . . . When I say pirates, of course it's an exaggeration, but the cultural background elsewhere is quite different . . . To me they seemed more fragile.

In addition to the arguments put forward by the former head of options, such as the functional importance of loyalty and morality, there is a real pleasure that comes from encountering people who share one's values and in whom one recognises personal qualities that one considers important. This phenomenon can also be seen in his description of the role of chess in the recruitment process, especially for young people who have not studied at a *Grande École*:

One particular quality that was a good indicator was whether or not they were good at chess and speed chess . . . So if people played speed chess well – we were a bit obsessed with the game – we'd say "Can you play speed chess?", and they'd say "Yes, I'm good". So I'd take out the chessboard and we'd have a game. I'd say, "If you beat me you're hired!"

This game enabled the head of options to identify a particular skill that he thought to be common to both speed chess players and successful market operators. But since that special skill might have been also present among candidates unfamiliar with chess, the unconventional recruitment test tended to reproduce identities and select certain social characteristics with a highly uneven distribution. At this point in time the derivatives activity was a niche market where no specialised qualifications existed, so the recruitment process was inevitably random ("Why me?" and "Why you?") and the endogamic processes used – speed chess, Ginette, *Grande École* – seemed to echo those doubts: "Because it was me" and "Because it was you".

Self-sustained rarity

Underemployment, barriers to entry and favours – even favouritism – limit people's access to the financial labour market. The rapid expulsion of inactive employees at the other end of the employment process ensures that the operators circulating in the market are a rare breed. The assets captured by the employees of a firm are only valuable if they are maintained. If employees are inactive for a long period, say one year, then the influence they have over their clients, their market share in a particular derivative, their team, or a particular financial innovation may disappear or at least be seriously weakened. Furthermore, if employees are inactive they quickly lose value on the employment market. There are two types of vacancies: first, resignations, retirements, departures negotiated amicably and time off; second, dismissals due to losses, inadequate performance or more generally an unfavourable economy.

In the first case, an employee's departure during a favourable economic period causes assets to devalue more slowly than in the second case. In the late 1990s, some employees tried to make the most of their sudden wealth by requesting time off to do something entirely different. If they wanted to keep their position in the firm, particularly in the case of heads of desk, a one-year break for personal reasons was considered too long. In order to keep their position open, they had to return to work within six months. It is generally thought that if people take a whole year off they will not return to work. There are exceptions, of course. The head of Securities Asia at Neptune Bank took early retirement in order to take care of his adopted children and breed horses. After four years he was bored and asked his former boss if he could return to work: "He didn't come back in the top spot because the job was taken, but he did come back." Generally speaking, if people are absent from the financial markets for more than one year, they are considered to be "out". They no longer receive calls from headhunters or requests from other firms and market partners to resume their activity.

Assets held by an employee depreciate far more rapidly when the individual has been fired. When employees are fired for professional errors or incompetence, for example if financial losses have been incurred (a type of dismissal that is less common than people think), those individuals are seriously handicapped in the micro-market in which they had been operating because their now bad reputation spreads quickly (thanks to brokers in particular). Other people start to question the quality of the assets they were trading, or even their ability to generate profit. One trader from Pluto Bank held on to his job after losing around 10 million euros in 1998 when Russia defaulted on its GKO bonds (government bonds). However, he quickly realised that he had become a pariah, not so much to his close colleagues, who were aware of the circumstances,[10] but to the rest of the bank and his market competitors. There seems to be very little chance of bouncing back in the financial markets if one is fired for incurring losses.

Nor is it easy to bounce back when the dismissal has taken place during an economic downturn in a sector of the financial market.[11] Structural difficulties in a market, a product or a sector (for instance, a fall in volumes or prices, a sudden unexpected shift in the market, a lack of activity, etc.) are the most common cause of redundancies. The markets follow irregular cycles with prosperous periods and low periods. In equity, for example, there were booms in 1984–1987, 1996–2000, and 2003–2007, and crashes in 1987–1988, 2000–2002 and 2007–2008. Periods of economic depression go hand in hand with waves of redundancies, sometimes on a major scale, in London or on Wall Street. After the Asian crisis, for example, the banks made vast numbers of operators redundant (Dahan 1997; Treanor 2001) – too many, even – and were forced to carry out a huge recruitment drive the following year to cope with the resumption of activity. However, when the situation was bad on the foreign exchange market (introduction of the euro, crisis in emerging currencies), the bond markets (rise in interest rates) and the emerging markets (rise in country risk), the climate remained good in the equity market and its derivative products. The banks preferred to make operators in the devalued sectors redundant and hire junior staff in equity products rather than trying to move foreign exchange operators across into the equity market. When the economic outlook for their product is bleak, in this mixed labour–assets market the dismissed employees find themselves with depreciated assets on their hands. Their professional aptitude is still of value, but the assets they hold are worth nothing. Their own value is no doubt slightly greater than that of a junior employee (on account of their general knowledge of finance) but it is not fundamentally higher. Recruitment consultants are often wary of salary expectations set when an employee was still managing valuable assets.

The career path taken by one former employee of a brokerage firm (foreign exchange) shows the impact of asset depreciation. He had entered the foreign exchange market in the mid-1970s when it was the primary niche market, and quickly progressed in his brokerage firm from telex operator to broker, becoming relatively well-off. In the second half of the 1980s, during his best years, he was earning 100,000 euros. However, foreign exchange brokerage was under threat from three sides: competition was increasing and reducing margins; the introduction of the euro in the mid-1990s first wiped out margins then currencies; and finally electronic brokerage systems were being installed in the Bloomberg and Reuters financial networks, bypassing the traditional brokers. In short, this particular broker held financial assets that were destined to depreciate. During the 1990s, his bonuses gradually fell. He was then asked to agree to a fixed pay cut. He accepted the first time "to save the firm" – letting his wages fall from 4,000 to 2,000 euros a month – but refused the second time. He was made redundant and never found another job in the finance industry.

This process of depreciation is far from isolated. It may be gradual or sudden. Employees usually leave the industry rather than moving into another sector of finance. In the collective imagination of financial actors, there are only ever two possible outcomes on the wheel of fortune: continuation or expulsion. It is a "survivor's job," explained one head of trading room. Exaggerating their situation in order to give it greater emphasis, operators claim there is no way forward in finance after a true dismissal. They collectively underestimate their chances of obtaining a new position in finance (which do exist), thereby reinforcing the rarity of such an occurrence through a self-fulfilling process (Bourdieu 1974).

One headhunter spoke with irony and condescension of her long list of contacts, people she had once pursued but who were now unemployed and came to her office crying and begging her to find them a job in finance. She would listen out of sympathy but had no illusions. She casually explained that they would probably end up working, "I don't know, in a pizza place or fast food restaurant, or be unemployed". These were not realistic scenarios but they effectively demonstrate that these people did indeed face a future outside the finance industry.

On the one hand, the industry expels people without really recycling them; on the other hand, it does its utmost to avoid cutting the wages of those who survive. When results for a trading room, department or bank are disappointing or negative, the management's primary response is to lower the bonuses of the least important people (i.e. newcomers, junior staff, operators at the end of their career) or even fire them if need be, in order to protect the bonuses of those it considers important whether or not they performed well that year. Banks consider it vital to prevent important people – generally speaking those who manage large portfolios (clients or securities) – from being poached by rival firms. These people may be capable of restarting an activity, particularly when the situation is bad in a trading room, department or bank but not in the market as a whole. Difficult years are those in which pay inequality within trading rooms is particularly acute. It is usually a year or two before bad results have a serious impact on the bonuses of major players. During a difficult period, ordinary operators may be fired and thus no longer feed the labour supply once they are out of the market; also, the bonuses of star actors are protected. Bonuses are therefore downwardly rigid and the financial market maintains its own particular rarity.

Headhunters and labour market segmentation

Seeing the labour market as a market of assets allows us to understand the reasons why the institutions that drive the labour market – headhunting firms and remuneration consultancy firms – divide the different markets into segments to such a degree (Gautié, Godechot and Sorignet 2005; Godechot 2006). Once operators' value is conceived in terms of the products in which they specialise and the value of the portfolio they manage, it is only to be expected that comparisons should be limited to peers holding similar portfolios and that replacements should be sought only among that same group. Likewise, it is clear that the strict segmentation of price comparisons made by remuneration consultancy firms is due to the fact that the assets held by actors cannot be transferred between one sector and another.

Headhunting firms[12] often receive urgent requests, either to find a replacement for an employee who has resigned and moved to a rival bank or else to develop a new sector in which the bank feels it is lagging behind its competitors. It is often said that headhunters only recruit "clones". The firm usually tries to replace the assets lost with exact equivalents, in other words people with similar abilities in terms of clients, market shares and know-how, or to capture the assets held by its competitors. The fastest way to achieve this is by poaching employees. The bank will often directly inform the headhunting firm of the candidates it wishes to meet; alternatively –and this is an even clearer indication that allocation matters more than individuality – it may specify the institution in which the headhunting firm is required to find candidates.[13] Usually the headhunting firm, with its flexible, practical structure that enables it to bypass HR, is not requested to actually select candidates (this will have been done already by the person making the request) but rather to approach them, negotiate with them and draw up a contract. This does not mean that the selection and assessment of candidates does not play an important role in the headhunting firm's activity. However, the evaluation made is not so much a professional assessment of individuals as one of individuals by professionals specialised in that particular activity.

The singularity and generality of skills matter less than the extension of financial capabilities and allocations, which are apparent from people's achievements and the place they already occupy in finance. In the executive branch of the headhunting industry, therefore, both in general headhunting firms and those specialised in finance, consultants in charge of the financial industry have always worked as financial operators in the past. Only rarely are they HR experts or professionals in personal assessment that have received specific training in psychology, HR management or sociology. Ultimately, knowing what is meant by a particular P&L for a product, a particular Sharpe ratio or a particular VaR quoted by a candidate is more important than being able to distinguish an egocentric or neurotic person, or any other character trait that might indicate a candidate's ability to work in a team. Having candidates assessed by a professional consultant familiar with the world of finance provides a far more informed appraisal of what the candidate is claiming to have achieved. A list of personal achievements is meticulously put together in a variety of forms, either by candidates themselves or by indirectly by "sources" or "advisors" who give consultants information on a candidate's career path.

One headhunting consultant specialised in finance described how they built up a database on all the traders who worked at Saturn Bank, detailing securities traded, bonuses, wages, P&Ls and even risk limits. This type of comprehensive tool allowed them to map the activity itself, and headhunters could transfer elements on the condition that they respected the divisions.

One of the aims of recruitment interviews is to evaluate what the candidate and the new organisation can offer. Of course, other approaches are also taken during the different phases of recruitment.[14] For example, one consultant always specified whether or not her candidates were "nice", "funny" or "good-looking", thus suggesting that the recruitment process depends on the empathy of both the person recruiting (heads of desk and heads of trading room) and the headhunter, who endeavours to use not only recruitment categories but also the client's personal preferences (Finlay and Coverdill 2002). However, in this technical, profit-driven world, social affinity is a necessary yet insufficient driving force.

Headhunters use selection categories that are both technical and social – in other words, designations of the division of labour and the relative value of the different segments of that division (Durkheim and Mauss 1963).

In the finance industry, assessments focus primarily on financial parameters, which can sometimes amount to tautology. In the absence of further information, consultants base their evaluations on candidates' bonuses in order to determine what they can contribute (and also to establish their starting salary). Transfers are thus particularly common during times of economic growth. Very high bonuses give candidates leverage in that they indicate a very high value signal and enable them to negotiate guarantees that they would not have obtained in their current position (up to two years of guaranteed bonus and often a higher fixed wage). As one HR professional stated, "In 2000 we gave out higher bonuses than ever before, and yet we also saw more resignations than ever before!" Another indication of the role of bonuses in assessing candidates' importance in finance (particularly as it has a direct impact on their negotiated wages) is the fact that some headhunters mention that candidates may bluff and lie about the bonus they received, which consultants try to guard against by cross-checking information with a number of different sources.

This game of assessment and relativisation applies to all financial indicators (P&L, sales credit, sales margin, gross profit, risk limits). During the recruitment process, candidates try to prove their own worth to the consultant by showing off their achievements and describing them in the first person singular: "I did this"; "I did that"; "That was my doing"; and even "That wasn't me". The area of activity covered by this "I" varies in order to win support. A share of the collective activity may be presented as a personal achievement. On the other hand, a share of the failures will be blamed on the economic situation, colleagues, management decisions or other external circumstances. When recounting the negotiation process with his future boss at Orion Bank, the trader who left the Titan brokerage firm told me that the two parties, both facing problems on the convertible bonds market in 2001, tried to talk about these difficulties without actually admitting to any losses: "No one wanted to say they'd made a loss. But at the same time, no one was fooled. 'We've had a hard time' or 'This year's been really tough' the guy from Orion Bank told me. But he was stating implicitly, 'No, no! We've never lost any money!'"

The key to recruitment interviews is making one's claimed achievements credible. The challenge is dividing up the area of appropriation so that it appears credible in relation to the position being offered. Some personal qualities generate support. It is therefore fairly common to suggest or request referees capable of verifying a candidate's track record in terms of P&L, sales credit or securities trades. In finance, social capital – a network of contacts ready to confirm the achievements a candidate is claiming – and symbolic capital thus serve as robust tools. The achievements of people with a strong reputation are obvious, and it seems unnecessary to verify them. For those without a reputation, it is vital to provide referees. According to one headhunter, however, checking references is often an indication that a recruitment process is underway, and is therefore a delicate process that may not be carried through. A headhunter may consider that simply having the option of checking a reference is proof enough. The task of crediting people with what they are claiming is therefore complex. It depends largely on whether the candidate, the client and the headhunter agree on the legitimate domain of appropriation.

Ultimately, because it is potentially inflationist and because it organises the transfer of assets through people's highly compartmentalised mobility, the mechanism that drives the labour market (headhunting, remuneration consultancy firms) promotes the Malthusianism that is particular to the financial labour market and the relatively high prices that prevail there.

***

In contrast with more material sectors such as the oil, car and chemical industries, assets in finance are much more readily appropriated, detached and transferred. Such transfers can be achieved to the advantage of the employees who organise them. Whereas industry employees cannot take the factory with them, in the finance industry employees can indeed leave with the cash register – not all of its contents but all the contents that give it value. True, they cannot leave with the firm's equity capital; however, once that capital has been stripped of everything that enabled it to increase above market levels, capital can no longer lay claim to the profits and must settle for normal remuneration: the compulsory interest rate plus a slight risk premium.

Notes

1 In case of failure, the hiring process usually resumes without extra financing (in the case of the most classic contracts). The phenomenon of opportunism on the part of the hiring manager should also be mentioned: the job interview is also a means of extracting information and finding out what competitors are doing, and it may be organised to this sole end rather than to offer any real job.

2 The difficulties of LTCM began when many financial institutions, learning of the fund's success, started imitating its arbitrage strategy (MacKenzie 2003).

3 For an in-depth analysis of these transfers, cf. Groysberg (2010).

4 Friendship plays a similar professional role in law firms (Lazega 1992).

5 Network sociology has explored organisational contexts in which certain ties afford advantages: when the point is to acquire information resources, weak ties and porous network structures are preferable, whereas strong, cohesive ties are important when it comes to cooperating and constructing a collective identity (Podolny and Baron 1997).

6 This phenomenon is also seen in law firms. Lazega writes: "As many managing partners in law firms know, the importance of constraint at the group level is not necessarily an encouragement for management to create dense and permanent work groups in collegial organizations. The existence of such groups is risky for the firm. They can threaten the firm with disintegration when entire teams consider themselves exploited . . . decide to defect, and take away with them part of the firm's human and social capital" (Lazega 1999, p. 262).

7 Similarly, the team that was working with John Meriwether on LTCM was made up primarily of former Salomon Brothers colleagues (MacKenzie 2003).

8　Goodwill is an intangible asset such as a label, a reputation, etc. that provides a competitive edge. During acquisition, goodwill appears on the acquirer's balance sheet as the difference between acquisition price and the price of the acquired firm's tangible assets.

9　Article 36 of the 1974 stockbrokers' collective agreement (*Convention collective de la Compagnie des Agents de Change*) stipulated that "the tenured employee can only be dismissed for a serious error recognised by the joint commission" on which the trade unions served (p. 12). According to a professional from the former company of stockbrokers, "no behaviour was seen as constituting a serious error – ever. The trade unions wouldn't allow it. There were always mitigating circumstances". Article 40 also established that in the event of a dismissal following job cuts or a merging of jobs, the company of stockbrokers must offer the dismissed employee an equivalent position within two years, and that if it failed to redeploy the employee within two years it would grant that individual two years' further compensation.

10　Pluto Bank's management had confirmed his positions and offered to double them the day before Russia defaulted.

11　The frequent redundancies on Wall Street and their impact on the way in which the corporation is represented as an object of continual restructuring has been analysed in detail by Ho (2009).

12　The paragraphs that follow on the subject of headhunting are also based on the results of a survey on headhunting (Gautié, Godechot and Sorignet 2006).

13　One firm that was ahead of its competitors was at risk of losing its advantage due to the intensive poaching carried out by its rivals. The former head of the options department at Saturn Bank explained, "The thing is that the British headhunters spent all their time poaching my guys, and I really resent them for it!" The considerable advantage enjoyed by Saturn Bank was largely lost. He joked that most of the derivatives trading rooms around the world were managed by his "exes", in other words, by some of his former employees who had moved over to rival banks.

14　An overview of the recruitment logic applied at each stage is given in Eymard-Duvernay and Marchal (1997).

References

Amossé, T 2003, 'Interne ou externe, deux visages de la mobilité professionnelle', *Insee Première*, n°921, pp. 1–4.

Bourdieu, P 1974, 'Avenir de classe et causalité du probable', *Revue française de sociologie*, vol. 15, n°1, pp. 3–42.

Bourdieu, P 1998, *The State Nobility: Elite Schools in the Field of Power*, Stanford University Press, Stanford CA.

Dahan, N 1997, 'La City entre valse des bonus et blues de l'emploi', *La Tribune*, December.

Demos, T 2010, 'Ex-SocGen Employee Convicted of Code Theft', *Financial Times*, 20 November.

Durkheim, E and Mauss, M 1963, *Primitive Classification*, The University of Chicago Press, Chicago IL.

Eymard-Duvernay, F and Marchal, E 1997, *Façons de recruter. Le jugement des compétences sur le marché du travail*, Métailié, Paris.

Finlay W, and Coverdill, J 2002, *Headhunters: Matchmaking in the Labor Market*, Cornell University Press, Ithaca CA.

Gautié, J, Godechot O and Sorignet, PE 2005, 'Arrangement institutionnel et fonctionne-ment du marché du travail. Le cas de la chasse de tête', *Sociologie du travail*, vol. 47, n°3, pp. 383–404.

Godechot, O 2001, *Les Traders. Essai de sociologie des marchés financiers*, La Découverte, Paris.

Godechot, O 2006, '"Quel est le salaire de marché?" Enquêtes de rémunération et mise en forme du marché du travail dans l'industrie financière', *Genèses*, n°63, pp. 108–127.

Godechot, O 2014, 'Getting a Job in Finance. The Role of Collaboration Ties', *European Journal of Sociology*, vol. 55, n°1, pp. 25–56.

Granovetter, M 1973, 'The Strength of Weak Ties', *American Journal of Sociology*, vol. 78, n°6, pp. 1360–1380.

Grout, P 1984, 'Investment and Wages in the Absence of Binding Contracts', *Econometrica*, vol. 52, n°2, pp. 755–785.

Groysberg, B 2010, *Chasing Stars: The Myth of Talent and the Portability of Performance*, Princeton University Press, Princeton NJ.

Groysberg, B, Lee, LE and Nanda, A 2008, 'Can They Take It with Them? The Portability of Star Knowledge Workers' Performance: Myth or Reality', *Management Science*, vol. 54, n°7, pp. 1213–1230.

Hamm, S and Burrows, P 2003, 'Inside Frank Quattrone's Money Machine', *Business Week*, 13 October.

Ho, K 2009, *Liquidated, An Ethnography of Wall Street*, Duke University Press, Durham NC.

Lazega, E 1992, 'Analyse de réseaux d'une organisation collégiale: les avocats d'affaires', *Revue française de sociologie*, vol. 33, n°4, pp. 559–589.

Lazega, E 1999, 'Generalized Exchange and Economic Performance: Multi-Level Embeddedness of Labor Contracts in a Corporate Law Firm' in *Corporate Social Capital and Liabilities*, eds R Leenders and S Gabbay, Springer, New York, pp. 237–265.

Lebecq, S 1990, *Les Origines franques, v^e-ixe siècles*, Seuil, Paris.

Lepetit, JF 2002, *Homme de marché*, Economica, Paris.

Lewis, M 1989, *Liar's Poker*, Hodder and Stoughton, Coronet Books, London.

Lewis, M 2014, *Flash Boys*, Hodder and Stoughton, London.

MacKenzie, D 2003, 'Long-Term Capital Management and the Sociology of Arbitrage', *Economy and Society*, vol. 32, n°3, pp. 349–380.

Malcomson, J 1997, 'Contracts, Hold-Up, and Labor Markets', *Journal of Economic Literature*, vol. 35, n°4, pp. 1916–1957.

Podolny J and Baron, J 1997, 'Resources and Relationships: Social Networks and Mobility in the Workplace' *American Sociological Review*, vol. 62, n°5, pp. 673–693.

Rozan, JM 1999, *Le Fric*, Michel Lafon, Paris.

Sanford, C 1996, 'Managing the Transformation of a Corporate Culture: Risks and Rewards' in *1996–1997 Musser-Schoemaker Leadership Lecture Series at the Wharton School*, University of Pennsylvania.

Treanor, J 2001, 'The Bull's Retreat', *The Guardian*, 24 October.

Zábojník, J 2002, 'A Theory of Trade Secrets in Firms', *International Economic Review*, vol. 43, n°3, pp. 831–856.

9   What do heads of trading room do?

Some employees acquire power over other employees and the firm itself once the collective they work for has allocated them assets that are both stable and transferable. Therefore, not all financial operator positions are equivalent, whether from a synchronic or diachronic point of view. Heads of trading room have a privileged position in financial trading rooms. Statistical analysis of pay in the finance sector has revealed their rising compensation (Chapter 1). In terms of legitimising the appropriation of profits, heads of trading or heads of sales running a financial products team, and to an even greater extent heads of a trading room, occupy a position akin to a first-tier contractor and original promoters of the activity (Chapter 4), and they can even be seen as "internal entrepreneurs". Changes in financial organisation have also tended to increase their power to capture profit by concentrating it in their hands.

It is more than a suggestive metaphor to call these heads entrepreneurs. In this border case, we may very well discover certain basic characteristics of entrepreneurship, traits that are more visible when the entrepreneurship is in its embryonic phase, that is, when other entrepreneur functions have not yet started to mask the prime function of capturing profit. It is thus possible to compare these internal entrepreneurs in the finance industry with those from the early stages of the Industrial Revolution.

Reading Mottez's history of the different forms of wage-earning, one is struck by the formal similarity between heads of trading room, who are technically employees, and the *hagglers* or subcontractors who used to practise *bargaining* in the early nineteenth century (Mottez 1960 & 1966). Before this practice was forbidden and criminalised[1] in the French industry, particularly in the construction sector, one encountered labour subcontractors:

> The haggler was a labour subcontractor who, with raw materials and major tools provided by the boss, outsourced tasks he received, either in the boss's workshop or building site, or else in his own home (depending on the type of industry) with the help of hired workers whom he paid by the day or by piece without the boss's intervention.[2]

Although heads of trading are legally just employees, they nevertheless have a number of points in common with the hagglers of the early nineteenth century.

Heads of trading room monopolise most of the power to recruit. They negotiate the bonus system for the whole of the room and preside over its distribution; they are therefore in the practical position of being able to directly determine, via a budget, how much subordinates will be paid. The firm provides capital, equipment and a back office, while the head of trading room provides a team of professionals. Mottez wrote: "The status of the haggler is ambiguous: on the one hand, he is a professional who organises labour; on the other hand, he is a labour entrepreneur who plays the part of an employer to those he hires, seeking to increase his profits at the expense of their salary" (Mottez 1960, p. 210). The nineteenth-century haggler was accused by labour organisations of forcing down wages and increasing poverty. This last point is not entirely proven, however. Nevertheless, this method of paying wages made it much easier to see how much of the value was being captured by the subcontractor, simply because of his position in the productive organisation, whereas in traditional entrepreneurship there could be multiple bases of support for that organisation (capital contributions, advances on wages, management and marketing work) which ultimately concealed the entrepreneur's activity.

Marglin, another astute observer of the early Industrial Revolution, has analysed the embryonic forms of capitalist firms under "the putting-out system" and characterised the essence of entrepreneurial activity in a famous article entitled "What Do Bosses Do?" (Marglin 1974). Reversing the technological determinism found in some of Marx's texts, he has tried to show how technology is a consequence of social order and not a cause thereof.[3] In his opinion, the division of labour was not adopted because of its greater efficiency but because it dispossessed workers of any control over their work and turned entrepreneurs into coordinators who, by becoming indispensable to production, acquired a situation of power in which they could earn greater profits and pursue a logic of capital accumulation. The entrepreneur's strategy is therefore to "divide and conquer".

> Why, then, did the division of labor under the putting-out system entail specialization as well as separation of tasks? In my view the reason lies in the fact that without specialization, the capitalist had no essential role to play in the production process. If each producer could himself integrate the component tasks of pin manufacture into a marketable product, he would soon discover that he had no need to deal with the market for pins through the intermediation of the putter-outer. He could sell directly and appropriate to himself the profit that the capitalist derived from mediating between the producer and the market. Separating the tasks assigned to each workman was the sole means by which the capitalist could, in the days preceding costly machinery, ensure that he would remain essential to the production process as integrator of these separate operations into a product for which a wide market existed . . . The capitalist division of labor, as developed under the putting-out system, embodied the same principle that "successful" imperial powers have utilized to rule their colonies: divide and conquer.
>
> (Marglin 1974, p. 70)

By transforming complex work into simple work, entrepreneurs shift the rent generated at the level of the individual self-employed craftsperson into the hands of the entrepreneur–coordinator. The division of labour is a strategic option, not so much because it makes it possible to produce things in a more technical fashion but because it modifies the locus where rent is captured. The entrepreneur who dispossesses the workers of their work can pay them less and force them into competition with less-skilled workers.[4]

This comparison of recent changes in the financial sector with the beginnings of the Industrial Revolution may appear odd and forced. It brackets employees in very different circumstances, such as the miserable conditions of manual industrial workers and the opulence of financial traders and managers who are empowered to conduct negotiations. However, there are suggestive similarities between the processes at work, despite the differences in context. In this case, it is not so much the capitalist entrepreneur per se who pursues the "divide and conquer" strategy but an employee, the head of trading room. The head of trading is tantamount to a labour subcontractor who appropriates some of the subordinates' rent by subdividing, recombining and managing the assigned workload to ensure her own indispensability. Pay in the finance sector may have globally increased in recent years due to a sharp rise in volumes, but this has been accompanied by greater hierarchical disparities. Basic financial traders or salespeople have been appropriating a relatively smaller share of increased profits, with team managers appropriating a relatively larger share.

I first show that these heads of trading room are internal entrepreneurs, similar to the proto-industrial "bosses" described by Marglin. Like the latter, heads try to create a central lynchpin role for themselves by subdividing and recombining work. However, they must, in addition to this organisational role, be able to persuade the whole group to move en masse. Hence, this chapter also analyses the relational structure underlying team moves and thus broadens our understanding of social capital. In recent years, many studies on social capital have tried to link two contradictory aspects of relational activities (Granovetter 1995; Godechot and Mariot 2004; Burt 2005): profits generated by the diversification and the non-redundancy of relationships (Burt 1992); and profits relating to network closure and group cohesion (Coleman 1988). Diversified relationships make it easier to build entities that are larger but more fragile in nature. Cohesive relationships create team spirit but also generate a lateral control system that makes it harder for a leader to emerge. To study these questions, I will analyse what heads of trading room do to produce a system of relationships that is profitable both in the workplace and also in the labour market.

Divide and recombine

The multiple effects that division of labour produces over the long run often become visible only in time. In a new activity in finance, people always start out with the idea of subdividing work so as to increase efficiency, occupy the terrain and mine the ore for as long they can before the competition attacks.

This division is organised, sometimes euphorically, and everyone is keen to take part. It is only at a much later stage that people notice that the division of labour has been a process for managing interpersonal competition and that it conveys predetermined forms of value sharing. The history of the division of financial labour is a recurring one of product discoveries by development teams, business start-ups (hedge funds) and back office reorganisations.

In the following two cases, the division of labour at first appears to have been established for its technical efficiency, but it also has a political dimension based on wealth-sharing, which is not necessarily intentional but is all the more effective because it is masked by the technical dimension.

The first example: one trader from Sirius Bank, a science graduate from the *École Normale Supérieure*, was on the verge of setting up a small hedge fund in 2002. He seemed keen to free himself from the division of labour. He intended to tell the people he hired: "It would be Communist! We're all going to be paid 3,000 euros a month and we'll share the firm's profits equally." When pressed for further details, he explained that this egalitarianism was limited to the traders in the small team he was setting up. Ultimately, the quant, the salesperson responsible for finding customers for the fund and the back office administrator, who were not promoted to partners and did not access capital, were not eligible for this generous and frugal equality.

The second example: the head of a sales team at Mars Bank became very successful in a short period of time by developing the marketing of a range of derivative products tailor-made for his customer's needs. However, the team he put together to build on this success was not comprised of peers or apprentices with whom he would share the business. The exceptions were team members located abroad, colleagues of equal seniority and peers he could not really control and whom he described as "free options". More generally, however, any newcomers brought in were specialists in fields such as tax, law, financial engineering and marketing, so that individuals had a particular skill set and undertook a series of tasks that the head of sales alone was in a position to recombine: "I've got guys now who are doing pure structuring so my sales staff can concentrate on sales and nothing else . . . What I've done is separate the work into two so that some guys' job is to have ideas and produce brochures, whereas others are supposed to become best friends with chief financial officers (CFOs) who are potential customers." By positioning himself in the middle of a division of labour that he orchestrated, the head of sales could keep the lion's share of a rent while enjoying the legitimisation of its distribution (as he said, "If you ask me, I've made a positive contribution").

The political division of labour

In other cases, however, the political division of labour is not merely an emerging effect but rather a project expressly embarked on. If we retrace the division of labour in the area of derivative products from the mid-1980s to the mid-1990s, reverberating as smaller movements in each period, we note that the division of labour has also been seen as a means of preventing independent financial actors from capturing an activity. The main organiser of Saturn Bank's options department designed its development in opposition to the "forex trader" model prevalent at the time in other banks such as Uranus Bank, which he criticised for managing the changeover poorly and for being incapable of devising a lasting activity. He explained that he always tried to avoid the kind of financial handicraft that relies on the juxtaposition of autonomous craftspersons:

> One thing was clear. There was an inherent weakness in the old way of doing things: these were individual performances, not group ones ... What was really bad was how this personalised the work. At times we had a star system, with just one person dominating the whole marketplace. But it's impossible for a single individual, lacking the support of a group or a particular methodology, to last.

One cannot rely on individual performance in the long term because it is neither safe from adverse economic conditions nor from the possibility that the person in question will leave one day. In our very first telephone conversation, the former head of options, recounting his experience at Saturn Bank, told me about his desire to create a "collective rent" (his words). He was an engineer educated at one of France's top universities who had started his career in a banking IT firm. After a conflict with the bank's management over issues of independence, he joined Saturn Bank in 1985. He continued developing finance-related IT systems for the bank, such as a system enabling agencies to give direct quotes of the exchange rate. He was given the opportunity in 1985 to construct an options trading room. He immediately realised that this new product "offered both leverage and safety" and sensed a chance to "build an empire". With a process background acquired during the reorganisation of the bank's information system, he came into this new product area firmly decided to create an entity that would be both technically and socially integrated: "Our policy was always to develop our own software and buy nothing. We wanted significant integration between our processes, back office, accounting, front office, etc. We also wanted to be responsible for sorting out any problems, if possible by applying a standard of maximum excellence."

To counter any departures that might have undermined his new structure, he tried to promote what Durkheim (1997) called *organic solidarity*, via an advanced division of labour – that is, a solidarity rooted in differentiation which is more robust than *mechanical solidarity* when social norms weaken.

In the end, it was this outsider to finance who began to promote an industrial conception of finance that could not really come from more traditional activities like stockbroking or portfolio management in equities or forex trading. His approach was based on starting from scratch with the models he wanted to use; creating his own software; training his own employees who were recruited directly upon graduation from the *Grandes Écoles*; and above all being sceptical about past techniques or actors, who were holders of individual rents that could not be merged with the collective rent he was trying to create. Describing Saturn

Bank's options department, the CEO of the rival Uranus Bank would later say: "They began to develop software that would allow them to manage forex options or any other kind of option. As a result, they took two years longer than we did to launch their options business. But when they finally got going in 1985–1986 they were quite successful." The goal for Saturn's head of options at the time was to create an "engineering bank" that unlike "commercial banks" or "marketing banks" would try to "have perfect control over the whole of the risk management and manufacturing process". Commercial activity was only established later on, when IT, modelling, trading and arbitrage processes were all ready. One symbol of such integration was that Saturn Bank was the first to set up rolling foreign exchange option books, traded 24 hours a day and passed from Paris to New York and on to Tokyo.

Some competitors such as Uranus Bank constructed their own options trading groups, opting to acquire blocks of activity that already had a large market presence (teams, software, etc.). It took less time for them to become productive, but they were easier to spin off and formed a less durable collective activity.

The strengths of Saturn Bank's integration and division of labour should not be exaggerated, however. Despite its advanced division of labour and in-house software and processes, the different elements comprising the entity managed by Saturn's head of trading room were easy to detach and there was always the threat that a significant proportion of the business could go missing at any point in time. The former manager spoke bitterly about American "arbitrage" banks (as opposed to the "innovative" bank he was running) systematically hiring away entire teams with the help of English headhunters. By taking his employees, they were eating into his collective rent.

Despite its imperfect efficiency, this is the kind of work organisation process that all of the banks surveyed would ultimately end up adopting, and it helped to shift the levels at which rents were being captured. The head of a trading room (and to a lesser degree, a head of desk) is there to subdivide, recombine and orchestrate, personally crystallising a lion's share of a trading division's total value creation. The specialists working below these heads are often more competent in their own area of specialisation but possess little awareness of what is being done on other desks, and even less knowledge of the back or middle offices.[5] Under the model of productive secrets described in the previous chapter, the head of a trading room is theoretically in a position to at least partially break a room's secret value down into simple elements, thanks to this divide and conquer strategy (Marglin 1974, p. 35). The manufacturing of these elements can be delegated, but the head is the only person in a position to combine them. This is why some, like Saturn Bank's head of equity derivatives group, under whose orders this particular product area had been developed, considered himself "lucky to have never had to specialise":

> It would have been completely counterproductive for me to get tied to one area, to settle into it, to say, "I need to read up on new models", etc. Others could do that. My job was to fit the pieces of the puzzle together so that things ran harmoniously and we could grow as quickly as possible.

Top-down coordination is, de facto, inevitable even when it is disputed. The head of a trading room ends up monopolising the rents that the traders used to split among themselves. Sometimes, as was the case with the former head of options, this is the first step towards accumulating capital. He of course denied any greed on his part ("Making a fortune? No, that was never it [my aim]!") The plans to create a collective rent, which he suddenly found himself overseeing, were used to service a morally superior project: creating France's biggest bank and showing the Americans that the French could do things much better than them. Looking to solve the problem of rival Anglo-American firms poaching his managers and to achieve his moral and financial project to establish a leading bank, he suggested to Saturn Bank's management in 1992 that they should establish a partnership venture – a subsidiary firm specialising in options, independent from the parent company and jointly owned by Saturn Bank and the heads of the trading room, who would be partners led by himself. The project did not come to anything (I will explain why later), but its very suggestion proves the extent of the power enjoyed by the head of options at the time. This is the perspective of one of the deputy chief executives, ten years later:

> His idea was to create a subsidiary and to play a direct role in that subsidiary. He did an excellent job of developing business but he didn't manage to convince Saturn completely – in other words to set up an organisation where he would be a shareholder, because that would have been a bloody stupid thing to do. It was stupid in terms of the guy's pay and level of responsibility. But mainly because they were contracting out a business that was needed by all the departments that served as underlying assets for those activities [options], be they equity, bonds, etc., and then all of a sudden everything fell into place because he buggered off, because he didn't want to . . .

Some said it was a coup . . . ?

> It was, because Saturn really depended on this guy. It wouldn't have taken much for him to become a multimillionaire if Saturn had given in. Also he'd contracted out a business at Saturn's expense, which is now probably Saturn's biggest business. It really would have been the hugest mistake.

The rationalisation of asset management

The derivatives industry followed the same process of division of labour, albeit less conspicuously, as the one used in the related sector of asset management on behalf of third parties (Kleiner 2000 & 2003). The asset management sector adopted a voluntarist policy for the division of labour that altered internal power relations. As Kleiner explains, in the mid-1980s finance work in that sector was highly unorganised:

> The organisation of labour in the French model of asset management is centred around the fund manager. Typically, when we look at the operation

method of management departments, we find that the workload – that is, the number of accounts and portfolios – is divided between the firm's fund managers. Each fund and each portfolio has its own dedicated manager. As a result, the department is highly segmented with people working individually: each manager looks after her fund or funds without concerning herself too much over what her colleagues are doing. Fund managers are responsible for all aspects of work and are monitored very little by the organisation that employs them. Each manager is responsible for making investment decisions, which means selecting the securities that are included in or excluded from her portfolios.

(Kleiner 2000, p. 14)

By the late 1990s, however, the activity was highly integrated and compartmentalised:

Thus, although the activity was managed by individuals in a non-systematic way, the new mode of organisation was based on a series of stages: economic research, buy-side analysis, investment committee, portfolio management, performance review and potential adjustments. This was called a "process" by French management professionals, who used the English term. It was a kind of assembly line where investment decisions were really made, just as one would produce cars, according to an entirely industrial logic . . . There was a major shift from highly personal investment decisions in the 1980s, taken by largely independent fund managers, to primarily collective decisions taken in the firm by 1999.

(Kleiner 2000, pp. 20–21)

The stakes involved in this transformation were perhaps lower due to the fact that asset management on behalf of third parties was less lucrative and more closely supervised than arbitrage or financial management for own account. By the end of that economic cycle, pay levels in asset management were generally lower than those commonly found in trading rooms.[6] However, the transformation was even more radical, both in the division of labour that prevailed, especially the division of financial decision-making, now tightly monitored, and in the inclusion in French law of the organisation of labour and its autonomy with respect to the parent bank (Kleiner 2003). The Anglo-American model was not adopted because it proved more efficient for savers in comparison with the "traditional" model (Kleiner 2000, pp. 33–40). Instead, it arose from the campaign to bring about greater legitimacy for the activity, led by the bosses of asset management teams who were keen to consecrate their new profession and new position, sometimes at the expense of fund managers' traditional autonomy. When constructing their rise, asset managers also wanted to establish a wage-payment method that was less favourable to their subordinates and thus more favourable to themselves. This is what the one portfolio manager implied, a clear-headed junior who had "a trump card to play: the process" and who would become a "soldier" of the new organisational methods:

That's why what really counts in this kind of management is the process. And we should talk about pay too, because the process consists in saying we're sick of star fund managers we're completely reliant on. If your star manager buggers off then you're in trouble. So what American institutions want for their pension funds aren't outstanding performances but consistent, regular performances. And for that you have to gradually push the value added up at firm level not just at on an individual level. What you need is for decision-making to be structured in such a way that each person is a pawn that can be moved. That's also a means of putting pressure on wages.

The sharp rise in the ten highest wages in an asset management firm like SGAM shows how successful this strategy was: average pay levels rose from 220,000 euros in 1997 – 8% of the wage bill – to 1.2 million euros in 2004 – 21% of the wage bill.

Collective moves

Hence organising work and managing subordinates is not only a technical process undertaken in order to enhance material productivity, it is also a way of managing social capital and building an indispensable position inside the group. This process of centralisation is to a certain extent similar to the structural hole aspect of social capital described by Ron Burt (1992). However, Burt focuses solely on the exercise of power within the group and ignores the power of the group itself when dealing with other groups. An understanding of social capital requires linking both dimensions.

Bourdieu is generally cited for his emphasis on group homogeneity because he stresses the durability and permanent nature of relationships and the strong interconnectivity of agents (Bourdieu 1980 and 1986). These are all factors that are likely to engender a strong group when it interacts with another group. When on the other hand Bourdieu affirms that "it is the same principle that produces a group instituted to enhance the concentration of capital and infra-group competition for the appropriation of social capital" (Bourdieu 1980, p. 3), he is distancing himself from the idea of a jointly owned form of capital and adopting a more balanced strategic perspective that is closer to Burt. Studying kinship inside Kabyl clans, Bourdieu showed that the homogeneity and the size of the group was for its leader both a positive strength for harvests and local wars against other clans, but also a threat because it generates costly consumption and risks of scission within the group and the resulting split of the clan's property (Bourdieu 1977). The leader of the clan tries to maintain an equilibrium favourable to his power by constraining its members to appropriate types of marriage (inside or outside the clan). In parallel, Burt's most recent studies seem to attribute a greater role to group cohesion (Burt 2005). He still sees diversification as the main vector of value added but now specifies that the group's cohesion enables trust to develop, reputations to stabilise and the group to line up behind an "entrepreneur".

In finance, heads of trading room are powerful not only because they can organise their primacy within the group but also because they build strong groups that can act in their favour. The most striking manifestation of their power is the fact that they can threaten to take all of their subordinates with them if ever they leave the firm. The possibility of redeploying collective assets in the finance business increases the power the heads acquire through a divide and conquer strategy. The head can therefore reallocate groups of individuals holding a range of tangible or intangible assets (market share, products, software, customers, etc.). The advantage inherent to the head of a trading room's position is organisational, structural and statutory.

Schematisation of the power to engineer a collective move

An analytical schema of networks can illustrate and clarify this point of view. In the following schema (for the example not based on data), the head of trading room is best placed to get the whole of the trading room to move (Figure 9.1). It would be much harder for a subordinate financial trader to offer a team for sale because coordination costs would be much higher; and it would be even harder to sell the head or the whole of the trading room because this would require a reversal in existing subordination and asset allocation relationships.

The head of a capital markets department is generally not well placed to organise a transfer of activities for several reasons relating to both the history of markets and the organisation of work. Department heads like Lepetit (2002) are

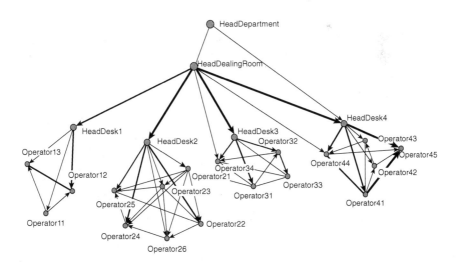

Figure 9.1 Collaborative relationships in a trading room

often individuals who supervise a market's development without doing any real trading themselves. They often suffer from a lack of legitimacy and above all from a lack of control over actual assets in the form of customers, market share, etc. For these individuals, it is more a case of approving subordinates' sharing of assets than of granting their own quasi-property rights. In addition, heads of department often supervise the activity from afar. They work in their own office, isolated and protected by their secretaries' desks. Their interactions with the heads of trading room remain sporadic. On the other hand, the head of trading room works directly in the trading room, interacting on a daily basis with all her employees, engaging in both business and informal discussions. The head of trading room forms ties that are both strong and diversified. The work organisation will ensure that the centrality lying at the heart of the organisational chart is effective. She becomes an indispensable intermediary between contacts separated by "structural holes", among whom she can develop competition in her favour (Burt 1992).

Strong ties give the head of trading room the capacity to move a group of employees, and avoiding any redundant ties increases their effectiveness. Ultimately, relational centrality puts the head of trading room in the best possible position to bring about a collective move. If an operator wanted to take a large number of staff with her, she would be forced to go through her head of desk and the head of trading room. Lacking close working relationships with subordinate employees on other desks (although these do sometimes develop), the operator is usually 4 degrees away from the operators at another desk (whereas the head of trading room is never more than 2 degrees from anyone in the room). The head of trading room cannot be totally "Burtian", however. She must take care to preserve some redundant contacts also, so as to circumvent, if need be, any second-in-command who may be insufficiently loyal or cooperative. For instance, the head of trading room on one of the floors I observed (Godechot 2001) cultivated all sorts of relationships beyond his direct subordinates. Moreover, an overly porous network could weaken the group dynamic and compromise the chances of a collective move. Close-knit, united teams are more likely to move en masse, since the group as a whole will put pressure on individual members. Employees will be all the more inclined to leave if they think that the bulk of the team is going, with little more than a skeleton activity being left behind.

Rising trading volumes have changed the balance of power in trading rooms. Where a financial activity is still being run by a small team of four or five traders, everyone interacts with everyone and the team manager has no significant structural advantage over anyone else. The manager has a kind of statutory privilege: if she moves along with the rest of the team, she is unlikely to accept a subordinate position at the new firm. At the same time, where a manager's style has displeased a team, its members may decide to leave without her. Larger activities encompassing several teams and levels in the hierarchy are marked by a more differentiated power structure. What can happen here is that a subordinate trader may well decide to jump ship along with a few colleagues, possibly accompanied by some outsiders. The head of desk may take a large fraction of her team with her and possibly another desk as well (if the individual in question has a good relationship with the other desk managers). The only person capable of moving the whole trading room, however, is the head of trading room, who becomes the key element in engineering collective moves due to the fact that she is the person who coordinates and subdivides the work.

During my investigations (based on nearly 100 interviews covering this and other topics), I heard many stories of collective moves, besides the hold-up described in detail in previous chapters, including:

- In 1990, after Drexel Burnham Lambert went bankrupt, its ex-head of futures negotiated the recruitment of a 60-person team with Indosuez.
- A market-making team resigned en masse from Neptune Bank because members refused new risk control measures.
- An equity derivatives team resigned en masse from a London investment bank, starting up a rival firm in Dublin where contractual non-competition clauses did not hold.

These stories are often casually exchanged and may be old or second-hand. To better understand the mechanisms by which the head of trading room will mobilise a group, it is also useful to undertake a detailed analysis of some failures.

The limits of the power to mobilise

Although possible, it is risky for the bank to replace the head of trading room. Either the head's successor finds it hard to get along with the teams under her orders and thus cannot prevent people from leaving and transferring the activity, or else she keeps her teams together but de facto replicates her predecessor's structural position including any associated bargaining power that she may be able to use in the future. When the head of equity derivatives at Neptune Bank helped bring about the departure of the head of fixed income and foreign exchange, and then took over all of his duties, he faced a wave of resignations, even before his former rival had found a new job. The operators involved had no faith in their new head of trading room, and took the opportunity to move elsewhere.

Although it is certainly difficult to replace the head of trading room, and the successor may well show similar secessionist tendencies in the future, the organisation of a succession often provides the bank with an opportunity to gain time and to lock in company assets.

This art of managing hold-ups can be illustrated by the contentious resignation of Saturn Bank's head of options. In 1990 and 1991, facing mass defections by traders headhunted by English and American banks, this manager's reaction was to try to invent a new institutional form, a partnership that would develop long-term incentives and stabilise staff levels (cf. boxed text).

The partnership project

When did this idea of a partnership first occur to you?

When I started . . . The English headhunters were the last straw for me. They have a special talent for destabilising people who've been working for two or three years after university and are extremely productive. At that point other banks noticed this. The American banks do very little research and development. For me it's really important that research and development forms the core of my activities . . .

Generally speaking, to solve this issue [of resignations and remuneration] a very important structural step had to be put into place. That step was the creation of Saturn Financial Products, which meant a proper partnership with an effective, modern partnership system, which I really liked because it aimed to resolve this question definitively. I know it created other problems, but I'd drawn up partnership statutes.

Was this partnership created because of remuneration issues?

It was more a question of commitment . . . We were treading on everyone's toes and it was a real source of conflict. I wanted to turn that conflict into a contractual opportunity, where we would reach the point of saying, "This is like a mushroom growing in every direction." We wanted to get things in order: "What are our rights? What are our obligations?" So that was the first thing to do: get things in order and make them durable. The second thing to do was refocus everyone's attention on the project. We needed to give it a name as well and to clearly define our position in relation to the rest of the bank, because our aim was not necessarily the same. There was some jealousy. When people wanted to flatter me they'd say, "You're taking Saturn to the top. You have a mission to lead Saturn!" And when they wanted to be unpleasant, they'd say, "Why don't you get on with anyone? Why is everyone against you?" So the idea was to establish our goal and a framework for the activity – to say that Saturn was a highly respectable commercial bank but we're going to have a different wage system and a different type of involvement. There is one clear framework in investment banking, and it's for the elite. And we're going to make sure the Americans are left in the dust. So Saturn Financial Products was born out of the partnership. I'd given a lot of thought to how we could develop the partnership system. When it comes to the wage system, I think that deep down everyone who does this job feels it isn't going to last. They think it can't last and that their luck will run out, so they have to make as much money as possible while they still can. As for the rest, well, what's gone is gone. They believe that the situation can't last and that the whole thing can fall apart at any moment. The idea was to reject that sense of fragility and set something up that would stand the test of time. And if we build something to last, people act more responsibly. I think it's more responsible to be an equity holder than a wage earner with a bonus, which infantilises people. All those bonus discussions were childish. The arguments were just infantile. So the idea was to move beyond that and put an end to that immaturity . . .

We wanted to create a partnership in which Saturn Financial Products was owned 75% by Saturn and 25% by the partners. The basic principle of any partnership is that people don't believe they have a right to any more than what is called the "bought value". That's fundamentally important. The bought value is the money that's been made and used as capital. The reason why all the partnerships are collapsing in the United States is because the market quotes two or three times the bought value . . . No partnership can function without following that principle. Why not? The idea is that it allows the partners to buy their share under reasonable terms . . . Do I calculate now what will be generated over the course of a lifetime and work out a kind of current value, and make that the firm's value? Or do I say, "No, the value of the firm will be determined little by little as it emerges!"?

Which employees would have become partners?

At the beginning there were about 20 employees who were partners. The idea was to have an open system. How would we manage the partnership's demography in the future? That remained to be seen, but I think we asked for a very high level of commitment from people in terms of personal involvement. And it was understandable that people couldn't keep that up their whole lives. We didn't want any cheating; everything had to be planned, organised and done properly. So we had people coming and going. When someone left, he'd sell. On the other hand, when someone joined they'd buy a share and make a financial commitment . . . The idea was for people to have a stake in the partnership and thereby become a capitalist . . . What I liked about having Saturn own 75% was that it meant they wouldn't start messing about. We had a framework, and I liked having that balance . . . People knew that within the partnership they would still get a bonus if they weren't a partner. We wanted it to be completely open with a status people envied and desired and would do anything to be a part of.

According to the head of options, the project's failure was due to several factors. The head of fixed income and head of equities were impatient rivals who wanted to break up his empire; the young co-chief executive officer, a newly appointed former government inspector, showed little understanding because he was primarily concerned with maintaining the unity of the bank he hoped to chair one day. Lastly, the head of options did not have the time to promote his project internally.

Trusting in his own power and empire, he tried to bulldoze his way through the opposition: "To me this was paramount so I threatened to resign if I didn't get what I wanted. I said, 'If you don't like it, I'll leave!'" His miscalculation may have been to think that his department's success was attributable to him personally, when his real power lay in his ability to engineer collective moves. To combat his impending resignation and stem the potential flow of resignations, the bank organised what its HR professionals described as "a full-scale putsch". HR allegedly made a surreptitious promise to promote all of the head of options' direct subordinates so as to prevent them from resigning along with their boss and leaving behind a field of ruins.[7] When the head of options finally did threaten to resign in 1992, he had not yet developed a credible project in another bank and could offer his team no other host structure if it followed him. It took him a year to put together an alternative project, finally concretising his partnership idea in the subsidiary of a German bank and taking around a dozen colleagues from Saturn Bank to this new venture. However, most of the financial power in the old options department, a total of around 300 or 400 employees, stayed put at Saturn.

The ex-head of options' rivals were the heads of equities, fixed income and foreign exchange, who split up the options department so that each ran the options teams associated with their own cash product. Some of the head of options' former subordinates were promoted to head of desk (and even trading room) and offered a chance to run a relatively autonomous derivative products section within the confines of departments defined by the underlying asset classes. More specifically, three direct subordinates of the ex-head of options[8] were put in charge of the equity derivative products group that would, by the late 1990s, become Saturn Bank's most profitable financial activity as the three rose up through the bank's hierarchy and revolutionised the pay scale. He still spoke of them with affection but others described them as "traitors". Clearly, the ex-head of options had taken too long to engineer a collective departure. By the time he made this move it was too late because the bank had already promoted the key figures he was counting on, realising that they would be less inclined to leave if they felt attached to the old structure. He had lost his ability to take Saturn Bank's assets with him to the new structure.

It is not true that the ability to engineer a collective move automatically increases proportionately with the size of the team involved or the volumes traded. Higher volumes imply the mobilisation of a bigger area but also diminish the intensity of mobilisation. Going further up the hierarchical scale and dealing with larger volumes connects activities that are more distant and heterogeneous with less intense links. Governance is done at a distance here and less time is spent with each individual. Leaders can easily fall prey to the counter-manoeuvring of direct subordinates who may hope that the boss will leave and make way for their own rise. In the late 1990s, the most strategic structural position for engineering collective moves seems to have been the head of trading room. After 2000, 15 or so years on from their arrival in the finance industry, these heads of trading room started wondering how they might secure their ascent by attaining a status that would finally legitimise their astounding economic success. Were they at risk of losing their power to rise up through the firm, or could they use it to acquire a position other than head of trading, whom those above consider little more than a head trader? The lack of any clear response to this meant that a whole array of career trajectories took shape. At Saturn Bank, for example, in the astute judgement of a R&D team manager, "no one questioned the hierarchy established in the 1990s" (at least not before 2001). After the head of options left in 1992, his second-in-command inherited the equity derivatives department, with the original number three becoming head of trading and the original number four head of sales. Two or three years later, the original second-in-command was promoted to run a financial products subsidiary in Asia, with the original number three replacing him as head of equity derivatives and the original number four becoming his deputy.

The career trajectory of the original third-in-command is particularly interesting. By late 1999, he had been promoted to co-manage, alongside an American, the whole of the equity and investment department (stock brokerage, equity derivatives, financial analysis, initial public offerings) and got onto the firm's executive committee. The doors to the bank's highest echelons, traditionally closed to market professionals in France, seemed to have finally opened. Yet this was a risky ascent since it meant that he was losing control over the equity derivatives group where his former deputy was now in charge. In other words, promotion put a distance between the manager and the entities that had first helped him to gain power. Two years later, the rise of the equity derivatives group was given a boost in a new reorganisation. It became a distinct and autonomous department at exactly the same level as the equity department that the original third-in-command headed. Hence, this manager definitively lost control over the equity derivatives group he had originally used as a springboard. He did take over some of the M&A activities that had heretofore escaped his authority but lost out on control of the more powerful department. His remaining activities, like stock brokerage or M&A, were generally smaller earners at Saturn Bank and made substantial losses during the 2001/2002 recession.

Financial traders describing this case talked about how the original third-in-command had been duped, since his former assistant "did him in" – a claim which one trader softened with the reminder that "it's the least that can happen in this business".

Others told me that the former head of options' third and fourth-in-command, "putschists" who were working together when the head left the firm, in actual fact loathed each other. The third-in-command, whom I met shortly after the reorganisation, appeared to see it as a "challenge". He made the following points: restructuring was a "breath of air"; he was "no longer the real boss [of equity derivatives]"; the equity derivatives he had been managing were now "their proper weight in the firm"; they had to "look beyond them"; "the pay is good, but at some point you have to do something with your life";[9] in his new job, where he was dealing with a "major structural readjustment", "everything could be reinvented", etc. He was a fierce critic of the trading world and opposed the trader he claimed he never was with the leader he hoped henceforth to embody:

Trading doesn't lead anywhere! You have to continue with your career, which means taking a step back then moving forward again. You have to go backwards in order to move in a new direction. There's no natural career development for traders. Your mind just atrophies because quite frankly it doesn't take much intelligence to quote a 4–2 [price range] all day. In terms of theoretical reflection you're just wasting away. Also in terms of your relationships with others, because you only ever communicate with people through a price scale. You only judge people by the prices they're quoting. You forget how to talk, convince, seduce. It's not a profession that lets you develop a sense of strategy. Being the boss of a big trading team doesn't really make you a leader. So it doesn't take you anywhere.

He argues that the management of trading rooms should be replaced by a new generation of leaders who are not necessarily market men but, rather, have proved their ability to lead:

A leader might not cost as much as a very good trader. But it might also mean that the next leader of the G8 [the trading room's group of managers] is a guy who's been recruited from Carrefour [a major firm in the retail sector] for his leadership qualities. That's how it'll be in the future . . . That's a real cultural revolution.[10]

Once his microphone was switched off, he finished with a fierce attack on the managers of the equity derivatives trading room. He told me that one boss had said "he saw no interesting jobs" outside of equity derivatives, which the third-in-command saw as a sign of necrosis, a lack of vision, a shortening of his intellectual horizon and the decision not to test himself elsewhere. He mocked financial operators who believe that their money makes them part of the bourgeoisie, oblivious to the fact that "outside the world of finance they're nobody!".

Switching between denial and clarity, he had developed a discourse aiming to transmute the loss of his external power (loss of control over the equity derivatives activity) as a sign of his fundamental decision (to remove himself from the vulgar world of trading, gain access at last to economic notability, perhaps at the cost of asceticism, by developing the fundamental quality of leadership and ultimately setting out on the path towards the bank's top echelons). A few months after this interview, I was surprised to see that he no longer featured in Saturn Bank's annual report. An HR professional informed me that he had left the bank. She suspected that the co-director of the department, a "real hit man", had done everything he could to oust him. Unable to control his assets, the former head of trading room had lost much of his power and legitimacy. He had been incapable, during the course of his risky rise, of converting market capital into a different kind of organisational capital.

***

By showing, through those two examples, both the circumstantial limitations (such as the bad timing of the outside option) and structural limitations (such as a professional ascension that weakens ties with the front office) of a head's power to engineer a collective move during the 1990s, I also define its strength. A head of trading room can *increase* her own *hold-up power*[11] by continually working to maintain strong, selective and hierarchised social relations. This way of managing *social capital* is original in that it exploits the strength of social ties as well their selectivity, density and porosity. If a manager wishes to bring a whole team along with her, strong ties are more effective than weak ones. In order to have time to develop these vital connections, she must select the most important relationships while delegating connections of secondary importance. Bringing on board a head of desk who in turn can bring all the members of her team may prove more economically sound than forming links with subordinate employees and even those below them (while also ensuring that one does not depend entirely on the former to recruit the latter). At the same time, the head of trading room must make sure the relationships between her contacts remain porous, thereby ensuring her own indispensability. If the heads of desk can coordinate without her help, they will have the capacity to take away a sector of the market and thus render her superfluous. The head of trading must protect her role of *tertius gaudens* – a third party who reaps the benefits by forcing her contacts into competition with one another (Burt 1992).

The head of trading room has to manage social capital in a way that is both practical and strategic: this is an art that cannot be reduced to a mere set of principles. Not only must heads of trading manage their social capital in a way that will enable them to engineer collective moves, but in their relationships with their own bosses they must transform it into a symbolic capital. They must get their own managers, top bank executives in the traditional sense, to believe that they are basically the delegates of a close-knit team of traders who are all ready to set sail if the conditions are not right; and that belief in cohesion is often more important than the actual cohesion of the team in question. The head of trading room appropriates the group's power when speaking with senior executives on behalf of the trading group. At the same time, and to maintain primacy, the head of trading room must increase the number of divisions, allocate privileges, force some employees to wait, reward them and avoid being replaced by some alternative coordinator.

In the end, the picture of financial activity that has emerged is highly political. The art of the head of trading room is similar to that of a war leader. It can be compared to that of the king in court society (Elias 2006), except that in this case the central position is ephemeral and has no guarantees. Much like a king, the head of a trading room must divide in order to govern. As Elias (2006) explained, fuelling tensions was for the king a critical strategy. A perfect understanding of his subjects constituted a dangerous threat for his power.

However, in view of a head's precarious position and her need to secure her team members' loyalty and the relative cohesion of the group as a whole in order to bring about a departure, the head is required to temper and conceal that division and counterbalance it with efforts to unite the group.

The group led by the head of a trading room has some points in common with the charismatic groups described by Weber and discussed by Elias. In these groups, "[Tensions] have to be suppressed. For what matters in this case, is to direct the strength, the aims and thus the social pressure of all the people united in this group outwards, against the disturbed social field, against the wider dominion that is to be conquered" (Elias 2006, p. 133). The head's power is all the greater when activities are on the rise, when she can both divide and downplay that division, finding enough booty to redistribute so as to turn that division into a collaboration. If she can skilfully navigate her way through this art of opposition, moving through the different stages in the partial redistribution of the collective production, she will gain full control over the mobilisation of that collective and its associated profits.

We therefore gain an understanding of the ways in which the appropriation of assets is concentrated in one focal point – an individual – and how internal entrepreneurs, who are salaried in status but fundamentally capitalist in practice, have emerged. The exceptional situation in which heads of trading room function explains their exceptional pay levels. However, beyond this, it also enables an analysis of wage relations and, more generally, interpersonal relations. It clarifies the conditions of possibility and effects of charisma in economic life.

Notes

1 Bargaining was banned in France by the Luxembourg Commission in 1848. It is still prohibited today (art. L 125–1 and 125–3 of the Labour Code) and is subject to serious criminal sanctions (art. 152–3).
2 Definition given in 1898 by the employment office, cited by Mottez (1960, p. 207).
3 He writes at the end of his article in 1974: "It was not the handmill that gave us feudalism, but the feudal lord that gave us the water mill" (Marglin 1974, p. 107).
4 Marglin alludes to imperfect competition, which probably plays a major role in this mechanism. The market for goods is protected by entry barriers, seemingly unlike an unqualified labour market. This means that entrepreneurs capture the rents previously held by self-employed craftspersons. At the same time, entry barriers protect entrepreneurs from the transfer of this rent to consumers via a price mechanism. Under these conditions, the resulting division of labour is politically optimal for the entrepreneurs alone: it is neither a technical optimum nor a social one.
5 "I can do any job in a trading room. That won't be the case soon. You have to specialise now," said one trader who had worked in the back office and middle office before becoming a trader.
6 According to the social reports of SGAM, a subsidiary of Société Générale specialised in asset management, the sum total of the ten highest wages reached 6.5 million euros in 2001. In the same period, the ten highest wages at Société Générale were eight to nine times higher.
7 This story was told at a lively lunch gathering. It may have been slightly exaggerated.
8 "I had three people: imagination [the future head of sales], energy [the future head of financial markets in Asia] and the one I called the Diesel [the future head of equity derivatives] because he'd have a huge stack of work in the morning but by evening

had processed the whole lot; he had such a high capacity to get things done well, it was marvellous," said the former head of capital markets at Saturn Bank.

9 He later continued, "You reach the age of 40, you've been making money for the past 15 years. You're sitting on a pile of dough. Have you made a success of your life? Really?"

10 The chances of a person from outside finance being appointed are extremely small, for the reasons cited earlier.

11 Bourdieu highlights the multiplier effect of social capital (Bourdieu 1980).

References

Bourdieu, P 1977, 'Case Study: Parallel-Cousin Marriage' in *An Outline of a Theory of Practice*, ed. P Bourdieu, Cambridge University Press, Cambridge MA, pp. 30–71.

Bourdieu, P 1980, 'Le capital social. Notes provisoires', *Actes de la recherche en sciences sociales*, n°31, pp. 2–3.

Bourdieu, P 1986, 'The Forms of Capital' in *Handbook of Theory and Research for the Sociology of Education*, ed. J Richardson, Greenwood, New York, pp. 241–258.

Burt, R 1992, *Structural Holes. The Social Structure of Competition*, University of Chicago Press, Chicago IL.

Burt, R, 2005, *Brokerage and Network Closure*, Oxford University Press, Oxford.

Coleman, J 1988, 'Social Capital in the Creation of Human Capital', *American Journal of Sociology*, vol. 94, Supplement 1, pp. 95–120.

Durkheim, E 1997, *The Division of Labor in Society*, Free Press, New York.

Elias, N 2006, *The Court Society*, University College Dublin Press, Dublin.

Godechot, O and Mariot, N 2004, 'Les deux formes du capital social. Structure relationnelle des jurys de thèse et recrutement en science politique', *Revue française de sociologie*, vol. 45, n°2, pp. 243–282.

Granovetter, M 1995, 'The Economic Sociology of Firms and Entrepreneurs', in *The Economic Sociology of Immigration*, ed. Alejandro Portes, Russell Sage Foundations Publications, New York, pp.128–165.

Kleiner, T 2000, 'D'un artisanat à une industrie: la transformation de l'industrie française de la gestion d'actifs par l'intégration de routines professionnelles depuis le système anglo-saxon', conference presentation delivered at the 'Journées d'études sociales de la finance', 21 April, École des Mines, Paris.

Kleiner, T 2003, 'La consécration des gestionnaires d'actifs sur la place de Paris', *Actes de la recherche en sciences sociales*, n°23, pp. 42–50.

Lepetit, JF 2002, *Homme de marché*, Economica, Paris.

Marglin, S 1974, 'What Do Bosses Do? The Origins and Functions of Hierarchy in Capitalist Production', *The Review of Radical Political Economy*, vol. 6, n°2, pp. 60–112.

Mottez, B 1960, 'Du marchandage au salaire au rendement', *Sociologie du travail*, vol. 2, n°3, pp. 206–215.

Mottez, B 1966, *Système de salaire et politiques patronales: essai sur l'évolution des pratiques et des idéologies patronales*, CNRS, Paris.

Conclusion

Value creation for wage earners?

My work can be summed up in very simple terms. Finance wage earners capture rents out of which they are paid exorbitant wages. Many scholars, even the most neoclassical ones, consider that market professionals exploit micro-inefficiencies in the securities market. I show that they also exploit organisational inefficiency. In the language of Bourdieu, over the course of their career in finance they accumulate "capital" from which they draw profits (Bourdieu 2005).

In order to uncover these rents, however, I had to look beyond the meritocratic, market-based denials that these professionals are so quick to make (It's the results! It's the market! It's the performance! It's the job!). To analyse this specific accumulation of an even more specific capital, I had to mobilise intermediary concepts from property right theory without which concepts (such as capital and profit) used in the classical analysis of capitalism would have run idle. I had to focus on the activity itself, including its organisation and division.

This shift led me to analyse how domains of activity in the workplace are, on a daily basis, allocated, confirmed, guaranteed, extended, stabilised and defended against attacks by rivals. These domains of activity are a means by which an actor can extend herself at work. She makes them her own. She acquires implicit property rights over them. And the fruits of those domains of activity become the fruits of that ownership and therefore of the wage earner. These tiny operations during which the rights to those domains of activity are allocated – operations that are particularly effective because they appear above all as technical ones – are the conditions of possibility for an attachment of a masterless profit to an individual. They enable a "this is mine" approach, which asserts its legitimacy both for oneself and for others. The differentials of volume and structure of those possessions allow us to conceive the differentials of capacity for the symbolic appropriation of profit.

The sources of legitimate appropriation of profit are also the sources of the forces that render that appropriation effective. The attribution of increasingly substantial and absolute rights over productive assets, clients, portfolios, knowledge, know-how, etc. is also a means of granting financial operators a monopoly over assets that are more and more detached and detachable. The owners of those assets feel justified in claiming the fruits for themselves (after all, are they not an extension of their own action and their own person?). They can also impose their conception of distribution on all wage earners who, during the productive process, require access to those profitable, monopolised, detachable assets. By threatening to redeploy those assets internally or externally in a hold-up, wage earners are able to appropriate effectively the multilateral rent associated with the productive collaboration.

This two-step analysis respectively mobilises the two polar principles of explanation in the social sciences: belief on the one hand, and opportunistic calculation on the other. How do you end up believing and making others believe that everything that has been done on the job was done "by you" and is "yours"? How do you threaten to break off relations in order to monopolise the lion's share of the profit? These two approaches, distinct in analytical terms, are in fact inextricably connected. The possibility of moving those assets seems to prove the individual origin of profit and strengthen people's belief in the legitimacy of their rights over assets and profit. In return, their belief in the legitimacy of those rights transforms any opportunistic strategy aimed at capturing profit into an operation of justice.

First of all, this incursion into the complex world of finance has theoretical merit. Analysing property rights within an organisation gives the tools for conceiving the symbolic in economic sociology otherwise than as an inspired antithesis of commercial venality.[1] By explaining how people mobilise property rights in order to justify and impose a particular division on others, I clarify the often-stated relationship between ownership and domination, and between capital and profit.[2] It then becomes possible to conceive that relationship as one of exploitation, without adopting, as Marx (1990) did, a theory of labour value, without using a metric to measure work quantity, and without carving up productive labour and unproductive labour, value production and the extortion of surplus value.

Some of these points overlap with the "Elements of a General Grammar of Exploitation" set out by Boltanski and Chiapello (2006, p. 373). They maintain that the characterisation of exploitation "presupposes establishing a vast mechanism of *accounting equivalences*" on the one hand, which enables an injustice to be highlighted, and on the other hand demonstrates "the strength on which the unequal division is based, and also what makes it invisible (otherwise unveiling it would be pointless)" (ibid., p. 374). Exploitation is an inversion of the justification proposed in the grammar of polities: it is no longer "the good fortune of great men [that] makes for the good fortune of the little people" but, conversely, "misfortune of the little people makes the fortune of the great men" (ibid., p. 375). This grammar allows for a plurality of modes of exploitation, particularly the connexionist exploitation that is characteristic of the "new spirit of capitalism", where "some people's immobility is necessary for other people's mobility" (ibid., p. 362). In a sense, this is a clarification of the mode of exploitation of the least mobile by the most mobile (ibid., p. 465).

In finance, exploitation is not a result of intrinsic mobility but of the extension of the mobility of people through the mobility of the assets with which they work. It is the "structure of capital", in this case the degree of transferability of the assets they hold, which then becomes a determining factor of that strength and that capacity to exploit others.

The exemplarity of finance

This incursion into the world of finance has a second merit. It not only enables theoretical sequences to be clarified but also allows us to reconsider the composite elements of wage labour, particularly its upper echelons. True, wage relations in the financial industry are exceptional. But they reveal general mechanisms that can also be found elsewhere. In other sectors we also find wage earners, particularly the heads of profit centres, who appropriate chunks of productive activity and thus lay claim to the symbolic and material profits of the property rights they seize. Finance is not the only sector in which wage earners have a chance to accumulate all kinds of products resulting from collective life – knowledge, know-how, software, colleagues, clients, capital – which they mobilise internally in order to establish their position or else move externally for their own profit. Thus, the extreme mechanisms found in finance are perhaps more general mechanisms that are liable to shape wage relations in other sectors in a more diffuse manner. I did not make a comparative study, but existing literature shows that these are highly suggestive leads.

Historians observe that during the Industrial Revolution, skilled English workers were hired by French businessmen for much higher wages on account of the new technologies they brought with them (Verley 1997). More recently, in his study of fast-growing businesses, Bhidé reports that 71% of the fastest-growing American companies that make the Inc. 500 list were set up by people who have replicated or modified an idea they encountered in their previous job (Bhidé 2000, p. 94). My study of the finance industry shows that the asset transfer phenomenon goes beyond innovation, industrial secrets and human capital, and also involves forms of material capital (computers, software, data bases) and, even more so, social capital.[3]

While it may appear general, the phenomenon of hold-up and asset transfer by wage earners varies in intensity according to sector, production type, robustness of legal protections in place and work organisation. In heavy industry, material assets protected by property rights are hard to move, and the technologies involved – themselves protected by patents and relatively specific to the particular production techniques used by the company in question – are not transferable either. In the services industry, immaterial assets are both easier to move physically and have weaker legal protection. The deterritorialisation of relations in the areas of production and commercialisation, which is often most pronounced in the flagship sectors of "globalisation", can make non-compete clauses ineffective. The consultancy industry is one economic sector known for group defections. Zingales describes a particularly striking case of a mass resignation in the advertising sector. In 1994, when Saatchi and Saatchi's main shareholder refused CEO Maurice Saatchi the right to award himself a generous stock options package, the Saatchi brothers left the firm with most of the staff and set up a rival company, leaving their former company, renamed Cordiant, severely weakened (Zingales 2000, p. 1641). However, as shown in Lazega's study of an American business law firm, some companies with a particularly high risk of mass defection have work organisation and social relations systems that significantly reduce this kind of threat (Lazega 2001, pp. 182–200). The administrative system of rotating clients and teams of employees between partners, as well as the relational dependence between partners who bring in clients and partners who run the firm, make it difficult to form close-knit teams that would have the capacity to leave together and take clients with them.

Inequalities and remuneration levels in finance can also be compared with those found in the show business world (Menger 2002). Admittedly, the main mechanisms differ markedly: there is a link between remuneration and the focusing of demand on a limited number of specific points (famous names). The show business "career" takes the form of a competition to acquire this star status as a personality with a famous name. This progression does not really take place in the context of traditional wage and organisational relations, but rather in a succession of prototype projects that bring together several actors. Despite significant differences between the entertainment industry and the finance sector, we can nonetheless observe a collective production that becomes individualised and leads to a person's success (or a very limited number of people). Artistic collaborations give rise to unequal and uncertain exchanges. Does a great film director establish the reputation of a great actor, or is it the other way round? The ones who achieve success are often those who have been able to take advantage of these ambiguous exchanges to further their own career (Lutter 2014).

The academic world is not entirely free of the mechanisms at work in the financial sector. In France, the remuneration of research professors depends essentially on their status and varies very little according to their academic work. The chances of appropriating financial profit are therefore limited. However, other forms of profit can be seized: prestige, sources of research funding, institutional power, employment positions, etc. Leaving one's laboratory with part of one's team is a very common strategy and this show of strength enables people to change the structure behind the distribution of academic profit.

This initial comparative, general outline invites us to go beyond the financial industry in order to analyse variations in forms of appropriation and the transfer by wage earners of collectively amassed assets.

Bonuses, inequalities and wage utopia

Lastly, finance is highly indicative in that it raises the open political question of wealth distribution. To finish the analysis, I shall shed my academic impartiality in order to consider that distribution. I summon entities – wage earners, capital – whose unity and reality are objectively questionable but whose invocation cannot fail to produce an effect. I shall take on two normative positions, both debatable and partial: "wage labour must be defended" and "inequalities must be reduced". Seen from these two angles, should the finance industry be considered exemplary? That exemplarity would bring new perspectives, certainly, but those perspectives are contradictory and aporetic. On the one hand, wage earners in the finance industry have, on the whole, established a remarkable system in defence of their own interests. On the other hand, that defence is organised at the expense of an explosion in wage inequality, the fragmentation of wage labour and even its dissolution. The finance industry does not offer any solutions. It merely draws attention to the political issues of our time.

The utopian exit from wage labour

In an ironic turnaround, we might wonder if finance wage earners are succeeding in achieving the old workers' watchword "abolition of wage labour". The individual who renounces wage labour usually has a private income or runs a private hedge fund. However, such exits from wage labour remain partly utopian horizons.

I was frequently asked the same question during my research: "Why don't these people stop working?" Financial operators themselves often say they do not intend to continue in their profession forever. They play with the idea of leaving, reinventing themselves, doing something else, but it usually remains a vague plan on the horizon and an option they continually put off. They think of it more as something that gives them a certain amount of freedom rather than an actual plan. Occasionally I would hear of employees who stopped working from one day to the next. I was also told that among the latter some were finally unhappy not working anymore: they became bored, depressed and they faced difficulties when returning to finance. When comparing people's successful and unsuccessful attempts to leave the finance industry permanently, one can reach the following conclusion: in order to be successful, the financial operator who wishes to leave must have invested sufficiently in an area outside finance in order for that alternative integration to give social meaning to her existence (Bourdieu 2000). For instance, I met a trader who became a theatre director. He was a former philosophy professor whose stint in trading was a mere digression for him – a means of ending a disappointing teaching career and transitioning towards achieving his dream of working in the world of theatre, in which he had already established a foothold before his career change.

Stopping work to live off one's private income may be problematic. People may well love travel and leisure activities. But will they love them the whole year round? Who will accompany them while they idle away their days? The greater a person's investment in the world of finance, the less meaning their social existence has outside of that field. To make their new life as a rentier enjoyable, they must have had a specific type of education (with a particular connection to money) and a rich social network among the high bourgeoisie or aristocracy, which these individuals do not have. That is why the desire to renounce wage labour and live off a private income does not really constitute a long-term plan ("I'll save up so much and then stop"), even if there are a few known cases. Giving up work and doing nothing are merely circumstances that financial operators go through. This includes heads of desk, heads of trading room or heads of capital markets departments who have been made redundant following a merger between two financial firms, for example. Inactivity is not seen as a permanent state, and even if it causes their assets to lose value, it is often seen as a temporary phase before they re-enter wage labour, usually in finance.

These operators may be able to free themselves from wage labour not by living off investments but by setting up a hedge fund. These hedge funds usually take the form of a partnership. The members, or at least the founding members, are managing partners who share profit directly among themselves in accordance with the rules they set out. The hedge fund has a mythical dimension for employees, for a number of reasons. First of all, it lures traders with the promise of completely independent trading, free of risk controllers, totally protected by stable, guaranteed boundaries (with an individual bonus formula, for example). It also has the utopian dimension of a financial firm free from both wage labour and capital, a kind of "temporary autonomous zone" (Bey 1991). Market finance, which is already largely an industry of wage earners, has a paradoxical utopian horizon on which it transforms completely into a firm of wage earners (who would no longer be wage earners) in the very unequal form of a partnership. While most financial partnerships (Goldman Sachs, Salomon Brothers, Merrill Lynch, etc.) were dismantled as a result of stock market inflation in the last quarter of a century, the partnership ideal was revived among the rank and file while managers became capitalist. In the mid-2000s, record bonuses allowed many financial operators to make the leap and free themselves from capital by leaving with their assets in hand and setting up small "cooperatives" – hedge funds run by a handful of financial operators who are all together wage earners, partners and peers as well as capitalist to some degree.

However, when taking a closer look, they are not entirely free from capital. Capital is not completely divested of its power to control to the extent that its role merely becomes that of equity provider whose ambition to hold the fund's assets and products is residual. Most hedge funds are attached to banks, both for financing purposes as well as for continuity as regards material operations, settlement, delivery, accounting, material resources (IT networks) in combination with HR (back office staff), which in a way constitute the bank's fixed assets which it succeeds in securing and rendering immoveable, and from which it extracts rent. The distinct cycles of hedge fund activity since 2000, which have alternated between phases of creation and phases of closure, show that wage earners who capture assets do not free themselves from capital altogether. Those that survive are often those with the strongest attachment to banks. Hedge fund members are monitored, sheltered, owned by the bank; they have slightly more autonomy than internal wage earners but, even when they are partners, they did not completely escape wage labour.

Value creation for wage earners

There are a number of examples of individuals leaving wage labour: financial operators who become rentiers, partners or capitalists. However, the financial industry as a whole has not abolished wage labour in structural terms (even dynamically). Even so, it displays characteristics that wage labour as a whole should consider. As such, finance is both a model to follow and a model to avoid.

It is an industry that in many ways is at the forefront when it comes to applying the rhetoric of value creation (Lordon 2000). The value creation imperative was put forward by consulting firms, starting with Stern and Stewart, which patented the idea of economic value added (EVA), and was quickly followed in its crusade by big consultancy firms like McKinsey. It was received with interest by the financial industry for several reasons. First, this idea resonated with financial analysts' need for monitoring economic activities. Second, the banks themselves were taking considerable risks on the financial markets and were looking for very accurate profit indicators, where the risk taken by capital could be discounted from the result that was effectively observed. Through this two-way movement, the concepts behind "shareholder value" became dominant in banking. With the introduction of risk-adjusted return on capital (RAROC), value at risk (VaR), analytical accounting, mark-to-market, the allocation of equity capital and current internal models for risk monitoring, the banking industry is in many ways ahead of other sectors when it comes to establishing value creation indicators.

However, value creation, repeated ad infinitum as customary justification for every economic decision, does not necessarily mean "value creation for shareholders", but perhaps above all "value creation for wage earners". The method for calculating bonuses by business line is fairly clear on this point (Chapter 2). The bonus is calculated on the basis of net profit before taxes and bonuses, but after equity capital has been remunerated for both its use (interest rate) and the risks incurred (risk premium). This net profit corresponds fairly well to created value. However, that created value is not just for shareholders: the bonus share is added to the one-third deducted by the state as corporation tax. In the equity derivatives business line, the bonus formula rate is as high as 35%. With Social Security contributions, that rate reaches around 50%. Value creation is therefore primarily value creation for wage earners. Claims that capital appropriates all created value, when it is already compensated for risk and capital contribution, are debatable. Indeed, is created value not chiefly the fruit of the activity of generations of wage earners? Finance thus presents a surprising paradox: by bringing about an accounting truth regime based on the unilateral allocation of profits to shareholders, finance enables wage earners to lay claim to a substantial share of those profits. From this perspective, finance can set an example for other economic sectors. It is possible to reconstruct in other management frameworks power relations that are more in favour of wage earners.

However, the analysis of the bonus distribution mechanism in detail shows that value creation can in no way be conceived as value creation for all wage earners. It amounts to value creation only for a few wage earners. This massive inequality and the presence of capitalism within wage labour challenge its claims of unity. What should wage labour do to counter this capturing of created value by a few individuals? Should it respect it as the entitlement of a particular group of wage earners? This question may seem irrelevant when that group merely comprises a handful of heads of trading room, but it is more pertinent when the group also includes traders and salespeople. Should trade unions disregard them, condemn them or support them? In the economic turnaround of 2001, the remuneration of

English CEOs (the "fat cats") was brought to public attention. Trade unions were quick to side with small shareholders and, at the general assembly, condemn executives' remuneration levels, vote in motions expressing disapproval or impose a cut in management pay when results were down. The problem of the positioning of wage earners in relation to finance employees is more difficult than in relation to CEOs. Financial operators cannot be reduced to a few dominant individuals. In a financial firm where most of the employees are affected directly or indirectly by bonuses, trade unions must know how to criticise a not-too-significant minority without causing an open split among wage earners. They can denounce the capture of created value by heads of trading room, but will generally show greater lenience when it comes to that captured by lower-level traders. In this case, their policies will focus less on calling for an alternative distribution system that may anger many and more on a hypothetical catch-up, because it is risky to criticise the system too aggressively. Instead of resulting in a more egalitarian distribution of created value, a denunciation might lead to the capturing of profit at even higher levels of the hierarchy, even to its distribution among shareholders themselves. What is more, although this point is debatable, the capturing of a large share of created value by a few may result in the capturing of a small share by the majority. From this perspective, it would seem that back office bonuses, which are modest in comparison with those of the front office but high in relation to retail banking and other sectors, originated partly thanks to the excessive bonuses of some front office traders and heads of trading room.

If they are to avoid debilitating levels of inequality, wage earners through trade unions must strive towards a policy that promotes the highest value creation for the majority by focusing on distribution and, above all, on methods of organising and dividing up work. However, this kind of policy is difficult to achieve. A utilitarian criterion must be defined beforehand (an instrumental definition of the highest value creation for the majority) and, above all, particularly complex levers must be activated: the division and organisation of labour, both of which are generally wrongly considered as being separate from collective bargaining and wage labour policies.

Let us advance a little further towards utopia. To avoid the appropriation of profit by a handful of people – those who manage the highest volume of detachable assets – a united, organised workforce can collectively appropriate the firm's assets and render them collectively detachable. Even if this were a viable solution, it would still pose a political problem for the workforce. If we take full account of the dissociation between the world of labour value and that of prices, created value is not just employee "overwork" in the Marxist sense of the term (Marx 1990). It may well be the fruit of generations of people managing a business, but it is far from being just "work"; rather, it is a highly lucrative activity in which people take advantage of competition imperfections on the securities market. Without going so far as to talk of a hypothetical "dictatorship of the financial markets", it is clear that other economic sectors (as well as households) pay a high price for intermediation on the securities market, regardless of the method – whether egalitarian or not – by which rent is distributed within the financial industry. Moreover, although this may be more debatable still, employees in the finance sector could impose high returns, costly price volatility and traumatic destabilisation on other sectors at a global level. This theme of a "dictatorship of the financial markets", first coined by the French Association for the Taxation of Financial Transactions and Citizen's Action (ATTAC) movement, fosters a new vision of class relations that differs significantly from that of Marx. According to this debatable sector approach, the finance sector and its employees have now replaced the bourgeoisie. As such, they exploit and distort the productive activity of the "useful" and "real" producers, new unity of wage earners and entrepreneurs of non-financial sectors.

Should other wage earners believe that the workforce of each sector must seek to establish a strong position, find the social entitlements of each sector equally worthy and refuse all arguments for interdependence that are liable to ruin the stabilising unity of wage labour? Or, rather, can they challenge the forms of appropriation of the value created by a sector because it would be detrimental to the appropriation of the value created by the majority?

Working rich, inequalities and taxes

The problems involved in seeking and imposing an alternative means of sharing created value leads to an exploration of other forms of redistribution. Is taxation not the ultimate redistribution tool? It may have the disadvantage of not giving back to wage earners the very thing that ultimately is a product of wage-earner activity, however, it has the undeniable advantage of not endorsing the heterogeneity of power relations from one sector to another and the unequal exchanges between companies or sectors. The generality of its implementation and the power of the state that supports its application are clear advantages. It becomes easier to justify if my interpretation of financial activity is accepted. The high wages of finance's working rich are not due to some exceptional innate skills. On the contrary, they are the result of a rent capture. Using taxation to correct these phenomena, which can then be categorised as unjust, becomes increasingly legitimate (Piketty 2014).

Adjustment through taxation certainly has its advantages, but if we put utopia to one side and return to reality, we also know that it comes up against significant obstacles that must be taken into account. Finance employees are, understandably, particularly indignant when it comes to income tax. The word "confiscatory" is frequently used: "In France, taxes are confiscatory!" They are quick to point out that two-thirds of their bonus is deducted as income tax or Social Security charges. Many try to avoid paying taxes, some by having their salaries paid in London where tax rates are lower; others by practising tax exemption, in other words investing in French overseas departments in exchange for tax cuts, which sometimes involves taking considerable risks, such as purchasing non-existent hotels. More rarely, people may have part of their compensation paid to offshore accounts. Yet not all of these financial operators lead a lavish lifestyle. Some say (perhaps as a way of boasting) that they do not know what to do with their money. However, whether they are prodigal or stingy, they usually seek financial advice in order to avoid this unbearable level of taxation. It is indicative that some left-wing financial operators admitted that they voted for Alain Madelin, the most libertarian candidate, in the first round of the 2002 French presidential elections (while intending to vote for the socialist candidate Lionel Jospin in the second round).

In France, the community of market professionals is still relatively small, with around 12,000 employees in 2007 (Godechot 2011). In London, there are far more. The Financial Services Authority register lists over 300,000 names for the period 2000–2013. As a result, employees' efforts to avoid taxation there have a far greater impact. If we expand this problem to the entire working rich category, we find that not only do they try generally to avoid paying taxes by exploiting tax loopholes, but also they seek to influence politics globally in order to steer economic and fiscal policy towards a lowering of tax rates. The high level of inequality then becomes a factor that undermines collective institutions based on forms of solidarity (universities, health insurance, pensions, public services, etc.). In London, French financial operators who have generally benefited from fully-funded higher education[4] in engineering *Grandes Écoles* are delighted with the excellent training they receive but deplore the overly dominant role played by the state and taxation in France, and are also becoming concerned by the exorbitant cost of private education in England. They promote the emergence of a highly neoliberal economy in order to reduce the tax burden, but they suffer the associated setbacks and costs. In a neoliberal world, the differentiation by quality and price of these privatised public services is much greater. As the working rich want the best quality in order to better flaunt their new status, they are even more attached to the income they earn, and taxes should not reduce their revenue, which may become "necessary". Fiscal redistribution of created value captured by the working rich thus faces challenges that cannot be underestimated. It is naive to rely on taxation alone to redistribute it. The emergence of this group and the rise in inequality have put pressure on politicians to lower taxes. This phenomenon is all the more self-sustaining because it leads to the deterioration of public services and the emergence of an alternative private sector with very different prices and quality of service.

***

The financial industry is often seen as being the heart of capitalism. However, it may actually be the sector that is least subject to the power of capital. Finally, the finance sector, with all its paradoxes and excesses, may be precisely the very sector that prompts wage earners to re-examine the sharing of value.

Notes

1 The sociological analysis of artistic spheres mainly focuses on this dominant opposition between an inspired pole (symbolic) and a commercial pole (material), at the risk of overlooking the symbolic order that lies within the commercial world (Bourdieu 1996).

2 The Bourdieusian model, which can be found in its purest form in *Language and Symbolic Power* (Bourdieu 1991), systematically links capital volume in a field, perception of profits and the exercise of domination without fully explaining the operating procedures of such an association.
3 Zingales (2000, p. 1643) believes that this capacity for appropriation, which he considers to be fundamentally connected to the growing role of human capital in economic life, can shift a company's boundaries and change relationships between shareholders and employees. The increasingly important role of social capital in business life, identified by many different authors, is even more likely to subvert a company's boundaries.
4 This education is free, and in some cases (*École Polytechnique*, *École Normale*, etc.) students are even paid.

References

Bey, H 1991, *TAZ: The Temporary Autonomous Zone, Ontological Anarchy, Poetic Terrorism*. New York, Autonomedia.
Bhidé, A 2000, *The Origin and Evolution of New Businesses*, New York, Oxford.
Boltanski, L and Chiapello, E 2006, *The New Spirit of Capitalism*, Verso, London.
Bourdieu, P 1991, *Language and Symbolic Power*, Harvard University Press, Cambridge MA.
Bourdieu, P 1996, *The Rules of Art: Genesis and Structure of the Literary Field*, Stanford University Press, Stanford CA.
Bourdieu, P 2000, *Pascalian Meditations*, Stanford University Press, Stanford CA.
Bourdieu, P 2005, *The Social Structures of the Economy*, Polity, Cambridge UK.
Godechot, O 2011, *Finance and the Rise in Inequalities in France*, Paris School of Economics, Working paper n°2011–13.
Lazega, E 2001, *The Collegial Phenomenon*, Oxford University Press, New York.
Lordon, F 2000, 'La "création de valeur" comme rhétorique et comme pratique. Généalogie et sociologie de la valeur actionariale', *Année de la régulation*, vol. 4, pp. 117–170.
Lutter, M 2014, *Creative Success and Network Embeddedness: Explaining Critical Recognition of Film Directors in Hollywood, 1900–2010*, MPIfG discussion paper, n°14/11, Cologne.
Marx, K 1990, *Capital. A Critique of Political Economy*, Penguin Books, London.
Menger, PM 2002, *Portrait de l'artiste en travailleur*, Seuil, Paris.
Piketty, T 2014, *Capital in the Twenty-First Century*, Harvard University Press, Cambridge MA.
Verley, P 1997, *La Révolution industrielle*, Gallimard, Paris.
Zingales, L 2000, 'In Search of New Foundations', *The Journal of Finance*, vol. 50, n°4, p. 1643–1653.

Index

remuneration consultancy firms 200, 203
renegotiation 174–5, 175–6, 180
rents 41, 43, 89–90, 226
res nullius 88–92, 111
research and development (R&D)
    engineers 32, 33; relations between
    traders and 134–8
residual claimant right 80
resignations 198; collective 152–4
responsibility 71, 76
results bonus criteria 56
results logic 50–1, 52, 148
retention: bonus distribution 57–61;
    devices for limiting defections 169–75
retirements 198
reward 57–61
risk xi-xii; calculations 48–9; limits 71
risk controllers 33, 34–6
risk-taking 27
role-based allowances 28
Roman law 69, 70, 85
Roth, L.-M. x, 12
Rousseau, J.J. 90, 94–5
Roy, D. 68, 85
Rozan, J.M. 6, 102, 112
Russian default on GKO bonds 198

Saatchi brothers 228
Saez, F. 2, 28
Saglio, J. 84–5
sales contracts 84
sales credit system 129–30, 132, 134
salespeople 32, 33, 37–8, 72, 85; allocation
    of client portfolios 79; career path
    165–7; mutual assistance 93–4; pay
    hierarchy 34–6; social differences from
    traders 121; traders, redeployability of
    assets and 120–34
Salomon Brothers 125–6, 231
Sandor, R. 187–8
Sanford, C. 181
'Saturn Bank' 11, 156–7, 194, 201;
    aftermath of partnership project 221–2;
    bonus distribution 47–8, 50–3, 53–4;
    bonus pool formula 47–8; derivatives
    149–50, 151; dispossession 83; head of
    options' partnership project 212, 217–20;
    initial contracts 169; non-compete
    clauses 171–2; political division of labour
    210–12; recruitment process 195, 196–7;
    relations between traders and salespeople
    128, 130–1, 133–4; sense of ownership
    of profit 97, 105, 107, 109; support
    functions and property rights 79, 80

Savigny, F.C. von 95
scarcity 58; redeployability, power and
    119–20
Schelling, T. 153
secrecy: about bonus size 60–1; divulging
    secrets 182–3
securities portfolios 70–6
segmentation of the labour market 200–3
self-sustained rarity 198–200
September 11 2001 58
service to business 29, 30
sex discrimination 60, 62
shareholder value 89–90, 232
shareholders xii, 70
simultaneous ownership 94
'Sirius Bank' 173
skilled labour 3, 4
smile 48
social capital 214, 223–4, 228, 236
Société Générale x, 38, 39–40, 183, 224;
    highest wages 20–2; wage inequality
    22–4
solidarity 210
specialisation 207
specification 102–3, 113
specificity of assets 116–20, 166–7
starting wage 167–9, 177
statistical trading 75–6
'stinkers' 68, 85
stockbrokers, traditional 194–5, 204
Stone, O. 5
strong ties 186, 203, 216, 223
structural holes 123–4, 138–9, 216
structural variations 79–80
subcontracting 50, 61; hagglers 206, 207
suitability of transactions 125–6
support functions 32, 33–4, 34–6, 54, 109;
    lease of work 101, 109–11; property
    rights 79–80; *see also* accounting,
    human resources (HR)
symbolic capital 223

Taleb, N. 6, 83–4
talent 8, 13
taxation 234–5
Taylorism 3
team moves *see* collective moves
team purchases 187–9
technical knowledge 183
technological change 3–4
ten highest wages, France 19–22
tertius gaudens 223
Thévenot, L. 56, 115
timing of hold-up 154

Taylor & Francis eBooks

Helping you to choose the right eBooks for your Library

Add Routledge titles to your library's digital collection today. Taylor and Francis ebooks contains over 50,000 titles in the Humanities, Social Sciences, Behavioural Sciences, Built Environment and Law.

Choose from a range of subject packages or create your own!

Benefits for you

» Free MARC records
» COUNTER-compliant usage statistics
» Flexible purchase and pricing options
» All titles DRM-free.

Benefits for your user

» Off-site, anytime access via Athens or referring URL
» Print or copy pages or chapters
» Full content search
» Bookmark, highlight and annotate text
» Access to thousands of pages of quality research at the click of a button.

REQUEST YOUR **FREE** INSTITUTIONAL TRIAL TODAY	**Free Trials Available** We offer free trials to qualifying academic, corporate and government customers.

eCollections – Choose from over 30 subject eCollections, including:

Archaeology	Language Learning
Architecture	Law
Asian Studies	Literature
Business & Management	Media & Communication
Classical Studies	Middle East Studies
Construction	Music
Creative & Media Arts	Philosophy
Criminology & Criminal Justice	Planning
Economics	Politics
Education	Psychology & Mental Health
Energy	Religion
Engineering	Security
English Language & Linguistics	Social Work
Environment & Sustainability	Sociology
Geography	Sport
Health Studies	Theatre & Performance
History	Tourism, Hospitality & Events

For more information, pricing enquiries or to order a free trial, please contact your local sales team: **www.tandfebooks.com/page/sales**

 Routledge
Taylor & Francis Group

The home of
Routledge books

www.tandfebooks.com